Mohandas

Revolutionary Lives

Series Editors: Sarah Irving, King's College, London;
Professor Paul Le Blanc, La Roche College, Pittsburgh

Revolutionary Lives is a series of short, critical biographies of radical figures from throughout history. The books are sympathetic but not sycophantic, and the intention is to present a balanced and, where necessary, critical evaluation of the individual's place in their political field, putting their actions and achievements in context and exploring issues raised by their lives, such as the use or rejection of violence, nationalism, or gender in political activism. While individuals are the subject of the books, their personal lives are dealt with lightly except insofar as they mesh with political concerns. The focus is on the contribution these revolutionaries made to history, an examination of how far they achieved their aims in improving the lives of the oppressed and exploited, and how they can continue to be an inspiration for many today.

Also available:

Salvador Allende:
Revolutionary Democrat
Victor Figueroa Clark

Hugo Chávez:
Socialist for the Twenty-first Century
Mike Gonzalez

W.E.B. Du Bois:
Revolutionary Across the Color Line
Bill V. Mullen

Frantz Fanon
Philosopher of the Barricades
Peter Hudis

Leila Khaled:
Icon of Palestinian Liberation
Sarah Irving

Jean Paul Marat:
Tribune of the French Revolution
Clifford D. Conner

John Maclean:
Hero of Red Clydeside
Henry Bell

Sylvia Pankhurst:
Suffragette, Socialist and Scourge of Empire
Katherine Connelly

Paul Robeson:
A Revolutionary Life
Gerald Horne

Percy Bysshe Shelley:
Poet and Revolutionary
Jacqueline Mulhallen

Toussaint Louverture:
A Black Jacobin in the Age of Revolutions
Charles Forsdick and
Christian Høgsbjerg

Ellen Wilkinson:
From Red Suffragist to Government Minister
Paula Bartley

Gerrard Winstanley:
The Digger's Life and Legacy
John Gurney

Mohandas Gandhi

Experiments in Civil Disobedience

Talat Ahmed

PLUTO PRESS

First published 2019 by Pluto Press
345 Archway Road, London N6 5AA

www.plutobooks.com

British Library Cataloguing in Publication Data
A catalogue record for this book is available from the British Library

ISBN 978 0 7453 3429 5 Hardback
ISBN 978 0 7453 3428 8 Paperback
ISBN 978 1 7837 1514 5 PDF eBook
ISBN 978 1 7837 1516 9 Kindle eBook
ISBN 978 1 7837 1515 2 EPUB eBook

This book is printed on paper suitable for recycling and made from fully managed and sustained forest sources. Logging, pulping and manufacturing processes are expected to conform to the environmental standards of the country of origin.

Typeset by Stanford DTP Services, Northampton, England

Simultaneously printed in the United Kingdom and United States of America

Contents

Illustrations

Maps

Figures

Acknowledgements

There are a great number of people to thank for the help and support I received in the writing of this biography of Mohandas Gandhi. First and foremost, I would like to pay a particular tribute to all those who have contributed – from a myriad of perspectives – to the very rich scholarship on Gandhi and South Asia that has been generated over the last forty or fifty years. For a popular biography such as this, a specific debt is owed to the many historians who have painstakingly mined and explored Gandhi's writings, probed a range of aspects of his life and investigated his impact on Indian nationalism and the varied meanings of his legacy for South Asia and beyond. Here special thanks are due to David Arnold, who as Professor of South Asian History at the School of Oriental and African Studies (SOAS) recommended that I teach on a course of his on Gandhi, while a research student. As a teacher, thanks are also owed to the many undergraduate students at SOAS, the University of Leeds, Goldsmiths College, and the University of Edinburgh, who subsequently took my own courses on Gandhi and participated avidly in seminars, contributing their own valuable ideas and questions. I am also grateful for the opportunity to present papers on Gandhi at the following institutions: the Mahatma Gandhi Centre for Global Nonviolence, James Madison University in 2009; the Centre for Social Change, University of Johannesburg in 2011, and the Department of History, University of the West Indies, St Augustine, Trinidad and Tobago in 2014.

This volume appears in 2019, and was written in part with the aim of making an intervention in the debates around the meaning and relevance of Gandhi's life, work and legacy which will accompany the commemoration of the 150th anniversary of his birth. The year 2019 also marks the centenary of the Amritsar Massacre, an event that exposed the darker side of British rule in India and made a forceful case, if one were needed, for why it was imperative to oppose imperialism more generally. Thousands of Indians fought valiantly to free

India from the yoke of the British Empire, and in this endeavour, they found common cause with anti-imperialists in Britain who became implacable foes of their own governments. This work is dedicated to the memory of two such individuals, Victor Kiernan (1913–2009) and Ralph Russell (1918–2008). As activists in the Communist Party of Great Britain, both worked to build solidarity with the Indian nationalist movement during the 1930s and 1940s and developed deep friendships with a generation of other young radical intellectuals in India, including those around the Progressive Writers' Movement. Both learnt and became fluent in Urdu and their love for the language and literature resulted in translations of the great Urdu poets – Mirza Ghalib, Muhammad Iqbal and Faiz Ahmad Faiz.

Victor, a one-time leading member of the Communist Party Historians Group, made an immense contribution to Marxist historiography in the post-war period, including his ground-breaking and superb work on *The Lords of Human Kind: European Attitudes to Other Cultures in the Imperial Age*, published in 1969, almost a decade before Edward Said's far more famous work, *Orientalism*. He taught Urdu and History at Aitchison College, Lahore and then was Professor of History at the University of Edinburgh until his retirement. Ralph taught in India and Pakistan and then was Professor of Urdu Literature and Language at SOAS until he retired. He remained an agitator and thorn in the side of university authorities over many decades, but also inspired students to great literary, linguistic and political heights. Whilst completing my PhD and beyond, I had the honour and pleasure of knowing both these remarkable men, who acted as very supportive but challenging intellectual mentors, with their deep knowledge and appreciation of South Asian history and their sharp analyses of Gandhi and nationalism. This little book comes out a decade after they both sadly passed, but it aims to pay tribute to both Victor and Ralph, and the wider tradition of radical, partisan scholarship that they both represented so well – one which always stands with, and champions, the oppressed and exploited. In the spirit of their memory, it is only fitting that this book is also dedicated to all those in the twenty-first century who are not only experimenting with, but also utilising, effective civil disobedience in the struggle to change the world for the better.

Thanks are also due to Peter Alexander, Rakesh Ankit, Des Barrow, Jane Bassett, Weyman Bennett, Kambiz Boomla, Ashwin Desai, Rehad Desai, Jackie and Phil Douglas, Uma Dephelia-Mesthrie, Zoya Economou, Ashley Fataar, Ursula Fataar, Bashabi Fraser, Alan Goatley, Siobhan Hawthorne, Ursla Hawthorne, Isabel Hofmeyr, Eric Itzkin, Kate Jelly, Gareth Jenkins, Despina Karayianni, Sayeed Hasan Khan, Yasmin Khan, Vivek Lehal, Anna Livingstone, Mac Maharaj, Dilip Menon, Kriti Menon, Meena Menon, Sandy Nicholl, Caroline O'Reilly, Basil and Elaine Palan, Shruti Patil, Yuri Prasad, Anju Ranjan, Kanchana Ruwanpura, Mike Simons, Sherry-Ann Singh, Urmila and Sunny Singh, Wilfried Swenden and Monique Vajifdar. Crispin Bates and Donny Gluckstein deserve special thanks for reading the draft and providing critical, valuable and helpful feedback.

I would also like to thank the archivists and library staff at the following institutions for their help and assistance: the British Library, SOAS library, University of Edinburgh library, Special Collections and Archives at Bishopsgate Institute, National Archives of India, National Library of Scotland, Nehru Memorial Museum Library, and the Gandhi-Luthuli Documentation Centre, at the University of KwaZulu-Natal. I am grateful to the guides in Johannesburg and Durban who made it possible for me to visit the Gandhi sites in those cities – this was a most educative exercise. I thank the School of History, Classics and Archaeology, University of Edinburgh for their support, particularly with securing the images in this book and to my colleagues in the Centre for South Asian Studies. Special thanks are due to the editors of the 'Revolutionary Lives' series and their anonymous readers, and particularly to David Castle, for his patience and support and to Jeanne Brady, Melanie Patrick, Robert Webb and the whole team at Pluto for their fine work with the production and publication.

Finally, to Chris and Christian. To Chris, for encouraging me to write on Gandhi in the first instance and for the constancy of his support, advice and love that remain inspirational. And to Christian, who alone knows the immeasurable contribution he made.

Glossary

adivasis	indigenous people
ahimsa	the principle of doing no harm
Baisakhi	both a harvest festival and the Sikh religious New Year in the Punjab
bania	merchants
bapu	father of the nation
bhangis	the lowest category of untouchable community, whose occupation is cleaning latrines
brahmins	priestly caste
charkha	spinning wheel
chowki	police station
chowkidar	local village guard
dalits	untouchables
dharma	duty
diwan	prime minister, combined with role of adviser; revenue collector
Durbar	lavish public reception held by Indian royalty or the British viceroy
gumasta	landlord's agents
harijans	children of God
hartal	a strike, but not in the conventional sense. It refers to a voluntary closure of workplaces, and can mean a total shutdown. But in most cases under Gandhi's leadership it does not imply picketing to achieve closure as this might lead to forceful action not aligned to peaceful protest.
jati	caste distinctions that are based upon occupational groupings, which are also held to be hereditary where members inter-marry and dine only with each other
khadi	handspun cloth
khaddar	home spinning

kshatriyas	warrior ruling caste
lathi	steel-tipped club
Nawab	Viceroy
panchayat	assembly of village elders
raiyots/ryot	peasants
Ramraj	the ideal rule of Ram, the hero of the *Ramayana*
Sahib	young prince
satyagraha	holding onto truth, truth force
satyagrahi	someone participating in a campaign of *satyagraha*
shudras	peasant worker caste
swadeshi	homemade
Swaraj	self-government
taluk	administrative area
tinkathia	tax system regarding indigo cultivation
vaisyas	merchant caste
varna	Hindu caste type, which divides society into four hereditary categories of priests, warriors, merchants and peasants
zamindars	landowning tax collectors

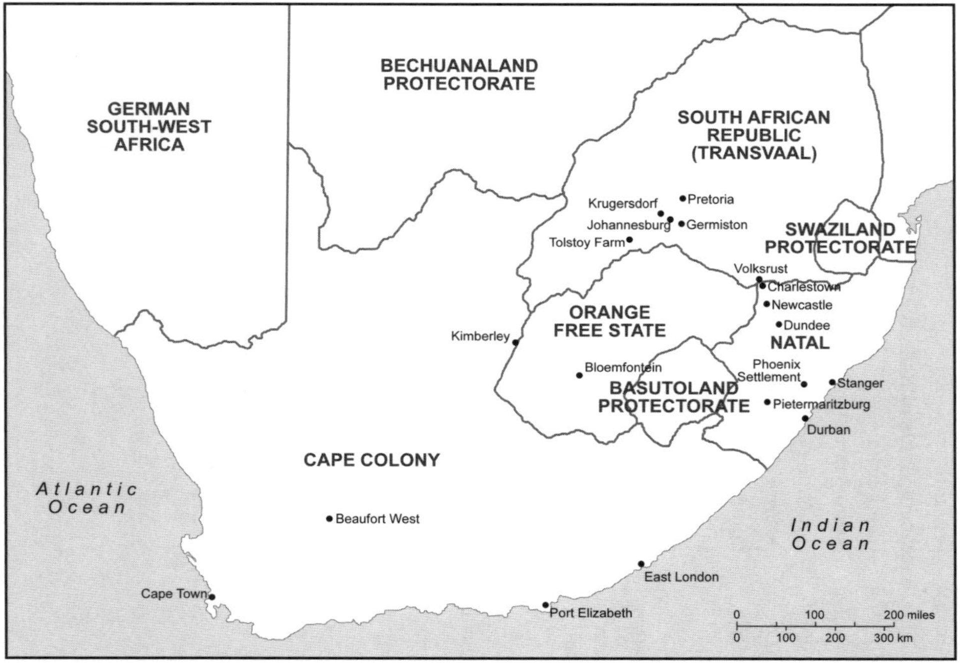

Map 1 Southern Africa, 1893

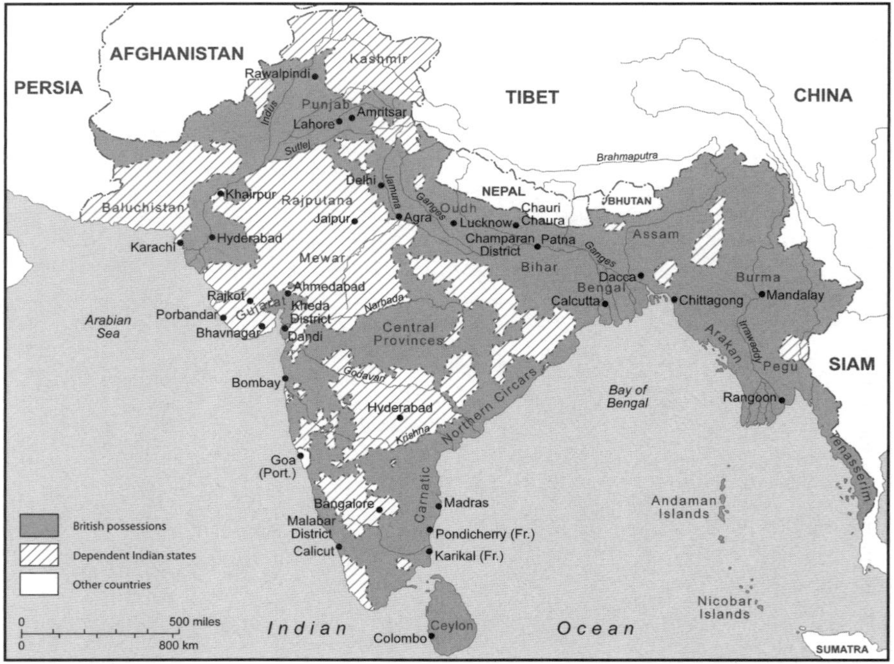

Map 2 India, 1914

In memory of Victor Kiernan and Ralph Russell

Introduction

Mohandas Karamchand Gandhi was one of the most photographed people of the twentieth century in his lifetime, and since his death he has become one of the most recognisable iconic figures of modern world history. Gandhi is not just simply the most famous 'founding father' of India; to use the language of Hegel, he is a 'world historical individual' whose impact on the twentieth century might be compared to Vladimir Lenin or Mao Zedong. His remarkable life has been captured on film – both fictional and documentary – and countless pamphlets, biographies and school texts continue to proliferate. Among the many forms of cultural representation of his life, which include plays, novels, and graphic novels, Richard Attenborough's Oscar-winning film *Gandhi* in 1982 made the greatest impact, providing a window into Gandhi the icon for many millions of people. The film was released at a momentous time when millions all over the world were fearful about the threat of nuclear holocaust during the Cold War, and peace movements were burgeoning internationally. In Britain, for example, the Campaign for Nuclear Disarmament organised mass demonstrations against the deployment of American Cruise missiles in Berkshire and opposition to NATO. A women's camp was set up at Greenham Common in an attempt to physically but peacefully prevent the Royal Air Force base in Berkshire from operating. Attenborough, himself a lifelong supporter of the Labour Party who later also opposed the Iraq War, stated in 1982 that 'Gandhi believed if we could but agree, simplistic though it be, that if we do not resort to violence then the route to solving problems would be much different than the one we take.'[1]

Such sentiments moved the United Nations General Assembly to vote unanimously on 15 June 2007 to declare 2 October – the date of Gandhi's birth in 1869 – 'International Day of Non-Violence'. Such a commemoration underlies Gandhi's global significance, and today, seventy years after his death in 1948, Gandhi remains an iconic and mesmerising figure. His stature as the father of modern India is undiminished; if anything, Gandhi continues to inspire awe in new generations of scholars, students and activists in all manner of social movements such as those against climate change, racism, imperialism and war. The protests in Gaza in May 2018, for example, on the seventieth year of the Nakba (the expulsion that accompanied the Israeli occupation), saw Palestinians using non-violence on their 'Great March of Return', with many explicitly stating how Gandhian methods and ideas were an inspiration. For example, one leading organiser of the 'Great March of Return', Abu Artema, stated 'I was inspired by Gandhi … I like the way he fought by peace. I think what is right is stronger than weapons, so I like the method of Gandhi, I liked the method of Martin Luther King.' It might be noted, however, that this change in tactics on the part of the Palestinians did not affect in the slightest how the Israeli state responded. At the time of writing, over a hundred Palestinians peacefully protesting have been shot dead and over 3,000 wounded.[2]

The Inspiration of 'the little brown saint of India'

Abu Artema's mention of Martin Luther King in the same breath as Gandhi is fitting, for King clearly understood the attraction of Gandhi's method during the Montgomery Bus Boycott of 1955–56. Bayard Rustin – a key organiser from New York – suggested how best to apply Gandhi's tenets of non-violence: 'Going to jail is precisely what we should be doing.'[3] As Harry Belafonte notes, 'Gandhi had preached this very form of civil disobedience; overwhelm the government's jails, he reasoned, and the government would have to compromise or collapse. "Jail, no bail" would become a rallying cry of the American civil rights movement, often to great effect ….'[4] In 1964, King noted in his Nobel Peace Prize acceptance speech how 'In the summer of 1956 the name of Mahatma Gandhi was well-known in Montgomery. People who had never heard of the little brown saint of India were now saying his name with an air of familiarity.'[5]

In the same speech, King also paid fervent tribute to Gandhi's strategy:

> Nonviolence is a powerful and just weapon ... a weapon unique in history, which cuts without wounding and ennobles the man who wields it ... He [Gandhi] struggled only with the weapons of truth, soul-force, non-injury and courage ... Nonviolent resistance had emerged as the technique of the movement, while love stood as the regulating ideal. In other words, Christ furnished the spirit and the motivation while Gandhi furnished the method.[6]

Aside from the American Civil Rights Movement, 'the little brown saint of India' clearly made a profound impact on a wide variety of people during his own lifetime. Perry Anderson captures well what set Gandhi apart from other leading Indian nationalist figures involved in the Indian National Congress (INC):

> He was a first-class organiser and fundraiser – diligent, efficient, meticulous – who rebuilt Congress from top to bottom, endowing it with a permanent executive at national level, vernacular units at provincial level, local bases at district level, and delegates proportionate to population, not to speak of an ample treasury. At the same time, though temperamentally in many ways an autocrat, politically he did not care about power in itself, and was an excellent mediator between different figures and groups both within Congress and among its variegated social supports. Finally, though no great orator, he was an exceptionally quick and fluent communicator, as the hundred volumes of his articles, books, letters, cables (far exceeding the output of Marx or Lenin, let alone Mao) testify. To these political gifts were added personal qualities of a ready warmth, impish wit and iron will. It is no surprise that so magnetic a force would attract such passionate admiration, at the time and since.[7]

Alongside passionate admiration, we should not forget that like any political radical he also inspired venom and mockery from conservatives and defenders of the imperial order. Winston Churchill famously scorned Gandhi as a 'half-naked *fakir* [ascetic]' in 1931.[8] Indeed, as early as 1914, the future South African Prime Minister Jan Christian Smuts was already remarking sardonically on the 'saint-like' qualities of Gandhi, when he noted that 'The Saint has left our shores, I sincerely hope forever.'[9] Nonetheless, aside from colonial officials like Smuts, Gandhi's 'saintliness' certainly came to characterise Gandhi's life and impact. In 1940, Albert Einstein stated 'Generations to come, it may be, will scarce believe that such a one as this ever in flesh and blood walked upon this earth.'[10] And of course, Gandhi's demise at the hands of an assassin's bullet on 30 January 1948 sealed his iconic status and sanctified Gandhi as the *Mahatma*, India's 'Great Soul'. King George VI described his death as 'an irreparable loss for mankind'. Labour Prime Minister Clement Attlee expressed 'profound distress' and Jawaharlal Nehru, first Prime Minister of India, immortalised him further with the now memorable words 'the light that shone in this country was no ordinary light'; it was 'something more than the immediate present' and would continue to 'illuminate this country for many years', giving 'solace to innumerable hearts'.[11] As the most revered figure of the Indian nationalist movement, Gandhi was affectionately referred to as *bapu* – father of the nation – seeming to offer India a unique path of development in the emerging Cold War world that was neither 'Western' nor 'Communist'.

Gandhi's admirers in the imperial metropolis of Britain itself were also legendary. Muriel Lester, a non-conformist social reformer from east London, went to India for the first time for three months in 1926. She thus writes of a British magistrate whom she meets at a dinner who explains what Gandhi had achieved for India:

> Ten years ago, if a coolie had suddenly crossed my path and frightened the horse I was riding, I would probably have sworn at him and shouted 'Get out of the way – you'. He would have cowered before me and disappeared. Now I should not shout at a coolie like that. But if I did, he wouldn't disappear. He'd stand facing me with complete assurance, look me full in the face and politely enquire, 'Why should *I* move?'[12]

Madeline Slade was the daughter of the distinguished Admiral Sir Edmond Slade, former commander-in-chief of the East Indies Station and a board member of the Anglo-Persian Oil Company. She had lived in India hosting local elite women at purdah parties and enjoyed horse-riding with the imperial elite.[13] Such was his personal charisma and appeal that, after reading of Gandhi's 21-day fast for Hindu-Muslim unity in October 1924, this quintessentially colonial white woman sold her diamond brooch and sent £20 along with a letter to Gandhi asking to join him. Gandhi invited her to come, but warned that the climate was challenging and the labour strenuous.[14] Nevertheless, she went, and stayed for many years. Yet Gandhi also made an impact on working-class women in Britain, and after his death helped inspire the leader of the Great Grunwick strike of 1976–78, Jayaben Desai, who defiantly invoked Gandhi in response to right-wing efforts to derail the magnificent strike action in the winter of 1976, telling a mass meeting of 130 strikers in Brent Town Hall, 'We must not give up ... Would Gandhi give up? Never!'[15]

The influence and inspiration of Gandhi on colonial subjects and anti-colonial activists internationally should also be briefly registered. Writing in 1931, one young supporter of 'West Indian Self-Government' in far-away colonial Trinidad, C.L.R. James – later a renowned revolutionary Marxist – noted:

> That Gandhi has the rich and middle-class Hindu with him is not surprising. But that the agricultural labourer in remote villages, the slum dwellers in the towns, should all be ready to face hardships, imprisonment, death; should understand and practise so successfully ideals as difficult as non-cooperation and non-violence, all this is something which to me is as miraculous as anything I have ever read.[16]

The Fifth Pan-African Congress, held in Manchester in 1945, saw organisers George Padmore and W.E.B. Du Bois laying a new stress on militant non-violence in the aftermath of Gandhi's successes, with armed revolt now only to be held as a tactic in reserve. A key Nigerian delegate noted 'we must take India as an example.'[17]

Kwame Nkrumah – one of those present at the Fifth Pan-African Congress – would lead the struggle for independence in Ghana in 1957 in no small part through the inspiration of Gandhi's tactics of civil disobedience, as his Convention People's Party carried mass agitation for 'Positive Action without Violence for Full Self-Government Now'.[18] In 1959, Eric Williams, leader of the People's National Movement in Trinidad and Tobago, who would in 1962 become the first prime minister of that independent nation, delivered a broadcast to mark the ninetieth anniversary of the birth of Gandhi.[19] Williams credited Gandhi as the one who 'led the revolt against British imperialism which led to the freedom of India', and whose tactics were now leading to successes in Africa thanks to Pan-Africanists like Nkrumah.[20] Williams emphasised the relevance of Gandhi for the peoples of the Caribbean and the Atlantic region more broadly in terms of the experience of indentured labour, but also saw Gandhi's passive resistance as a 'new method of political struggle' that placed its inventor Gandhi on a par with the 'tradition of revolutionists, with men of the French Revolution, with Marx'.[21]

In South Africa, Nelson Mandela held Gandhi as the 'archetypal anticolonial revolutionary', noting that his strategy of non-violent resistance and his assertion that a people can only be dominated if they cooperate with the dominators, had inspired anti-colonial and anti-racist movements internationally. Explaining the military dimension of Umkhonto we Sizwe, the armed wing of the African National Congress, Mandela added that 'even then, we chose sabotage because it did not involve the loss of life.' Mandela also rightly stressed the importance of Gandhi's time in South Africa for Gandhi's own political development, once remarking on a visit to India 'You gave us Mohandas, we returned him to you as Mahatma … No ordinary leader – divinely inspired.'[22]

The theme of Gandhi as a 'saint', and 'divinely inspired' became manifest after his death. To again take a perhaps less familiar example from the Caribbean, the great pioneering Trinidadian calypsonian Raymond Quevedo, also known as Atilla the Hun, penned the following 'Panegyric to Gandhi' in 1948 on hearing of his death:

> The whole civilized world must mourn
> For Mahatma Gandhi who is dead and gone
> Recognized internationally by the world
> As a great and noble soul
> I declare his death is undoubtedly
> The greatest tragedy of the century

Born over seventy-eight years ago
His life of selflessness we all know
Although he preached civil disobedience
He was an advocate of non-violence
He said Humanity their problems could solve
By embracing a policy of love
Laudation to his glory will never cease
The wonderfully great Apostle of Peace

In the death of the Mahatma
The world has lost a great spiritual leader
A real true saint, good upright and
A beautiful soul and a noble man
Millions are weeping in sympathy
Over this terrifying tragedy
So let us join with them and sing R.I.P.
May he rest in peace in eternity.'[23]

The above all testify to Gandhi's enduring impact and appeal. He is held as an uncompromising opponent of injustice and imperialism and a champion for the oppressed and exploited the world over. This is why he is often viewed as a great revolutionary figure – albeit a non-violent one. Indeed, Gandhi himself made this claim about himself in 1931: 'I believe myself to be a revolutionary – a non-violent revolutionary … my means are non-co-operation.'[24] Fifteen years later, he further elaborated the essence of his non-violent revolution: 'A non-violent revolution is not a programme of "seizure of power". It is a programme of transformation of relationships ending in peaceful transfer of power.'[25]

The Contradictions of a 'Non-Violent Revolutionary'

Such an enigmatic figure as Gandhi, who inspired – and continues to inspire – such forces and passions, has led to a proliferation of literature both scholarly and popular which attempts to try and make sense of the man himself. Indeed, the vibrancy of interest in Gandhi is most clearly evident in the tremendous amount of scholarship that engages his writings and life. The earliest biographies by the English missionary Joseph Doke, the French writer Romain Rolland and the American journalist Louis Fischer were written by people who knew Gandhi and had deep respect for his ideas. Doke, a Baptist minister from Devon born in 1861 had met Gandhi in Johannesburg while working as a Christian missionary in 1907 and the two became kindred spirits, with Doke's biographical sketch appearing in 1909.[26] Doke's work was written with Gandhi's permission and essentially represents an oral testimony told by Gandhi to him through several conversations, and published with the aim of helping British people to understand him better and not just dismiss him as an anarchist or troublemaker. Rolland had been drawn towards Eastern mysticism philosophically through the works of the poet, Rabindranath Tagore, and the religious guru, Swami Vivekananda, and eventually, Gandhi. Rolland's biography appeared in 1924, though he did not meet Gandhi until 1931, in Switzerland.[27] Both books are faithful, but perhaps inevitably as they were written while Gandhi was still alive, in the midst of his campaigning and with his star in the ascendancy, they are quite hagiographic in tone. Louis Fischer's *Life of Mahatma Gandhi*, written after Gandhi's death and published in 1950, was a pioneering, more comprehensive, scholarly overview, and it proved hugely influential, helping provide the material for Attenborough's film.[28] Similarly, the radical British Quaker Reginald Reynold's *To Live in Mankind: A Quest for Gandhi* (1951) provided a valuable first-hand account of Gandhi's life drawn from Reynolds's time in India in 1929.[29] Many of the above had extensive correspondence with Gandhi going back some thirty years and they provide perceptive and thoughtful insights into Gandhi himself and how he was viewed by early twentieth-century radicals, Quakers, theosophists and non-conformists who detested imperialism and looked towards a better world.

If these early books based on first-hand knowledge of Gandhi helped introduce audiences in the West to Gandhi's remarkable life, they have inevitably since been supplemented by a host of serious academic studies. Many *Gandhi Readers* have been published over the decades, demonstrating the emergence of a vibrant field of 'Gandhi Studies', with scholars mining new sources through which to interpret Gandhi.[30] The man himself was a prolific writer; he corresponded with family and close associates, journalists and intellectuals, dignitaries and politicians, friends and adversaries. Many scholars, working meticulously and tirelessly, have collected, edited and made available to the public Gandhi's *Collected Works* in both print form and electronically.[31]

Perhaps some of the most notable studies of Gandhi's politics have been by historians such as Judith Brown,[32] David Arnold,[33] David Hardiman[34] and Geoffrey Ashe.[35] In differing ways, they have probed Gandhi's life and his ideas to offer varying interpretations ranging from the sympathetic, to those striking a more critical note and challenging some of the long-standing myths – nationalist and otherwise – which have arisen about him. Alongside these works, writers have highlighted and explored the specificities of Gandhian thought in philosophy and religion.[36] Recently, Ramachandra Guha's work has emphasised the importance of Gandhi's time in South Africa,[37] whilst Kathryn Tidrick argues that his student days in London were much more central to the formation of Gandhi's political project.[38] Both Guha and Tidrick have been particularly significant in terms of (re)examining new material and acting as a corrective to the over-simplified interpretations of Gandhi as quintessentially Indic: 'I do not want my house to be walled on all sides nor my windows to be shut. I want the culture of all lands to blow about my house as freely as possible: but I refuse to be blown off my feet by any of them.' These words of Gandhi's, inscribed on the foundation stone of the Indian YMCA in London, capture well his cosmopolitanism, as well as locating him firmly within an indigenous context. Memoirs and biographies by relatives have also been valuable in affording an opportunity to see Gandhi through the family archive.[39] Scholarship from South Africa has been vital in questioning the notion of Gandhi as catalyst for change amongst Indians in South Africa and more recently the excellent book by Ashwin Desai and Goolam Vahed has persuasively contested the nationalist myth of Gandhi as the saviour of South Africa's Indian community.[40]

Other recent trends in Gandhi scholarship have challenged the accepted wisdom that Gandhi and non-violence were the defining feature of modern India. Faisal Devji has sought to recast Gandhi as a very mortal individual, who was pragmatic and willing to entertain notions of violence to achieve the emancipation of the ethical self.[41] Scholars now increasingly view Gandhi's life within the analytic framework of transnationalism, exploring the life and afterlives of 'the Mahatma Overseas', with respect to travel and the circulation of ideas.[42] Other recent scholarship – no doubt in part written with an eye on what kind of books might attract publicity, controversy and sell well to a wider popular audience – have focused on certain more unusual aspects of his life, such as his so-called 'sexual experiments'.[43]

Controversies about aspects of Gandhi's life and political views inevitably continue to provoke media comment, debate and argument.[44] Gandhi's life was clearly one of complexities, contradictions and ironies: the apostle of non-violence who was mowed down by an assassin's bullet; a deeply religious individual who fought passionately for Hindu-Muslim unity only to see India free but partitioned; a man who was seen as a religious zealot and imprisoned as a dangerous subversive nine times by colonial governments, and yet every British viceroy from 1916 onwards had to deal with him, and a 'saintly' figure who never held political office and is seen to be above the grubby business of political horse-trading and yet was a shrewd political operator who weighed every action and word in a calculated manner. This is the enigma of Gandhi – how could this little man from a small town in India, a London-trained barrister, with a penchant for elocution, dancing classes and French lessons, come to dominate Indian politics in the first half of the twentieth century and inspire a variety of social movements and liberation struggles ever since?

This political biography will chart Gandhi's life chronologically to try and unravel this enigmatic 'non-violent revolutionary' through an examination of his activism and ideas in their concrete historical context. In contrast to the elitist mainstream political currents of Indian nationalism at the time, which were focused on gentlemanly requests for gradual constitutional reform, Gandhi's capacity to mobilise and lead masses of people into struggle against British rule was indeed radical and revolutionary. By challenging the might of the largest and most powerful empire in the world, Gandhi's campaigns to demand serious reform and self-government opened the door for social forces from below that would aim to go beyond mere constitutional niceties. However, other forces – both more conservative on the right and more radical on the left of Gandhi – also exercised their pull on the momentum of the independence struggle in India. In some ways, Gandhi was at the crossroads of such tensions, and his appeal can be assessed in the distinction between his intent and its actual objective impact.

By campaigning in such a militant fashion for the bourgeois democratic demand of national independence – *purna swaraj* (self-rule) – Gandhi opened the way for forces that went far beyond him, despite his intentions. The objective achievement of independence for the 'brightest jewel in the crown of the British Empire', to use Disraeli's phrase, was revolutionary in the sense of shattering any hope of maintaining Britain's place as a great power in the world – far more than, say, the impact of Irish independence in 1922, even though James Connolly, leader of the Easter Rising of 1916, was a conscious socialist revolutionary. Gandhi's legacy as a 'non-violent revolutionary' has always been contested and it remains so today. Both within the international radical left and the Indian left, Gandhi's ideas have been engaged with, tested and contested, in his times and since.

Given the hope that Gandhi seems to embody to new generations of activists wishing to change a world scarred by permanent war, grotesque inequality, and the racist legacies of colonialism, it is imperative to reflect on Gandhi's life in order to gain insights into his strategy – and also its limitations. It would be tempting to simply valorise Gandhi as a great 'non-violent revolutionary', place him at the helm of a great radical tradition, and leave matters there. After all, Gandhi was hailed as such by a range of figures including Eric Williams and Nelson Mandela. Many young radicals today would surely agree with the anti-capitalist comedian Russell Brand, who in his 2014 book *Revolution* playfully describes Gandhi as a 'mad-looking little Indian bloke all dressed up in a nappy', but more seriously hails him as an 'extremely efficient revolutionary'.[45] This efficiency, according to Brand, lies in the simplicity of Gandhi's mathematical application of his non-violent creed, as evidenced in the iconic 1982 film, with Ben Kingsley's Gandhi delivering the following riposte to a British brigadier: 'In the end, you will walk out. Because 100,000 Englishmen simply cannot control 350 million Indians, if those

Indians refuse to cooperate.'[46] This is a simple quote, but it neatly encompasses Gandhi's philosophy.

For many people, including Brand, the question of why Gandhi was a 'revolutionary' is self-evident, since it rests on the argument that if Gandhi's pacifist and non-violent approach liberated India from British colonial rule, therefore his method and tactics must have 'worked' and he therefore deserves to be acclaimed as a 'revolutionary'. However, the story of India's struggle for independence was anything but non-violent – as any cursory glance at Indian resistance to British rule over two centuries will attest. To credit Gandhi and his tactics alone with delivering independence is to arguably fall into an elitist nationalist 'great man' narrative of history – a view which is almost as erroneous as explanations of decolonisation which romanticise the 1945–51 reforming Labour government of Clement Attlee. This book will then locate Gandhi's life, ideas and work within a larger process and examine the contradictions of how he stimulated mass movements for political and social change, but then strove to limit their impact within certain bounds. He deserves a place in a series on 'Revolutionary Lives' because it could be argued that Gandhi 'weaponised' non-violence into a revolutionary strategy, in a not dissimilar way to his utilisation of fasting, vegetarianism, vows of silence and even sexual abstinence.

This book's subtitle, 'Experiments in Civil Disobedience', is inspired by the sub-title of Gandhi's own autobiography, *The Story of My Experiments with Truth*. In many ways, it is a fitting one, for Gandhi's whole life was littered with experiments, whether relating to diet and vegetarianism; communal living, or sexual abstinence. They all represented Gandhi's struggles with his most intimate demons and were a challenge in the process of becoming the master of one's *karma* (destiny). Gandhi believed that deep social change could only result from individual spiritual transformation. Yet only by focusing on the historical reality of Gandhi's 'experiments in civil disobedience' in their concrete context will it be possible to examine and assess the effectiveness of his approach, and draw conclusions about his actual relationship to revolutionary politics.

1

Early Life: 1869–93

A small insignificant princely state in north-western India seems an unlikely place from where the father of Indian nationalism might emerge. Yet it was precisely such a place that was home to Gandhi's beginnings. Mohandas Karamchand Gandhi was born on 2 October 1869 into a middle-caste family of *Modh banias*, a trading and money-lending community who had a reputation for being thrifty and wily businessmen. His birthplace was the small town of Porbandar, in a semi-independent princely state – the Rana of Porbandar – on the south-west coast of Gujarat, where his father's family had been *diwans* (prime ministers/advisers) to the princes and kings.[1] Though clearly comfortable, his background was not aristocratic or upper class. He was not from a staunch nationalist family, like Jawaharlal Nehru, nor was he from the professional urban elite like Mohammad Ali Jinnah, founder of Pakistan. Though lacking a patrician background, Gandhi's childhood was firmly middle class and middle caste. Caste is a hereditary form of social class by which Hinduism prescribed the division of labour in India through a hierarchical system that has led to the subjugation of millions of people for centuries. The Hindi term *bania* broadly translates as merchants and traditionally refers to an occupational community comprising traders, bankers, money-lenders and dealers in grains or spices, and in modern times, numerous commercial enterprises. It has evolved from the *vaisyas* caste, which is third in hierarchy of the traditional caste structure, where, to use the Hindu lexicon of the *varna*, the educated priestly *brahmins* provided religious legitimacy to the warriors and rulers – the *kshatriyas* at the top – and both groups together with the farmer and merchant *vaisyas* hold supposed superiority over the mass of toilers including peasants (the *shudras*).

Gandhi was the youngest of four siblings and the product of his father Karamchand's fourth marriage. Karamchand had lost his first two wives whilst they were very young and each after giving birth to a daughter. Female mortality rates were high in provincial Porbandar and Karamchand would have felt obliged to marry again and produce sons, as was the custom and expectation across India and more globally. Sadly, for him his third marriage was childless and so Karamchand sought permission to take another wife, Putlibai, whom he married in 1857.[2]

The Princely State of Porbandar

Porbandar lies in the peninsula in western India and its coastline borders the Gulf of Kutch to the west, the Arabian Sea to the south and the Gulf of Khambhat to the south-east. The rest of the peninsula, chiefly in the east along the Gulf of Cambay, were districts ruled directly by the British as part of the Bombay Presidency. Instead of direct rule by the British, the Rana of Porbandar, with its capital as the harbour town of Porbandar, became a British Protectorate in 1809 and under the Raj, the princely state covered an area of 1,663 square kilometres comprising 106 villages with a population, in 1921, of over 100,000 people. It was not as opulent as Kashmir or Hyderabad states, but neither was it impoverished. It was one of the few princely states with a coastline, providing vital transportation links to the Arabian Peninsula and East and Southern Africa. Porbandar's strategic geography made it quite central as a site of transnational migrations as historically, the sea provided great routes for trade, pilgrimage and diplomatic missions.

Porbandar was one of some two hundred small princely states. This backwater contained tiny kingdoms, the size of many contemporary Gulf States, which were ruled by local potentates who acknowledged British suzerainty in return for local sovereignty. As British Protectorates, they ceded responsibilities for defence, external affairs and communications, but exercised relative autonomy over civil and court governance. Two-fifths of India was comprised of such princely or 'Native' states. This region was home to a large number of communities, castes and settlements and the agency's headquarters were at Rajkot, the town where the Political Agent used to reside and from where he reported to the Political Department office in Bombay.

As a princely state, Porbandar was ruled by a feudal despotic dynasty of Rajputs called Jethwas who claimed martial and spiritual lineage from a range of deities in the epic *Ramayana*. These Rajput Hindu states originated in the thirteenth century through a mixture of warfare and domination, but also through incorporation, adaptation and evolving claims of genealogy and kinship ritual. It is precisely because these were evolving social and political formations that they were judiciously incorporated into sixteenth- and seventeenth-century Mughal administration and military structures and later found accommodation with the British Empire.[3] It is tempting to think that princely states were either mere puppets of British imperial domination or represented some indigenous autonomous entity. In reality, the truth lies somewhere in between. To be sure, they were feudal polities that exercised considerable power and enjoyed autonomy within their domains, able to discipline their ministers on the whim of the royal household. However, they did lose major privileges and the British and nationalist leaders were somewhat ambivalent in their dealings with princely states. British officials saw them as loyal military allies whilst denouncing them as autocrats; praised them as natural leaders of their subjects but also chided them as profligate playboys. Above all, the British envied, admired and took full advantage of their lavish hospitality. Likewise, Indian nationalists, initially pointed to native princely kingdoms as evidence of effective indigenous government. Some were happy to seek their financial backing for political organisations and collaborated with them during constitutional negotiations. However, they were also lambasted as – in the words of Nehru – 'very backward … and in the feudal age'.[4] What this ambivalence demonstrates is that indigenous polities were conveniently used for whatever purpose suited either the British or Indian nationalists.

In spite of feudal pretensions, princely states were not static. Long before Europeans arrived in India, dynamic processes of state formation and transformation had been under way as in any other part of the world. War, famine, invasion all contributed over several centuries and more to new and different political formations.

Similarly, the onset of British rule affected developments within these semi-autonomous entities. As such, they constituted continuing processes of state formation right through to independence, when all were eventually incorporated into the successor states of India and Pakistan. The British had no clear policy, but officers acted pragmatically and/or opportunistically, depending on circumstances. The general pattern, however, was from treaties to subsidiary alliances to indirect rule. Consequently, an intellectual framework of indirect rule was constructed to provide legitimacy for British imperial rule within an indigenous framework.[5] British officials felt keenly the need to produce documents which would explain what they had been doing and what precedents they could follow. As a result, imperial rituals such as the Assemblage of 1877 and the Durbars of 1903 and 1911 played a significant role as British officers attempted both to express and to create the desired political order. They wanted a 'feudal hierarchy' and to set the princes off as 'natural' leaders, who were to support the paramount power and benefit the imperial state economically.[6] Accordingly, the process of compiling documents and forming legal arguments had the advantage of providing the imperial government with an inexpensive means of governing areas of relatively low agricultural productivity and often inaccessible populations.

As British rule deepened, it used a combination of co-option, repression and setting religious and ethnic groups off against each other – tactics varied according to situation and switched sides as to who was favoured at any particular time. British Orientalist constructions rooted in colonial sociology impacted on mapping and census-taking. The latter played a critical role in stimulating ethnic mobilisation in the production of censuses, gazetteers, religious writings and newspapers. But princes also contributed to ethnic mobilisation through patronage of caste histories and religious translations. Caste, religious and linguistic identities became more tightly defined in the princely states. Yet Porbandar, like most princely states, had been unscathed by the great revolt of 1857 – the high point of Indian resistance to British rule in the nineteenth century – and remained loyal to the East India Company and its feudatory elites. It was not until the late 1920s that local popular movements began to emerge with the formation of the All-India States Peoples' Conference (AISPC).

Gandhi's Family Background

Being born into a *diwan* family provided a certain status for the Gandhi clan and, though not wealthy, they were able to command respect and courtly airs from the local population. Growing up in a princely state resulted in Gandhi having very little contact with or experience of direct British imperial rule. This had the advantage in that it instilled a deep conviction in him that Indians could and should rule themselves. But it also shielded him from the full might of the empire and its oppressive state apparatus. A sense of family loyalty to the principality but also an independent spirit can be gleaned from Joseph Doke's 1909 biographical sketch, as related to him by Gandhi in 1908–09. Gandhi's grandfather, Uttamchand, was dismissed for apparently displeasing the Queen Regent, and obtained sanctuary in neighbouring Junagadh state. The *Nawab*[7] here was astounded when Uttamchand gave a salute with his left hand, a sign viewed as disrespectful and punishable by death. But when asked to explain himself by the *Nawab*, the elder Gandhi replied, 'in spite of all that he had suffered, he kept his right hand for Porbandar still.' According to this story, the *Nawab* of Junagadh was impressed by Gandhi's patriotism and continued to give him protection until the brouhaha blew over and Uttamchand was recalled to the Porbandar court.[8]

A similar story of bravery was recounted by Gandhi about his father, Karamchand. Like the grandfather, the father too had been dismissed by the Porbandar court and moved his family to Rajkot. All princely regents were subordinate to the British agent in Kathiawar agency and this could lead to ministers being dismissed under their orders. Karamchand had apparently heard a rude remark made by the British agent about his prince and took objection to it. The agent demanded an apology that Karamchand refused. His penalty was to be arrested and detained for a few hours. Such an affront to British authority was unthinkable in parochial Gujarat and caused much excitement. After a few hours, the agent relented and the apology waived.[9]

According to Doke's account, both the grandfather and father displayed acts of great courage that were the epitome of what was to become 'passive resistance', and thus left a lasting impression upon the young Gandhi (see Figure 1).

Karamchand, though clearly a loving father, does appear to be quite a remote figure in Gandhi's childhood. But family life also included people from other faith communities. Jain monks, family friends who were Muslim and Parsis, were all regular visitors to the Gandhi home and his father would 'listen to them always with respect, and often with interest'. This Gandhi recalls is how 'I got an early grounding in toleration for all branches of Hinduism and sister religions.'[10]

Gandhi's mother Putlibai was a pious woman who though a caste Hindu, was part of the *Pranami* sect, a reforming tradition that fused aspects of Hindu mythology with Sufi Islam and aspects of emergent

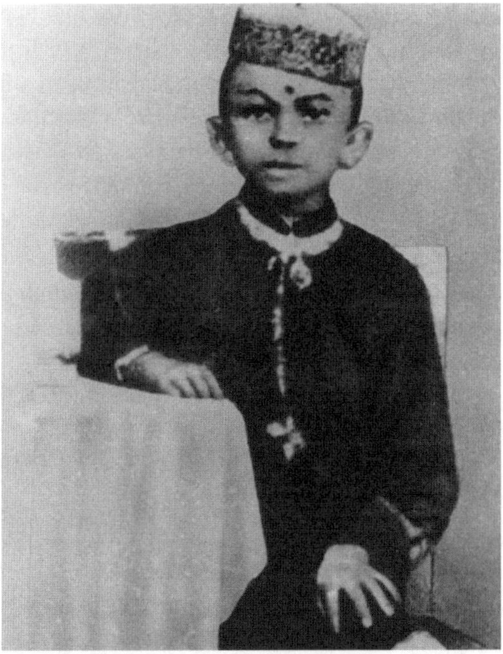

Figure 1 Young Gandhi, at the age of 7, in 1876. It is the only existing picture of Gandhi as a child.

Source: Wikimedia Commons, the free media repository.

Sikhism. As well as providing a synthesising component, this sect baulked at traditional hierarchical religious dogma and placed great emphasis on charity and peaceful coexistence, as well as chastity and abstinence from meat, alcohol, tobacco and any other intoxicating drugs. She spent much of her time in observing fasts and prayers. Her comparative saintliness is emphasised repeatedly in Gandhi's own account of his mother, as well as by Doke describing her as the 'Holy of Holies'.[11] Putlibai was keen to provide charitable support to the sick and needy and so she opened her house to ensure alms or a cup of whey were provided daily to any person in need. If anyone was ill, she was on hand to administer and look after them. Though these acts of charity appear to be applicable to all the community, and no discrimination was applied in terms of religion, interestingly, Doke's warm and affectionate account only mentions her care applying to 'Brahmin or Sudra';[12] the 'untouchables' – those landless agricultural labourers whose work was seen as so dirty that they were deemed below even the lowest caste – are conspicuous by their absence. This in no way implies that Putlibai was anti-low caste or untouchable but it does indicate the societal and cultural limits of her reforming sect traditions. Nevertheless, family life emphasised religious tolerance, simplicity and strong moral values. Gandhi had a close relationship with his mother. She was warm, affectionate and very protective. Her liberal attitude impacted upon him. The deep emotional bond Gandhi had for his mother is evident in her final advice to him before leaving for London, and he vowed to abjure from wine, women and meat, thus indicating Gandhi's desire to be a dutiful, obedient and respectful son.

If Porbandar was the Gandhi ancestral family home, Karamchand's nuclear family made their home in Rajkot, some 125 miles away. It took five days to travel between the two by ox-wagon and so return visits were few and far between, and reserved only for special occasions. Both the distance and mode of travel underlines the relative isolation and backwardness of this region. Porbandar was a unitary princely statelet, but Rajkot was divided into the old and new town. The old wing was governed by the *Sahib* [young prince] of Rajkot and the site of the Gandhi home, whereas the new town was located within the Bombay presidency and so under British rule. If

Porbandar had the sea and was quite picturesque if parochial, Rajkot was not blessed with such scenery. It had 'more of the squalor of the Orient about it',[13] but its proximity to the Bombay presidency meant it had better transport links to major cities and the education system was far superior to anything available in Porbandar state. Gandhi was schooled in Rajkot, initially at a vernacular school and then at the Alfred High, an English-medium school where he successfully matriculated at age 17–18.

Gandhi was not a particularly scholarly or intellectual student. He professed to having 'a distaste for any reading beyond my school books'[14] and accordingly did not have any high regard for his own academic ability.[15] He did not excel in the classroom or on the sports field, though Rajmohan Gandhi, his great-grandson, suggests that this view comes from a misreading of his 'self-deprecating' autobiography. Out of 38 students who had passed the high school entrance examination, Gandhi was one of only two students in his year to matriculate.[16] He also occasionally won prizes and scholarships, and following graduation he enrolled at the Samaldas College in Bhavnagar, where he stayed for one term before travelling to London.

His childhood was typical of most children in that he was playful, mischievous and sufficiently curious to try new experiences. Experiments with meat eating were one such example. Gandhi's best friends at high school were Muslims and Parsis, and with them he engaged in furtive meat eating, believing this is what made the English physically strong and able to dominate Indians. As an observant caste Hindu, who was vegetarian, this proved to be a mortifying experience for Gandhi, as the texture and taste were difficult for his palate to take. But he continued to participate in preparing tasty meat snacks that became nightly feasts to be enjoyed in secret, for 'it was [a] feast … and it was enjoyed.'[17] One of his close friends, Sheikh Mehtab, also took Gandhi to a brothel one day. Again, Gandhi's curiosity got the better of him as on entering the brothel he 'was struck blind and dumb in this den of vice', rebuffing the prostitutes' advances and was promptly ejected from the brothel.[18] One other childhood experience scarred him and that was theft. Aged 15, he had taken a gold bracelet from his brother, Laxmidas or Karsandas, in order to help clear a debt for that sibling. Mortified and guilt-ridden, he decided to come clean and make a full confession to his father. But he could not do this directly and so he wrote of his wrongdoing in a letter to his father. He fully expected to be punished but his embarrassment and humiliation were complete when he saw his father's eyes swell up as he tore the note and realised that there would be no conventional penalty for him as his father accepted the sin. Gandhi's own account states this is when he learnt the lesson and art of *ahimsa*.[19]

As the youngest son after his father's death, he was chosen to be chief breadwinner for the family. This meant studying law abroad. The decision to send him to London was not an easy one for the family. It entailed a breach in custom and ritual that some high-caste Hindus held dear. To travel such great distances and to cross the 'black waters' (the open ocean) was akin to a state of apostasy for high-caste Hindus. Reassurances and ceremonial blessings were sought and after much fracas, granted. He was of course married before embarking on his journey to London. In 1883, at the age of 13, he underwent a classic arranged marriage to Kasturbai, who was 14. The children were betrothed at the age of eight and had no say in the matter – it was an arrangement between families – but Kasturbai did spend a little time in Rakjot before the wedding and the bride and groom did have time to play together as children. This was a traditional ceremony befitting caste Hindus. Gandhi had become a father by the time he was 16, but the baby only survived a few days. The couple were more fortunate after that as his first son, Harilal was born in 1888. In Doke's account, Gandhi initially approached the British administrator in Porbandar, Sir F.S.P. Lely for help towards funding his law studies. Hoping that his family's history of loyal service would predispose the administrator to grant a scholarship for him, Gandhi sought an interview with him. He was turned down curtly, as Lely advised him to 'graduate first, then you can come to me, and I will consider it.'[20] It should be evident that Gandhi's world was both parochial and international. As Yasmin Khan observes, he was able to look outwards to broader oceanic networks and inwards to localised pre-colonial traditions.[21] These insights would prove to be invaluable to the young Gandhi as he embarked upon his first journey abroad.

In Victorian London

'The home of philosophers and poets, the very centre of civilisation'[22] is how Gandhi perceived London. Coming from a conservative, small-town family, it is not difficult to imagine his excitement when he was sent there in 1888 to train as a barrister. In 1890, there were only 207 Indians in London and Gandhi initially found life quite isolating and perplexing. He was living alone, having to manage his own expenses, pay for lodgings, wear a new set of clothes, familiarise himself with new and strange smells of food, and mingle with people whose mores were quite alien to him. He did not have an army of servants, as he lacked a patrician urban background, had not been raised in a Western liberal environment, did not have the benefit of English public schooling or Oxbridge, and so did not possess the self-confidence of an upper-class Nehru or wealthy Jinnah. When he docked at Tilbury (not Southampton, as mentioned in his autobiography) dressed in a white flannel suit that no one else was wearing, he stood out and his self-consciousness and embarrassment mortified him. Even on board ship, he had taken his meals in his cabin, as eating with cutlery, or examining a menu that he could not make head or tail of, were a challenge to him and he faced constant embarrassment over his vegetarianism and poor command of English. On top of this, he had contracted ringworm. He travelled with two other Indians, one of whom was a doctor. They took the train together to Fenchurch Street Station; while on the train, Gandhi picked up the doctor's top hat and stroked it against the grain, as it were, and 'disturbed the fur'. The doctor responded 'somewhat angrily'. This, Gandhi later wrote, was his 'first lesson in European etiquette'. The doctor explained that in England he should not, as he might in India, touch people's possessions, or talk loudly, or ask questions of a new acquaintance.[23] The doctor then prescribed him acetic acid for ringworm and suggested he move out of his hotel immediately, and into an English home.

Wearing western suits and closed shoes proved enormously challenging. Gandhi really was a fish out of water in many respects. In order to overcome these handicaps, Gandhi decided to turn himself into a typical English gentleman. He bought his clothes at the Army and Navy Store, evening suits from Bond Street, learnt to wear a tie, and sported a double watch-chain of gold. Not content with this, he began to take lessons in dancing, French and elocution. In spite of his shyness, he spent a huge amount on clothes that his budget could not take, and a revealing vanity typical of teenagers was clearly evident as he 'wasted ten minutes every day before a huge mirror, watching myself arranging my tie and parting my hair in the correct fashion'.[24] In these endeavours, Gandhi found it hard to remain true to his vows to his mother of abjuring from meat, wine and women. He was awkward in his dealings with English women, such as his landlady's daughter, whom he found difficult to engage with. Initially, he did not talk about his wife or the fact that he was a father, but his shyness kept him from fooling around with young women and eventually he did own up to his marriage and fatherhood. He managed to avoid alcohol and intimate dealings with women, but his diet and vegetarianism proved to be troublesome for a while.

Acculturation aside, Gandhi was exposed to two main influences in London that would begin to shape his philosophical outlook. Though London was the heart of the British Empire, it was also home to a generation of counter-cultural critics, who often followed a non-conformist, semi-anarchist, and bohemian alternative life-style. Victorian London may have been the imperial capital, but it was full of urban squalor, poverty and poor sanitation. The industrial age had brought about mass social change, with many people migrating from small towns and rural areas to large cities. Urbanisation, greater literacy and mass culture were producing a fervent atmosphere in cosmopolitan London. The imperial centre was the site of transnational debates with lively discussion groups and societies debating the great questions of their age. With an increasing print press, these democratic spaces became vehicles for animated debates on women's suffrage, unrest in Ireland and the colonies, and the politics of vegetarianism.

Vegetarianism

Gandhi eventually found a vegetarian restaurant on Farringdon Street. It was here that he came across Henry Salt's book *Plea for Vegetarianism*, published in 1886 by the Vegetarian Society. This transformed his views on diet and food. His vow of abjuring meat was no longer a vow given to his illiterate mother, but had become a philosophic moral principle that he had *chosen*. He became a member of the Vegetarian Society, the goals of which were not mere dietary concerns but to 'seek the conditions necessary to reach a human ideal that valued the spiritual, physical, mental and moral aspects of human life' (see Figure 2). He was attracted by the ideas of the strong protecting the weak – hence his belief that human supremacy over the animal world was not about control and hunting, but the mutual benefit of all living things. It was also here that he encountered the view that eating was not designed for enjoyment but for survival and therefore he concluded that 'man was not meant to be a cooking but a frugivorous animal.'[25]

Figure 2 Gandhi with the Vegetarian Society, 1891. The photo was taken in Portsmouth at one of their May Meetings. Back row (l–r): Rev. James Clark, E. Dolby Shelton, W. Chudley, William Harrison, Peter Foxcroft, Joseph Knight. Middle row (l–r): Miss May Yates, G. Cosens Prior, Mrs William Harrison and Mrs Peter Foxcroft. Front row (l–r): T.T. Mozumdar, Josiah Oldfield, Mohandas K. Gandhi.

Source: *The Vegetarian Messenger and Health Review*, September 1936; British Library, London, UK© British Library Board. All rights reserved/Bridgeman Images.

Gandhi's membership of this society provided introduction into the circle of middle-class non-conformists and dissenters of late nineteenth-century England. He became friends with Henry Salt, who introduced him to the writings of the American philosopher, Henry David Thoreau, author of the seminal 1849 essay 'Civil Disobedience', originally referred to as 'Resistance to Civil Government'. Thoreau was an abolitionist and environmentalist; he was influenced by transcendentalism as a means of personal salvation and renowned for his espousal of simple living.[26] His opposition to the Mexican-American War and slavery led to his refusing to pay taxes to what he labelled an unjust government. He was imprisoned for this, but still refused to pay. Thoreau's famous essay articulated vehement opposition to the American government and questioned the necessity of a state. His essay would have a transformative impact on Gandhi as he became a member of the executive committee of the Vegetarian Society and made his very tentative debut at public speaking. Being shy and diffident, Gandhi's initial forays into public speaking were awkward and stilted. He was more successful at writing articles on Indian vegetarians for the newspaper.[27] Here he provided some in-depth accounts of regional diets in India and how it was that many Indians lived on just 1 *pie* (1/3*d*) per day.

Gandhi used the pages of the *Vegetarian* to argue against child marriage, declaring how the 'wretched custom of infant marriages and its attendant evils' were responsible for Indian weakness.[28] He also believed that Indian weakness was the result of moral slackness that required inner regeneration. Members of the Vegetarian Society believed the consumption of flesh contaminated the human body with violence and the only political response was total abstinence from a meat diet. Vegetarianism was aligned to the advocacy of temperance, and concerns over the lack of a nutritional diet for manual labourers and the poor. This appealed to the young Gandhi as it fused with his childhood caste beliefs whilst expanding his scope for further thinking on these matters. Now a vegetarian by conviction, he shared a flat briefly with Josiah Oldfield, with whom he helped found the Bayswater branch of the Vegetarian Society.

In London, many Indians of all faith backgrounds adapted to cultural and dietary conditions in order to fit in, and thus consumed meats of all types, drank alcohol and dressed as English gentlemen. But Gandhi felt he had wasted some three months and the little money he had on acclimatising to English mores. He abandoned the elocution and dancing classes and sold his violin. And in matters of diet, he became a steadfast vegetarian. An early measure of Gandhi's commitment is provided by the following anecdote. He was invited to a fine restaurant in Holborn with other Indian students. The friend who had invited him was the same man who had taken Gandhi under his wing since their journey to England and had advised him on all manner of things English, including telling the young, 'country bumpkin' from Porbandar that he had no business coming to London if he was committed to irrational, superstitious oaths. Hoping that modesty and manners would fix these parochial tendencies, the friend observed the young law student. As the soup course was served, Gandhi asked the waiter what was in it. His friend was so embarrassed that he said, 'You are not fit for decent society; if you cannot act like a gentleman you had better go.' And Gandhi went.[29] This example too illustrates a certain self-sufficiency and determination in relation to what were fast becoming deep convictions.

Gandhi would return again to the Vegetarian Society on his trip to London in 1931, where he was invited to address a meeting. Here he made the case for morality as the basis for vegetarianism.[30] For him, vegetarianism was not to be adopted if it was purely for health or medical reasons: 'If anybody said that I should die if I did not take beef tea or mutton, even on medical advice, I would prefer death. That is the basis of my vegetarianism.'[31] In childhood, he had absorbed the common fallacy that a meat diet had made the British invincible and Indians weak, but in London he discovered the opposite.

The vegetarian movement was largely white, male and middle class. Henry Salt was an Old Etonian born in India. But it was also part of a larger movement of radical reformers who were anti-urban, anti-industrial and critical of the commercialisation of Victorian Britain. They were concerned with nature conservation and the protection of the environment. They were bourgeois and interested in change through individual effort and moral fibre. It was this individualism and the simplicity of their message that appealed to Gandhi.

Theosophy

The other group that was important to Gandhi's evolution was the Theosophical Society. Founded in New York in 1875 by Madame Helena Petrovna Blavatsky, it drew heavily on Hinduism and Buddhism for its intellectual heritage, encouraging the reading of Sanskrit texts and seeking to reconcile new developments in Western science with organised religions. Blavatsky thought all religions of the world had sprung from the same source and therefore a cross-fertilisation of aspects of these traditions could produce new and inventive ways of being. In this sense, Theosophists offered a modernised reformed form of Hinduism fused with elements of Christianity and other belief systems, a sort of scientific spirituality. Thus far, Gandhi had viewed religion as a series of superstitions and meaningless rituals. On reading Blavatsky's *The Key to Theosophy*, Gandhi observed how it 'stimulated in me the desire to read books on Hinduism' and disabused him 'of the notion fostered by missionaries that Hinduism was rife with superstition'.[32] He was introduced to the *Bhagavad Gita* and other religious texts that he had never read or given much thought to before. Two English brothers whom Gandhi had met through the Theosophical Society were interested in learning and understanding the meaning of the *Gita*, which they had read. They were both familiar with Edwin Arnold's poetic rendering of the *Gita* – *The Song Celestial* – and they invited Gandhi to read this with them. They hoped Gandhi would be able to do this and to provide detailed explanation of these texts. In the attempt to do so, Gandhi realised that he was not able to explain anything. He felt ashamed for not having read the classic poem either in Sanskrit or in Gujarati. And he was mortified to tell them that he had not read the *Gita*, but that he would gladly read it with them in spite of his limited knowledge of Sanskrit.[33] So it was that Gandhi set about a close reading and study of the *Gita*, which opened him to a 'new view of life … that touched my spirit as perhaps it can only touch a child of the East; I had found at last, as I believed, the light I needed.'[34] Gandhi also read Edwin Arnold's *Light of Asia*, with 'even greater interest'.[35]

At the same time, Gandhi read the Old Testament, which he found nauseating. However, the New Testament enthralled him, especially the Sermon on the Mount. The combination of these texts pointed to an alternative way of being religious, one that synthesised a variety of texts and influences but simultaneously emphasised a similar message: that renunciation was the highest form of religion, the imperative of offering the other cheek and love to an opponent. This curious mixture of Christian suffering, Hindu mythology and Jainism-inspired asceticism and denial would come to epitomise the adult Gandhi. Through such exposure and engagement with European social reformers and non-conformists, Gandhi began to conceive of how religious ideas could be expressed in different ways and for a much wider use than mere personal faith.

In between immersing himself in the study of the law and religious texts, Gandhi took a short trip to Paris during the Great Exhibition in 1890. Gandhi was not impressed by the Eiffel Tower which he felt had 'no art' despite its tremendous feat of modern engineering. For Gandhi, it represented 'the toy of the Exhibition. So long as we are children we are attracted by toys, and the Tower was a good demonstration of the fact that we are all children attracted by trinkets.'[36] But he was quite taken by churches and began to see that in Catholicism, 'all this kneeling and prayer could not be mere superstition.' Instead worshippers 'were fired with genuine devotion and they worshipped not stone, but the divinity of which it was symbolic. I have an impression that I felt then that by this worship they were not detracting from, but increasing, the glory of God.'[37] Gandhi's engagement with religious ideas in London and his encounters with European non-conformist Christians would have a fundamental impact upon his notions of theology and his evolving political outlook.

Conclusion

Gandhi's London experience demonstrates that he was not fearful of borrowing 'western' ideas and that 'Gandhism' far from being a uniquely Indian creed is the product of contemporary transnational debates taking place in metropolitan London. It fused global concerns of mysticism, non-conformism and moral indignation wrapped up in a philosophy of personal salvation. London represented a free metropolis in which to engage in lively debates on the impact of urbanisation and industrialisation, demands for suffrage for women and workers, Ireland and the colonies. The participants in these discussions came from a range of places and backgrounds, and brought a variety of ideas and issues to the table as new ideas challenged old ones. Gandhi's writings on his time in London are important for what they tell us about his evolving ideas and capacity for self-reflection. They are the product of accumulated experience and exposure to a wealth of contemporary radical ideas that posed serious questions about the oppressive nature of society. The urban blight of modern civilisation would become a central theme in Gandhi's thought. The London years demonstrate the extent to which Gandhi was able to transcend earlier limitations on experience and free thinking and begin to explore remedies for a stained world.

On completing his law studies, Gandhi was called to the bar in 1891 and set sail for home, armed with his professional qualification and Bond Street suits, but also with his new-found zeal. Gandhi's affection for London never withered. In 1909, he admitted to Doke, that 'even now, next to India, I would rather live in London than any other place in the world.'[38] Porbandar, however, proved to be a dead end for the young barrister, as he failed to secure employment to support his family. Instead, he went to Bombay to practice Indian law but again with little success. In Porbandar, he was the victim of his own naïvete. Unaccustomed to small-town politics, on one occasion, he called on the British agent to intercede in a case involving one of his brothers. In London, Gandhi had enjoyed friendships and made acquaintances with many Europeans, including with this officer. However, Gandhi was dismissed with the abruptness in which British officials excelled and found that 'an officer on leave was not the same as an officer on duty.'[39] Mortified, Gandhi was advised by his fellow barristers to 'pocket the insult'. There would be many more insults to pocket, as Gandhi accepted an offer to act as a legal adviser to an Indian firm in South Africa. He was provided with a first-class fare and £105, which was more than enough to keep his family whilst he went away for what he assumed would be no more than a year.

2

South Africa and the Birth of *Satyagraha*: 1893–1915

Richard Attenborough's 1982 film *Gandhi* has the famous scene of a 23-year-old Gandhi being forcefully ejected from a first-class compartment by a ticket inspector on his way from Durban to Pretoria in 1893. After being humiliated at Pietermaritzburg, Gandhi finally arrived in the Transvaal, where he had to take a coach, sitting on the box with the guard. On this occasion, a big Dutchman insisted on Gandhi not only giving up his seat to him as he wanted to smoke, but that Gandhi sit at his feet! Gandhi refused and was beaten by the Dutchman until fellow passengers intervened, allowing him to continue his journey. An indication of his naïvete regarding white racism – which was far more intense in South Africa than in either India or Britain – can be seen by the fact that when he arrived in Johannesburg he went straight to the Grand National Hotel to find a room and was of course told there was 'no room' for the likes of him.[1] In spite of these humiliations, he later claimed the Pietermaritzburg episode to be the 'most creative experience' of his life.[2] This was one of numerous racist insults that Gandhi encountered, as racial segregation, discrimination and violence characterised the lives of all non-whites in South Africa.

Gandhi was in South Africa because he had been commissioned by the Gujarati firm of Dada Abdulla and Sons, to represent them in a case against their cousin, another Gujarati trading company located in Pretoria, Transvaal. On his arrival at Durban port, Gandhi made the following observation in his autobiography that 'Indians were not held in much respect. I could not fail to notice a sort of snobbishness about the manner in which those who knew Abdulla Sheth behaved towards him, and it stung me.'[3] But Gandhi had not previously experienced direct racism in London, where he had been accepted without prejudice in the circles in which he moved. Both his childhood and his three years in London had sheltered him from the worst excesses of imperial racism at home and abroad. To be treated as a 'coolie' (a common term for an Indian labourer) barrister shook Gandhi to his foundations. He firmly believed that as subjects of the empire, Indians had a right to equal treatment before the law. And coming from an ancient and proud tradition, he was the equal of whites.

By the time Gandhi arrived in Durban on 24 May 1893, South Africa was already home to an established Indian community made up predominantly of indentured labourers and their descendants. After the abolition of slavery in the British Empire in 1834, the practice of indentured labour was utilised widely across British colonies to replace the loss of slave labour. These labourers were used to work the sugar plantations of Fiji and Mauritius in the Indian Ocean region, to Guyana and the plantations of Trinidad, Jamaica and Barbados in the Western Hemisphere. Between 1860 and 1891, the British colony of Natal was home to 41,000 Indians. By comparison, Europeans numbered 47,000 and Africans 456,000. More Indian migrants arrived to service the ever-increasing rapacious desire for cheap labour and by 1904 Natal had just over 100,000 Indians. A smaller minority of Indians arrived in the Transvaal, not as indentured labour but as merchants and traders. Though their population was much smaller, by 1904 there were 11,000 Indians in the Transvaal, compared to 229,000 Europeans and 945,000 Africans.[4]

Indentured labourers came predominantly from the Madras Presidency and were Tamil and Telegu speaking. The majority of this labour force was Hindu, but some were Christian and were referred to as 'coolies'. They came on short-term contracts for five years which could be extended up to a further two years as contract labour. After this, they were free to either return home or to live and work in British territories within South Africa. While Chinese labour was also imported under the system of indenture, it was mostly Indians who furnished this labour source. The second group of Indians to arrive in Natal came from Gujarat. They were predominantly Muslim merchants; similar trading groups also came from Bombay, comprised of Parsis and Hindus, as well as Muslims. This community was referred to as 'Arabs', being predominantly Muslim, but they formed a group of what were termed 'passenger migrants' as they paid their own travel fare to South Africa. In addition to being urban, they were educated, professional groups engaged in commerce, law, journalism and the medical practice.

The class differences between the Indian populace was a major cause of friction for both Indians and also European settlers. The latter resented Indian traders as competitors for the retail trade and those former indentured workers who chose to stay were seen as competitors in the labour market and so all were labelled 'coolies' or 'samis', an Afrikaans vulgarisation of *Swami* meaning 'teacher' or 'leader', and an epithet sometimes thrown at educated Indians. The economic basis of this antipathy framed racial animosity towards all Indians, who were despised as outsiders with alien customs of language, religion, marriage practices and food. Middle-class Indians from Gujarat insisted on calling themselves 'Arabs', or Bombay Parsis preferred 'Persian' to try to avoid the pejorative 'coolie', but to no avail as Gandhi's train experience demonstrates. Racism was also used to label all Indians unhygienic, responsible for importing disease and spreading unsanitary conditions. Demands to halt the 'Asiatic horde' were reflected in letters and newspaper articles of the time which demanded that 'coolie immigration has to be stopped', and insisted that if immigrants and cultivators were to be permitted, 'we want them white ... let us not become suffocated with the native scum of the streets of Bombay and Madras.'[5]

Building on his experience on writing for the *Vegetarian*, Gandhi fired off an earnest but typical response to the *Natal Advertiser*:

> It seems, on the whole, that their simplicity, their total abstinence from intoxicants, their peaceful and, above all, their business-like and frugal habits, which should serve as a recommendation, are really at the bottom of all this contempt and hatred of the poor Indian traders. And they are British subjects. Is this Christian-like, is this fair play, is this justice, is this civilization?[6]

When Gandhi first visited the Durban courthouse with his employer Dada Abdulla in 1893, the local magistrate asked him to remove his turban. Gandhi refused on the grounds that removing headgear was a sign of disrespect in India, and left the court in protest. The *Natal Advertiser* reported the incident under the banner headline: 'An Unwelcome Visitor':

> An Indian entered the Court House yesterday afternoon and took a seat at the horseshoe. He was well-dressed ... He entered the Court without removing his head-covering or salaaming, and the Magistrate looked at him with disapproval. The new arrival was courteously asked his business, and he replied that he was an English barrister. He did not attempt to present his credentials, and, on returning to the horseshoe was quietly told that the proper course for him to pursue, before taking up his position at the Bar, was to gain admission to the Supreme Court.[7]

Clearly just a curtain-raiser to the more famous train incident, Gandhi was becoming rapidly and acutely aware of the petty, deep racist indignities that Indians confronted. This was further compounded by his increasing self-belief and national pride in being Indian. The English Bar had trained him well as he eventually won the case and concluded matters between two warring cousins amicably. He was apparently all set to return home to India. But Gandhi remained and turned to political activism, and we will now examine the three significant campaigns that he waged in South Africa which demonstrate the radical and insurrectionary nature of his activism, as well as pointing to some of the emerging complexities and contradictions of what would soon become known as 'Gandhism'.

Gandhi's First Campaign: 1894–96

White resentment at Indians compelled politicians to pass legislation aimed at containing the 'merchant menace'. The Natal government promptly introduced two bills restricting the freedom of Indians. The Immigration Law Amendment Bill stated that all Indians had to return to India at the end of a five-year indenture period or, be re-indentured for a further two years. If they refused, £3 annual tax had to be paid. According to Arnold, this was equivalent to six months' wages for plantation workers, so was a heavy disincentive to stay.[8] The bill came into law in 1895. A Franchise Amendment Bill also made an appearance in 1894, designed to limit the number of Indians who had the vote.

Although there were only 300 of them, in comparison to 10,000 white voters, the Bill caused outrage among the Indian leadership. They decided to contest the measure by any means available to them. On the eve of his intended departure, Abdulla hosted a farewell party for Gandhi at his home in Grey Street in Durban. The guests at the farewell dinner, mostly Indian merchants, appealed to Gandhi to stay and fight the legislation on their behalf, offering to pay him an annual retainer to do so. Gandhi wrote later, 'The farewell party was turned into a working committee ... thus God laid the foundations of my life in South Africa and sowed the seed of the fight for national self-respect.'[9] Before the night was out, Gandhi had drawn up a petition and set up a temporary committee. Within a fortnight the petition had 10,000 signatures and the plight of Indians was also publicised within India and Britain with the *Times of India* and the London *Times* both supporting the right of Indians to stay on in South Africa if they wished, and to vote.

Gandhi's first campaign was to demand the retention of the Indian franchise. He played a prominent role, as he was a talented letter-writer and meticulous planner. He was tasked with compiling all petitions, arranging meetings with politicians and addressing letters to newspapers. His methods were constitutional and reflected the professional middle-class community he served and identified with. In June 1894, he helped mobilise Natal's Indians to petition the legislature to retain the franchise. He sent letters to the Governor, the Legislative Council and the Secretary of State for the Colonies. As part of this campaign, he wrote and published a pamphlet on Indian grievances to help raise public awareness in India and hopefully to force both London and Delhi to intervene in the Natal legislation. The pamphlet documents in painstaking detail the affronts to Indians at the hands of Europeans in South Africa: 'The man in the street hates him, curses him, spits upon him, and often pushes him off the foot-path.' He informs his readers how the local press refers to Indians as 'parasites', 'wily, wretched semi-barbarous Asiatics', and as 'black and lean and a long way from clean, which they call the accursed Hindoo'.[10] This document was signed by the same group of people at the farewell party indicating those whose grievances and interests he was championing. Indentured labourers do not get a mention.

Gandhi travelled back to India to meet with nationalist leaders and petition the Indian government. This embarrassed the British government in London and as the petition was presented to the Colonial Secretary, Lord Ripon, he had the bill temporarily set aside. Nevertheless, a law was passed in 1896 by the Natal authorities, who had been granted self-government in 1893 and thus disqualified voters who were not of European origin. Despite this setback, by 1896, Gandhi had established himself as a political leader and on his return from India that year he decided to take his family back with him to South Africa. And so he set sail from Bombay aboard the SS *Courtland* with his wife, Kasturbai, and now his two sons, Harilal and Manilal. When the ship docked, Gandhi and 800 fellow passengers were kept from disembarking for nearly a month as a result of daily dockside demonstrations and government quarantine regulations. As white hostility against Indians was verging on the violent, Gandhi was assaulted by a group of protesters as he tried to leave the port. The intervention of the Durban police commissioner's wife saved him from serious injury and he had to be smuggled from her home disguised as a policeman in order to prevent further incidents. In Gandhi's absence, anti-Indian sentiment had intensified in Natal to prevent further Indian immigration. This resulted in further legislation stipulating that prospective immigrants had to possess £25, speak and write English, and also empowered municipal authorities to refuse trading licences on the ground of 'insanitation'. Authorities began refusing to grant licences to any Indian applicants, and many merchants accused Gandhi of having pushed the authorities too far.

In spite of the defeat, the formation of the Natal Indian Committee on 22 August 1894 marked the birth of the first permanent political organisation to strive to maintain and protect the rights of Indians in South Africa. This committee eventually evolved into the Natal Indian Congress (NIC) and in June 1903 Gandhi launched the journal *Indian*

Figure 3 Gandhi as a lawyer in South Africa, 1906.
Source: Wikimedia Commons, the free media repository.

Opinion in Durban. Both were essentially vehicles for the Gujarati and Bombay elites with whom Gandhi identified. The NIC had an annual membership fee of £3 and even though *Indian Opinion* was initially published in Tamil, Hindi and Gujarati as well as English, it only enjoyed about 900 subscribers; three years after its launch, the Tamil and Hindi sections ceased to publish, clearly indicating poor readership but also underlining the narrow and elite nature of its audience. Nonetheless, Gandhi's political involvement, philosophy and influence grew. He had begun to attract the ire of Natal's white population and in 1903 decided to move his legal business to Johannesburg, where he gained in stature as a campaigner for the rights of the Asian community. Though many Indians continued to experience material, social and political deprivation, this was in stark contrast to Gandhi's own material circumstances that improved dramatically from his position in 1893. Arnold points to how a penniless barrister went on to earn an annual income of £5,000 with a large household in Durban; by February 1903, he had a law office in Johannesburg with two clerks and a secretary (see Figure 3).[11]

Gandhi's Second Campaign: 1906–09

A second campaign came in 1906 in Transvaal, now under Boer self-government. The Boer government introduced the Asiatic Law Amendment Ordinance, a piece of legislation designed not only to restrict Indian immigration but to allow for deportations. It required all Indians and Chinese in Transvaal over the age of eight to report to the Registrar of Asiatics, provide full personal details, be finger-printed and carry an identification pass at all times. Failure to comply on any aspect of the requirements would result in either a £100 fine, three months' imprisonment, or deportation. At the same time, the Natal government sought to curtail the activities and rights of Arab traders and those who were free after their compulsory period of indenture. A further item of new legislation – the 1906 Asiatic Registration Act – affected *all* Indians in the Transvaal and Gandhi referred to it as the 'Black Act'. Thus it was not surprising that at a packed meeting of 3,000 people at the Empire Theatre on 11 September 1906, Gandhi was able to launch a resolution condemning the proposal and gain mass approval to disobey its provisions. It was here that Gandhi called for some of the tactics we are now familiar with. He declared 'wisdom lies in pledging ourselves on the understanding that we shall have to suffer things like all that and worse ... if the entire community manfully stands the test, the end will be near.'[12] He called on Indians to make a solemn pledge to oppose the ordinance even if it meant fines, imprisonment, loss of property, or deportation.

Such a militant stand perhaps owed something to the inspiration Gandhi received from the recent Russian Revolution of 1905, which, although defeated, had shaken the Tsarist empire. Writing in November 1905, in *Young India*, Gandhi had noted 'the Russian workers and all the other servants declared a general strike and stopped all work', forcing the Tsar to make some concessions for 'it is not within the power of even the Tsar of Russia to force strikers to return at the point of the bayonet ... For even the powerful cannot rule without the cooperation of the ruled.'[13] As Vijay Prashad comments, 'the lesson of non-cooperation came from Russia. It was not the politics of the elite or even merely of urban areas. It was the politics – as far as Gandhi could make out – of the masses, including the peasantry.'[14]

Gandhi had again visited London in October 1906 to petition for the rights of Indians. This time, he met with the Secretary of State for the Colonies, Lord Elgin, and John Morley, Secretary of State for India and addressed MPs in a committee room of the House of Commons. He appealed to them to abolish the Black Act in the crown colony of Transvaal. Again, London was embarrassed and the British vetoed the law in December 1906, while Gandhi was on a ship returning to South Africa. But again, the British had granted the Transvaal self-government from 1 January 1907, leaving the new administration under General Louis Botha free to re-enact the law, this time as the Transvaal Registration Act. The law eventually came into force on 31 July 1907, after the British government approved the Act on 9 May 1907.

Anger at this law provoked popular agitation: January 1908 saw 155 Indians imprisoned for refusing to register and from that date until May 1909, Gandhi himself had been imprisoned three times, totalling six months in all (see Figure 4). As provisions of the Act affected all peoples of Asiatic origin, Chinese settlers also become involved and the initial action had galvanised and united the Indians of Transvaal. Pressure on the Transvaal government led the Colonial Secretary, General Jan Christian Smuts to contemplate a compromise. And so, on 28 January 1908, Gandhi and two of his colleagues, Leung Quinn, leader of the Chinese community of Johannesburg and Thambi Naidoo, a Tamil businessman from Mauritius, wrote from prison to Smuts, agreeing to a compromise proposal brought by Albert Cartwright, the editor of the *Transvaal Leader*. Two days later, Gandhi was taken from prison in Johannesburg to meet Smuts in Pretoria, where a compromise was agreed, stipulating that Indians would register voluntarily, after which the government would repeal that aspect of the law which made registration compulsory. Gandhi justified this compromise in the following terms: 'we are sincerely anxious to prove to the Government that we are loyal and law-abiding, and that we are willing to adopt any course which will lead out of the present difficulty without violating our consciences, inflicting any indignity or casting any stigma on us.'[15]

Figure 4 Gandhi outside a South African prison with fellow non-violent resisters, January 1908. This was the old Fort Prison Complex at what is now known as Constitution Hill, Johannesburg.

Gandhi was imprisoned four separate times in South Africa, and incarcerated for a total time of seven months and ten days. In India, he was imprisoned a further five times by the British colonial state, meaning that it has been estimated he spent a total of 2,338 days (nearly 6½ years) in jail across the course of his life.

Source: Wikimedia Commons, the free media repository.

Smuts, for his part, agreed to keep negotiations going with passive resisters, but secured an undertaking from the imperial government to stop the flow of indentured labourers to Natal – a demand he first made in 1908. By April 1909, the government began to deport some who took part in the campaign. Although Gandhi was the first to register, the compromise aroused criticism from many Indians who accused Gandhi of selling out. When Gandhi went to register, an angry Indian attacked him and was promptly arrested, but Gandhi called for his release, saying he had no desire to prosecute as they had acted in the belief that what they were doing was the right course. However, Smuts had no intention of keeping to the bargain and the Act remained in force in full. This is what led to some 2,000 resisters burning their registration documents at the Hamidia Mosque on 16 August 1908. Indians also began engaging in other forms of resistance such as trading without licences, and crossing over from one province to another without permits.

Throughout the campaign, 3,000 people were arrested. Fifty-nine people were deported to India in April, and a further 26 in June 1910. Six thousand Indians left the province. Ultimately, the campaign had failed to halt the Transvaal government's plans to limit immigration and to secure the general rights of Indian citizens. However, the campaign was markedly different from the previous one, as mass participation of Indians had shifted tactics away from a purely constitutional approach towards one focused upon the active participation of ordinary people. Gandhi's initiation of this activity went beyond the confines of the Arab traders; the mass appeal of direct action certainly took the authorities by surprise, and it is here that we see the beginnings of Gandhi's particular strategy and tactics evolving. *Satyagraha* was defined by Gandhi as holding on to 'truth', hence the literal translation is 'truth-force'. He also referred to it as 'love-force' or 'soul-force'. For Gandhi, *satyagraha* went beyond mere passive resistance and became a strength in the practice of non-violent methods. For him, 'pursuit of truth did not admit of violence being inflicted on one's opponent but that he must be weaned from error by patience and sympathy ... And patience means self-suffering.'[16] The main function of *satyagraha* is not to injure the enemy by any means. It is an appeal to the enemy either through reason or by gentle rational argument. It is something like a sacrifice of the self. Gandhi's biographer Louis Fischer states *satyagraha* 'means to be strong not with the strength of the brute but with the strength of the spark of God'.[17] It emphasised pity, tenderness and mercy, but entailed the use of moral pressure in situations of conflict.[18] To make this *swaraj* (act of self-governance) possible, Indians must engage in a form of non-violent (*ahimsa*) struggle that brought to the fore the 'moral dimension of all action',[19] thus demonstrating the influence of the religious principles Gandhi had imbibed in London and in his dealings with Christians in South Africa.

The apparently noble sentiment behind the method of *satyagraha* assumes that both parties are playing by the same rules. The fact that Smuts had ulterior motives suggests he was playing a different game. The tactics of passive resistance and *satyagraha* entailed the politics of compromise and reconciliation, and the unity achieved by Indians in the Transvaal in 1908 was ruptured by the agreement between Gandhi and Smuts. Nonetheless, 1907–09 is seen as the birth of 'passive resistance' as *satyagrahis* now became eager to be arrested, and were imprisoned when they tried to cross provincial boundaries. Gandhi was again imprisoned, from 10 October to 13 December 1908. He took up cooking duties for his 75 fellow *satyagrahis* in prison and performed various laborious tasks, including cleaning toilets, a task normally considered unthinkable for someone of the middle-class background from which he had emerged.[20]

Gandhi's Third Campaign: 1913–14

Gandhi's third campaign in South Africa – which was to be the largest and most popular act of resistance in this period – came in 1913 after the Union of South Africa had been declared in 1910. The hated Black Act of Transvaal had lapsed but the £3 annual tax remained, as did restrictions on movement and entry. In March 1913, the South African Supreme Court ruled that Hindu, Muslim and Parsi marriages were invalid, rendering wives little better than concubines and children as illegitimate in the eyes of the law. The government upheld this ruling and although Gandhi pleaded with Smuts to remove the £3 tax and overturn the marriage ruling, he did not respond. At a meeting on 28 April 1913, Gandhi called for a strike and a renewed passive resistance campaign against the £3 tax. There were other demands: the right of Indians to travel between provinces, fair trading laws, recognition of marriages conducted under Hindu and Muslim rites, and the right to bring wives and children from India to South Africa. Under Gandhi's guidance, the campaign was launched in September 1913 with the first resisters being women who crossed over from the Transvaal into Natal, while women from Natal crossed over into the Transvaal. The Natal women were the first to be arrested, and Indian anger led to many more flocking to join the cause. The Transvaal women were not arrested, so they went to Newcastle and persuaded workers to go on strike. Strikes had been initiated in the mines and Gandhi went to Newcastle and spoke to the striking miners, whose employers had turned off the water and lights in their compounds as punishment.

On 13 October 1913, a meeting was held in Newcastle which resulted in the formation of a passive resistance committee; Thambi Naidoo tried to get workers at the railways to go on strike, but failed. He was arrested, but was released on 15 October, when the committee addressed 78 workers at the Farleigh colliery. The workers went on strike, were arrested and ordered to return to work on 17 October. They refused, and within a week the number of strikers had swelled to 2,000. Within two weeks, between 4,000 and 5,000 workers were on strike. Gandhi, Naidoo and labour activist C.R. Naidoo moved around the area, urging workers to join the strike.

On 23 October 1913, Gandhi led a march of workers out of the compounds. The plan was to lead more than 2,000 strikers across the border into the Transvaal, stopping at Charleston. On the appointed day, 6 November 1913, Gandhi led 200 strikers and their families on the march to Charleston. The next day, Naidoo led a further 300 strikers towards the border. Another column of 250 left the next day, and after a few days some 4,000 strikers were on the move. The strike spread to the south of Natal and by 7 November the strike was effectively under way, joined by a further 15,000 workers. Workers at South African Refineries, Hulett's Refinery, Chemical Works, Wright's Cement and Pottery Works, and African Boating, among others, joined. These strikes by industrial workers raised the stakes and further galvanised the marchers. They went first to Charleston, on the Transvaal–Natal border 60 kilometres from Newcastle. They were given 1.5 pounds of bread and some sugar, and told to submit to the police if they were beaten, to behave hygienically and peacefully, and not to resist arrest. They arrived without incident, and were fed with food donated by local businessmen and cooked by Gandhi.

Gandhi informed the government of their intention to continue into the Transvaal, and called on them to arrest the strikers before they arrived, but Smuts calculated that the strike would dissolve before long, and opted to wait and see. Gandhi decided that if the strikers were not arrested, they would march to Tolstoy Farm in Lawley, 35 kilometres south-west of Johannesburg, covering 30–40 kilometres a day. As the marchers crossed the border into Volksrust, just 2 kilometres from Charleston, Gandhi was arrested. He appeared in court in Volksrust but was released on bail, leaving him free to join the marchers. Altogether, Gandhi was arrested on three occasions during the march, and on 11 November 1913, he was sentenced to nine months' hard labour.

The strike, by about 20,000 Indian workers in total, paralysed sections of Natal's economy. By the end of November 1913, produce markets of Durban and Pietermaritzburg were paralysed, sugar mills were closed, and hotels, restaurants and homes were left without domestic workers. The coal fields were also affected, as mine workers sought to enter the Transvaal illegally and whole fields of sugar cane were burned. Rumours that black workers were poised to join the strike sent shivers throughout the province. Police were sent in and some workers were shot and killed. Reactions to the strike and march stung the government, especially in Britain. Lord Harding, the British Viceroy in India, lashed out at the South African government and demanded an inquiry. Gandhi was released on 18 December 1913, and the government of the Union of South Africa announced the establishment of a commission of inquiry.

Gandhi's chief concern was the plight of Indians. Any notion of inter-racial unity amongst the Indian and black workers was a million miles from his thinking, as he stated, 'I saw it reported that we might even ask the Kaffirs to strike. But such is not our intention at all. We do not believe in such methods.'[21] Similarly, when Gandhi announced that he would lead a mass march on 1 January 1914, white railway workers went on strike. Gandhi immediately withdrew his threat, reasoning that to continue would be against the spirit of *satyagraha*. Smuts and Gandhi entered into a series of negotiations and on 30 June 1914, they concluded an agreement, which became the Indian Relief Bill 1914. The agreement gave recognition to Indian marriages, abolished the £3 tax and all arrears accruing from it, set 1920 as the deadline for new Indian immigrants and eased the movement of Indians from one province to another and abolished the system of indenture. Though restrictions on trade and movement from province to province remained on Indians, Gandhi had won a victory, and was welcomed as a hero, the *Mahatma*, when he returned to India in 1915.

Literary and Political Influences: Thoreau, Tolstoy and Ruskin

As we have seen, Gandhi had first come across Henry David Thoreau's writings whilst in London, but South Africa afforded the opportunity to put them into practice. In a letter dated 12 October 1929, Gandhi stated that Thoreau's 'Civil Disobedience' had 'left a deep impression' upon him.[22] During his second campaign in 1906 against the 'Black Act', he set about translating portions of Thoreau's famous 1849 essay, immediately publishing it in instalments in *Indian Opinion*. In introducing Thoreau to the Indians of South Africa, Gandhi argued that he was one of the greatest and most moral men to hail from America. This greatness lay in the simple fact that Thoreau 'taught nothing he was not prepared to practice in himself', risking imprisonment 'for the sake of his principles and suffering humanity'. As such the essay had 'been sanctified by suffering. Moreover, it is written for all time. Its incisive logic is unanswerable.'[23] And that 'his example and writings are at present exactly applicable to the Indians in the Transvaal.'[24]

As an abolitionist, Thoreau had castigated the US government for its enslavement of African Americans and its brutal war with Mexico. For him, it was not enough to champion soldiers who refused to fight an unjust war, if individuals themselves were willing to fund such a war through taxation. He argued that payment of taxes was a means of popular collusion with state authorities and so insisted on non-payment of taxes. His ideas unsettled the bourgeois notion of 'no taxation without representation'. If governments and laws were unjust, then modern democracy was a sham and non-cooperation with it was a moral imperative.

Gandhi was mesmerised by Thoreau's example. In his passive resistance campaign over Asian registration, Gandhi both invoked and practiced Thoreauvian ideology to its fullest. The pages of *Indian Opinion* were used to popularise, inspire and educate his embryonic passive resisters:

> Under a government which imprisons any unjustly, the true place for a just man is also a prison ... where the State places those who are not with her, but against her, the only house in a slave State

> in which a free man can abide with honour ... If the alternative is to keep all just men in prison, or give up war and slavery, the State will not hesitate which to choose. If a thousand men were not to pay their tax bills this year, that would not be a violent and bloody measure, as it would be to pay them, and enable the State to commit violence and shed innocent blood. This is ... the definition of a peaceable revolution ....[25]

Applying the force of Thoreau's ideas to the South African context, Gandhi led a call to arms, declaring of the Asiatic Registration Act of 1906, that 'British Indians have not only a law which has some evil in it ... but it is evil legalised ... Resistance to such an evil is a divine duty ....'[26] The insurrectionary implications of this strategy was not lost on Gandhi. In addition to the American Thoreau, Leo Tolstoy, the great doyen of Russian literature who, as a Christian pacifist bemoaned large-scale industrialisation and the violence he believed attended this development, also exercised considerable influence on Gandhi. Tolstoy's *The Kingdom of God is Within You* overwhelmed Gandhi as a 25-year-old. A philosophical treatise, the book was first published in Germany in 1894 after being banned in Tsarist Russia. Tolstoy was a devout Christian and believed that a literal interpretation of Christian Scriptures enjoined non-violence. The book became a key text for Tolstoyan, non-violent resistance, particularly appealing to Christian anarchist movements.

For Gandhi, it 'left an abiding impression ... Before the independent thinking, profound morality, and the truthfulness of this book ... seemed to pale into insignificance.'[27] Under Gandhi's influence, it would be transformed into a global text to challenge oppression and economic exploitation. As a Christian anarchist, Tolstoy accepted the authority of the Sermon on the Mount, as supreme. Consequently, any human institution claiming to be authoritative over human society was anathema to him. In his essay, 'Patriotism and Christianity', Tolstoy explains at length his doctrine of resistance and how a new stateless society can be realised:

> No feats of heroism are needed to bring about the greatest and most important changes in the life of humanity; neither the

> arming of millions of men, not the construction of new railways and machines, nor the organization of exhibitions or trade unions nor dynamite outrages, nor perfection of aerial navigation, and so forth. All that is necessary is a change of public opinion.[28]

Here again, we have some of the ingredients that contributed to Gandhi's thought process in terms of challenging unjust power. Following this logic, Gandhi stated, 'The best, quickest and most efficient way is to build up from the bottom … Every village has to become a self-sufficient republic. This does not require brave resolutions. It requires brave, corporate, intelligent work ….'[29]

In 1908, Tolstoy wrote 'Letter to a Hindoo', which outlined the notion that only by using love as a weapon through passive resistance could the native Indian overthrow the British Empire. Taraknath Das, editor of the revolutionary paper *Free Hindustan*, had written to Tolstoy in 1908, asking him, as a great champion of the oppressed, to write something for them attacking the British. Tolstoy was more than happy to condemn British imperialism but rebuked the young firebrand by insisting that his ilk was repeating 'the amazing stupidity indoctrinated in you by the advocates of the use of violence … your European teachers'.[30] He went on to insist that if the 'Hindoos had been enslaved by violence it is because they themselves have lived by violence, live by violence, and do not recognize the eternal law of love, inherent in humanity'.[31] And he instructed his young would-be Indian disciples to 'free your minds from those overgrown, mountainous imbecilities which hinder your recognition of [the law of love], and at once the truth will emerge from amid the pseudo-religious nonsense that has been smothering it.' He urged them instead to remain steadfast in the traditions of non-violence rather than 'adopting the irreligious and profoundly immoral social arrangements under which the English and other pseudo-Christian nations live today'.[32]

This was music to Gandhi's ears. After reading 'Letter to a Hindoo', Gandhi wrote to Tolstoy on 1 October 1909 informing him of the conditions in the Transvaal and seeking permission to reprint his letter in his native language, Gujarati. Permission was granted, and Tolstoy wrote a letter to Vladimir G. Chertkov, his intimate friend and, later, the editor of his collected works, saying, 'The letter of the

Transvaal Hindu has touched me.'[33] Their mutual admiration and respect was deep, and the two now struck up and continued a correspondence. When Tolstoy died in November 1910, Gandhi wrote an obituary, 'The Late Lamented Tolstoy the Great': 'In India, we would have described him as a *maharshi* [great seer] or fakir. He renounced his wealth, gave up a life of comfort to embrace that of a simple peasant … he himself put into practice what he preached.'[34] The influence of Tolstoy's ideas about the need to generate mass change in public opinion ultimately came to fruition in India through Gandhi's organisation of nationwide non-violent strikes and protests. Alongside his reading of Thoreau and Tolstoy, it was perhaps however Gandhi's reading of the English social critic John Ruskin's *Unto this Last* that most helped him begin to break from his early elitism. As Gandhi recalled, reading it made him 'determined to change my life', influencing his concept of 'soul-force' as a substitute for physical force. He discovered the book in March 1904 through Henry Polak, whom he had met in a vegetarian restaurant in South Africa. He read Ruskin's work on a train journey from Johannesburg to Durban and translated it into Gujarati with the title *Sarvodaya* (*Well Being of All*). He learnt from it that 'The good of the individual is contained in the good of all … the lawyer's work has the same value as the barber's … a life of labour, i.e., the life of a tiller of the soil and the handicraftsman, is the life worth living.'[35] Gandhi tells that he 'arose with the dawn, ready to reduce these principles to practice'.[36] His literary readings about the worth of manual labour led him to think about the way Indian middle classes treated their fellow indentured countrymen. He slowly found their condescension towards this community to be contemptible. Equally important was the relatively paltry state of Indian political organisation, in the grip of conservative merchant politics which prevented the raising of issues that would build and retain a broad base of support. Gandhi saw that businessmen were incapable of seeing beyond their narrow selfish interests and this was the result of a kind of 'moral degradation'. Ruskin's ideas would also provide the inspiration behind the Phoenix settlement outside Durban and later Tolstoy Farm on the outskirts of Johannesburg, where Gandhi trained passive resisters or *satyagrahis*, as he now termed them.

Hind Swaraj

Written in less than ten days in November 1908, on his way back to South Africa from London, Gandhi's *Hind Swaraj* – or *Indian Home Rule* – appeared first in instalments in the pages of *Indian Opinion*. It was published as a book in 1909, though the government of Bombay proscribed it at once. Less than a hundred pages long, and comprised of twenty short chapters, *Hind Swaraj* is cast in the form of a dialogue between Gandhi, 'The Editor', and his interlocutor, 'The Reader'. This structure conforms to religious and teacher-student imagery, as Gandhi sought to flesh out his thinking distilled through close readings of Thoreau, Tolstoy and Ruskin. It is the closest thing we have to a personal manifesto in which Gandhi expounds his views on British rule in India, Indian civilisation, passive resistance and Hindu-Muslim relations. He is most critical of Western-style industrial development and makes scathing attacks on the idea of 'modern civilisation' as the only supposed path to progress. He chastises Britain as 'a civilisation in name only', castigating the trappings of modern capitalism with its factories and mines and stating that the fate of workers 'is worse than that of beasts', as they are 'enslaved by temptation of money of the luxuries that money can buy'.[37] Such a vision is obviously very attractive to the many people dissatisfied with rapacious capitalism and its soulless, heartless existence.

Commenting on modernisation, Gandhi complained that lawyers, doctors and railways have impoverished the country,[38] claiming medicine to be a 'European' science where doctors have 'almost unhinged us' designed to keep Indians enslaved through reliance on conventional drugs,[39] and regarding his own profession, he firmly believed that individuals became lawyers 'not in order to help others out of their miseries, but to enrich themselves ... they are glad when men have disputes' and 'lawyers, therefore, will as a rule, advance quarrels instead of repressing them.'[40] Gandhi held rail infrastructure to be a critical means of allowing the British to control India as it facilitated troop movement. Further, he argued that railways were 'carriers of plague germs' spreading the 'bubonic plague' as people and goods could move around more freely so distributing illnesses.[41]

His explanation for why a 'degraded and ruined' nation like Britain could rule India was not because they had conquered it by physical and mental superiority or meat eating but because 'we gave it to them. They are not in India because of their strength, but because we keep them.'[42] He was merciless to those who believed that India should follow British-style democracy with parliamentary representation. He held the 'Mother of all Parliaments' to be 'a sterile woman', comparing it to 'a prostitute because it is under the control of ministers who change from time to time'.[43] To those elite Indian nationalists who argued that imitating the British system of parliamentary representation was a good model to follow, Gandhi replied, 'English rule without Englishman … you would make India English. And when it becomes English it will be called not Hindustan but Englistan. This is not the *Swaraj* that I want.'[44]

The *Swaraj* – self-government – that Gandhi wanted was not the mere replacement of British colonial rule for the rule of the brown *sahibs*. For Gandhi, self-rule meant a complete mental and psychological break with existing society. The Martiniquan revolutionary Frantz Fanon's understanding of the impact of colonialism on the colonised was not dissimilar to Gandhi's in one respect. Fanon argued that colonial structure and its ideology had nurtured a deep inferiority complex that produced 'the wish to be white' on the part of the colonised. The colonised individual 'lives in a society that makes his inferiority complex possible, in a society that derives its stability from the perpetuation of this complex, in a society that proclaims the superiority of one race; to the identical degree to which that society creates difficulties for him …'.[45]

Fanon described powerfully the way in which racism corrodes the lives of the colonised physically, mentally and emotionally, as the colonised is compelled to 'pawn some of his own intellectual possessions in order to assimilate the culture of the oppressor'.[46] Much earlier than Fanon, Gandhi had made similar points in terms of language when he insisted that Indians needed to pride themselves on their heritage, and not adopt the language of an alien power:

> And what is our condition? We write to each other in faulty English … our best thoughts are expressed in English; the proceedings of

> our Congress are conducted in English; our best newspapers are printed in English. If this state of things continues for a long time posterity will – it is my firm opinion – condemn and curse us.[47]

On Indian lawyers having to speak in English he observed, 'Is not this absolutely absurd? Is it not a sign of slavery? Am I to blame the English for it or myself? It is we, the English-knowing men, that have enslaved India.'[48]

Hind Swaraj allows us to understand how Gandhi could command such authority and popularity that he would be catapulted to national prominence. Thoreau, Tolstoy and Ruskin were serious critics of existing society. Their ideas represented a radical and arguably a revolutionary critique of injustice, oppression and the materialism that blighted much of humanity. Gandhi imbibed their ideas thoroughly and began to develop his strategy of *satyagraha* based on non-cooperation with an unjust system. After reading *Hind Swaraj* shortly before his death, Tolstoy wrote in his diary on 19 April 1910, 'This morning two Japanese arrived. Wild men in ecstasy over Europe and its civilization. On the other hand, the book and the letter of the Hindu [Gandhi] reveal an understanding of all the shortcomings of European civilization and even of its total inadequacy.'[49] However, Gandhi's political vision with respect to what alternative form of society was possible and how it might be achieved contained inherent limitations and contradictions, and his experience in South Africa would also bear this out.

The British Empire's Loyal Stretcher-Bearer

Whilst Gandhi's philosophical and political thought grew ever more radical, his approach towards the British Empire remained cautious and even supportive of the status quo. Thus, on 17 October 1899, a few days after the outbreak of the Anglo-Boer War (and before his second campaign in the Transvaal), Gandhi convened a meeting to persuade Indians to sign up for an ambulance corps. He argued that Indians could not demand their rights as British citizens if they were not willing to show loyalty to the Empire. By January 1900, five hundred Indians had signed up for the Indian Ambulance Corps, including

Gandhi who was duly rewarded with a medal for 'chivalry' and loyalty to the monarch on the day. Gandhi abhorred those aspects of imperial authority that treated Indians as second class. He wanted all Her Majesty's subjects to be accorded equal status under the Empire, as can be gleaned from this positive endorsement of 'Empress of India' Queen Victoria: 'the memory of that noble lady remains as fresh as ever. Her interest in India and its people was intense, and in return, she received the whole-hearted affection of India's millions.'

Further inviting Indians to celebrate the royal proclamation for its 'feelings of generosity, benevolence, and religious toleration', Gandhi noted that

> India is a vast storehouse of wealth to Great Britain, whilst thousands of its inhabitants are dying of starvation with scarcely a murmur. We venture to suggest that, if there were more of Queen Victoria's spirit of enlightenment put into the affairs of the Empire, we should be worthier followers of so great an Empire Builder.[50]

Similarly, the outbreak of inter-imperialist conflict with the Great War in 1914 saw Gandhi call on Indians to fight on the Allied side. 'We are, above all, British citizens of the Great British Empire,' he told them. As war broke out, Gandhi circulated a letter to Indians in Britain that declared, 'we, the undersigned have, after mature deliberation decided for the sake of the motherland and the empire to place our services unconditionally, during this crisis, at the disposal of the authorities.'[51] Gandhi was not alone in this. Many early nationalists were conservative minded and shared many of the liberal ideals of the British Empire, and found it difficult to imagine a world without it. Thus it was that in an open letter to the Indian public, the former Liberal MP and Indian nationalist, Dadabhai Naoroji, perhaps best known for his development of the anti-imperialist economic 'drain of wealth' theory of Indian poverty, wrote: 'Fighting as the British people are ... in a righteous cause to the good and glory of human dignity and civilisation, and moreover, being the beneficent instrument of our own progress and civilisation, our duty is clear – to do everyone our best to support the British fight with our life and property.'[52] Gandhi's proven loyalty to the British Empire at this critical moment did not go unnoticed, and he appeared in the 1915 New Year's Honours list having been awarded a Kaiser-i-Hind gold medal.

In explaining Gandhi's evolution in these years he has been described as a 'collaborationist nationalist',[53] whereas others have referred to Gandhi as the 'stretcher-bearer of Empire', and perhaps this more accurately captures the essence of Gandhi's political evolution, as it was arguably the failure of his original constitutional strategy that led Gandhi to take a more decisive turn to activism[54] and not a pivotal break with the liberal imperialism.

Race, Caste and Class

The politics of race dominated the history of South Africa and relations between Africans and Indians were defined in accordance with strict racial laws governing Natal, the Transvaal and the Orange Free State. Gandhi's own attitudes led him to instinctively stand in opposition to these laws, but he did not extend his sympathy to the majority black African population of South Africa – whom he called the 'kaffirs' – and was initially horrified that Indians were placed on the same level as Africans. In a speech delivered in Bombay on 26 September 1896, he complained that Europeans wanted to 'degrade us to the level of the raw Kaffir whose occupation is hunting, and whose sole ambition is to collect a certain number of cattle to buy a wife with and, then, pass his life in indolence and nakedness'.[55] In an open letter to the Natal Parliament in 1893, Gandhi wrote: 'I venture to point out that both the English and the Indians spring from a common stock, called the Indo-Aryan.' Pointing to these connections demonstrates the extent to which Gandhi identified with European notions of culture and civilisation, even if the majority of whites in South Africa saw no such connection.

One of Gandhi's early battles was over separate entrances for whites and blacks at the Durban post office. Gandhi objected that Indians were 'classed with the natives of South Africa' and demanded a separate entrance for Indians: 'We felt the indignity too much and … petitioned the authorities to do away with the invidious distinction, and they have now provided three separate entrances for natives, Asiatics and Europeans.'[56]

Gandhi wrote in 1908 about his prison experience:

> We were marched off to a prison intended for Kaffirs. There, our garments were stamped with the letter 'N', which meant that we were being classed with the Natives. We were all prepared for hardships, but not quite for this experience. We could understand not being classed with the whites, but to be placed on the same level with the Natives seemed too much to put up with.[57]

The politics of race and skin colour was so institutionalised within South Africa that even before official apartheid, Africans and Indians both suffered at the hands of white domination. But as Desai and Vahed argue, this was exacerbated by 'the way in which Gandhi decided to challenge the afflictions facing Indians'.[58]

The agitation he built was based upon the gap he perceived in the provision of British culture and its constitution on the one hand, and their application to the Indians in the colony on the other. But his initial instincts as a campaigner lay with the urban professional middle classes. He identified with their social, economic and political concerns and his first political action was to reflect their interests. As a result, in spite of Gandhi's leadership and political mobilisations the above quotation highlights some uncomfortable truths about his time in South Africa. As Maureen Swan has noted, Indian political consciousness and organisation in South Africa pre-dated Gandhi's arrival:

> Indian politics in Natal and the Transvaal were crucially shaped by the social and economic stratification of the Indian population and that these politics were dominated by merchants, traders and western-educated white-collar workers seeking to maintain their relatively privileged position in the economic hierarchy.[59]

She challenges the highly romanticised idea of Gandhi as the saviour and natural leader of an unorganised, apolitical and unconscious people. She draws attention to individuals such as Haji Ojer Ally and Sheth Haji Habib, who had been involved in opposing discrimination since the mid-1880s.[60] Gandhi had little knowledge or contact with the mass of labouring Indians. An indication of Gandhi's own sense of self-importance can be gleaned from his observations in *Satyagraha in South Africa*:

> there were hardly any free and well-educated Indians in South Africa capable of espousing the Indian cause. English-knowing Indians were mostly clerks whose knowledge of English was only commensurate with the needs of their occupation and not adequate to drafting representations, and who, again, must give all their time to their employers.[61]

For most of Gandhi's time in South Africa, the problems of the indentured labourers and the underclass were never on the political agenda, except as an opportunistic ploy to safeguard trader interests. As Swan points out, 'Their politics, far from unifying the Indian community as has been asserted in the past, were directed specifically towards attaining white recognition of the fundamental differences between the two major social groups in the community, merchants and workers.'[62] The preoccupation of the NIC's merchant leadership with their own business affairs, and the legal and constitutional nature of its political activity together set the stage for a 'full-time organiser, preferably fluent in Gujarati and English and with a legal training'.[63] So Gandhi in many respects was the right person in the right place at the right time. It is clear that the oppressed Indian community did have political awareness and a political culture that Gandhi was able to tap into. However, to over-emphasise his special qualities risks denying agency to the Indian masses and dovetails into an elitist approach that privileges the role of a middle-class individual.

Conclusion

At this stage of his life, Gandhi was very much in the mould of a 'Victorian' Indian who sought accommodation and acceptance into the British Empire. His caste background and education reflected middle-class aspirations and meant that he shared the upper-class prejudices of Europeans on many issues. Indians in South Africa were a heterogeneous, fragmented community with many different interests. The diversity of religious interests amongst the middle classes was something with which Gandhi could easily associate. However, the strikes that were critical to his third campaign demonstrate a break with elitism. Although the professional middle classes were his starting point, to have any chance of success required mass action, which militated against the safe constitutional strategy he had hitherto been pursuing. The fact that Gandhi was continually being thrown in jail by the very Empire he lauded must have helped Gandhi conclude – as he did in *Hind Swaraj* – that there was something very wrong with British imperial society at a deep, systematic level. It also brought to the fore tensions between his reformist intentions and their more radical potentialities unleashed by his movements. Gandhi's time in South Africa is generally held to be his apprenticeship and the testing ground of his ideas and practice for the battles to come in India. South Africa provided Gandhi with a world stage on which to campaign for Indian rights. As such, the South African experience – where Gandhi learnt many of his skills as an organiser of mass politics – was pivotal to the evolution of *satyagraha*.

3

The Champion of the Oppressed Returns: 1915–19

Gandhi as the champion of the oppressed has been a constant image and one that his admirers often point to as evidence of his radicalism and revolutionary spirit. Russell Brand affectionately refers to Gandhi as the 'little Indian man in nappies'. But more importantly he describes the meeting between Gandhi and women textile workers of Lancashire in 1931 by stating, 'you can see the workers really dig him'.[1] The explanation for Brand is all too obvious:

> the women know a kindred spirit when they see one. They know that Gandhi is fighting for the rights of the oppressed against the powerful, a struggle they know well. The insight of these women, the inherent connection shared between the world's exploited people in the struggle for autonomy, matters now more than ever.[2]

At the time, Gandhi was in Britain for negotiations over constitutional reform (at the Second Round Table Conference), but in London he stayed in the East End as opposed to a fancy hotel in the West End. His host was Muriel Lester, social reformer and pacifist who had travelled to India and was a supporter of the Friends of India Society. Lester recalls Gandhi stating, 'I will not sleep one night in London away from Bow. Here I am doing the real Round Table work, getting to know the people of England.'[3] He met with local children and one essay from an 11-year-old boy, which was published in India, refers to Gandhi as an Indian educated in law in London but who chose to give this up to help India 'get better conditions'. The description continues, 'He has given up all his belongings and is trying to be one of the poorest Indians. That is why he wears a loin cloth.'[4] It describes Gandhi's meeting at the Second Round Table Conference and how this is about '6,000,000 peoples who do not know what a good meal is'. The reference was to the vast army of the untouchable community whom Congress had ignored for too long. The essay concludes that Gandhi is 'an Indian Christian'. In May 1933, Lester, appealing for Gandhi's release, insists that Gandhi 'stands for the poor, works for the poor, half starves himself for the poor' and that he has become a symbol for and of the poor.[5] Statements such as these point to how Gandhi has been lionised as the hero of the dispossessed and exploited, and this image dominates global narratives about him. This chapter will focus on four critical groups to examine this aspect of Gandhi's life and work in more detail – peasants, workers, untouchables and women – and it will also assess his concept of 'trusteeship'.

The Politics of Indian Nationalism

On his return to India in 1915, Gandhi cut a very different figure compared to the established leaders of Indian nationalism, which had been dominated by two contrasting forces. Firstly, there were those wedded to a constitutional approach who sought reform through accommodation with British rulers within the imperial hierarchy – a strategy whose interests were represented and articulated by the Indian National Congress (INC). The second strand was much more militant in its approach and used direct action by force to ambush colonial interests in a bid to help oust British rule. This latter approach is sometimes referred to as the 'terrorist wing' of Indian nationalism. Originally established in 1885 as an association representing the interests of upper-class Indian men to the colonial state, the Indian National Congress was the brainchild of two retired British civil servants, Allan Octavian Hume and William Wedderburn, who felt Indians had a right to expect some representation. It was a highly select, exclusive club, including such notables as Gopal Krishna Gokhale, a Bombay leader and close associate of Gandhi; Dadabhai Naoroji, a Parsi intellectual and cotton trader who became a Liberal MP for Finsbury Central in 1892, and Romesh Chandra Dutt, an economic historian and writer from Calcutta. Under their leadership, the INC was the epitome of elite, upper-class, liberal-minded would-be parliamentarians. This social milieu defined the INC's goals and strategy. Congress initially did not demand independence, instead lobbying for consultation and representation behind closed doors to try and achieve the gradual 'Indianisation' of the regime. This narrow base was also to include Motilal Nehru, the father of India's first prime minister, Jawaharlal Nehru, and, originally, Mohammad Ali Jinnah, who was later to become the first governor-general of Pakistan.

This 'moderate' wing was challenged by the so-called 'extremists' (as defined by the British), centred around the fiery nationalism of the Maharashtra-based Brahmin, Bal Gangadhar Tilak, who had led peasants in a successful revenue strike during a famine in Maharashtra in 1896, and the Bengali nationalist leader Aurobindo Ghose. They demanded outright independence – *swaraj* – and were prepared to use violence to achieve this. In spite of obvious differences in goals and tactics, the common element in both wings of nationalism was their elitism and substitutionism. INC leaders believed that the enlightened and educated, i.e. themselves, should speak for the masses; the colonial regime could thus easily placate them with vague talk of reform and future consultation. Those espousing a revolutionary armed assault saw change as coming from a dedicated minority brave enough to 'carry out' a revolution on behalf of the majority. But the colonial government was easily able to marginalise and outmanoeuvre them through arrest, assassination and deportation. Gandhi was of course highly critical of the Congress high command whom he viewed as elitist, condescending and arrogant. And we have seen how in *Hind Swaraj* he castigates parliamentarians, for wanting to mimic the British and demean their fellow Indians. In both instances, the absence of a genuine mass movement was the fundamental weakness. It was Gandhi's intervention at this juncture that was decisive in shifting the goals and parameters of the freedom movement. He first followed the advice of his mentor, Gokhale, to travel and *see* India in order to learn more about the country. So, he travelled third class, walked everywhere, gave up wearing suits and took to wearing *khadi* (homespun) clothing. It was under these conditions that he became involved in his first localised campaigns: Champaran, Kheda and Ahmedabad from 1917–18, and they illustrate his attitude towards the peasantry and workers.

Gandhi and Mass Action

India is overwhelmingly rural today and was even more so in Gandhi's day. In the 1931 census survey, the total population was about 350 million out of which the rural population comprised 310 million.[6] Literacy levels were below 30 million.[7] On 6 February 1916, Gandhi made a speech at the opening of Benares Hindu University lambasting the use of English at public meetings, deriding the Indian rich and princes for their lack of concern for the poor, and demanding a forthright but peaceful protest against the British.[8] The next year, he initiated campaigns based on mass action that would fundamentally change the character of the nationalist movement.

Champaran was in the north-eastern province of Bihar, bordering Bengal. Here the Bengal Tenancy Act of 1885 secured a system of indigo cultivation which resulted in the imposition of a system called *tinkathia*. Indigo, a plant that yielded a prized blue dye, was a very profitable crop under colonial rule; in 1788, 30 percent of the indigo imported to Britain was from India and by 1810, it was 95 percent. Indigo could only be cultivated on fertile lands. But these areas were densely populated and hence, only small plots could be acquired. This made it difficult to expand the area under cultivation and attempts to do this to boost indigo cultivation often resulted in peasants' eviction and so always created conflict and tension. Under this system, the tenant farmers were forced to grow indigo in three *kathas* of every *bigha* (three out of twenty parts of their land). In April 1917, Gandhi visited the district of Champaran, where only 2 percent of the population lived in towns and the remainder in rural villages (see Figure 5). There were three powerful land-owning *zamindaris* of Champaran, who all operated under the *tinkathia* system. *Zamindars* were a hereditary class – a nobility – and had control over their peasants, from whom they reserved the right to collect tax on behalf of imperial courts or for military purposes. They existed under Mughal rule and survived under the British, who rewarded supportive *zamindars* by recognising them as princes.

In Champaran, as in many districts, peasants were then at the mercy of ruthless, greedy plantation owners. The farmers were poorly compensated for their indigo crops and if they refused to plant

Figure 5 Gandhi at the Champaran *satyagraha*, Bihar district, April 1917.
Source: © Photo Division, Ministry of Information & Broadcasting, Government of India, New Delhi.

indigo, they faced heavy taxation. The landlords (mostly British) would enforce this system through their agents, called *gumasta*, who brutally executed the terms of employment. As a result, the reduced production of much-needed food crops and exclusive indigo farming (peasants were not allowed to grow any other crop even during the indigo off-season) had led to untold sufferings for the *raiyots* (peasant cultivators), including famine-like conditions. The daily routine of peasant life was further blighted by poor sanitation, ignorance, stifling caste oppression and imposed purdah for women. Sporadic rebellions in 1914 were effectively crushed by militias working for landlords. Champaran's poverty can be gleaned from the fact that in 1921 only 4 percent of those aged 20 and over could read and write. Judith Brown states that distress in 1917 was not simply the result of the pattern of landholding, but more fundamentally lay in the economic changes which underlined the power of the planters and the weakness of the *raiyots*.[9] So, when the news of Gandhi's arrival reached Champaran, it spread in the region like wildfire and he was greeted by large crowds of peasants at railway stations.

Though a court order meant Gandhi had been instantly arrested when he arrived, the British magistrate was compelled to release him due to mass support from villagers. Gandhi instituted a campaign of recording peasant grievances and drawing up a charge sheet against plantation owners, effectively establishing his own court to plead on behalf of cultivators. His efforts eventually resulted in a commission of inquiry, with him as a member, which negotiated a settlement that abolished the century-old *tinkathia* system and reduced the revenue paid to the planters by 20–25 percent. This was a spectacular victory in the face of the intransigent planters and the provincial government.

Word of this victory quickly spread, as Gandhi's magic seemed vindicated on Indian soil. Gandhi led a *satyagraha* (non-violent protest) a year later in Kheda district outside Ahmedabad in his native Gujarat province. This was a highly developed region with thriving agriculture. But a combination of plague, famine and poor harvests resulting from severe flooding left some of the more prosperous peasant elite, let alone landless peasants, facing severe hardship. Peasants were forced to buy vital food items which were sold at inflated prices following the Great War. They faced a demand from colonial officials that they pay full taxes, but also a 23 percent increase. Consequently, the peasants appealed for a remission of their land revenues, but this request was immediately ignored by the colonial government. According to Gandhi, if crops were less than one-fourth of the normal yield, peasants were entitled under the revenue code to a total remission of the land revenue.

Peasants in Kheda started a payment boycott under Gandhi's leadership. Some 3,000 signed a pledge not to pay the taxes and to conduct themselves as *satyagrahis* (non-violent protesters). The revolt was astounding in terms of discipline and unity. In spite of government provocation and the seizure of property and cattle by hired thugs, the majority of peasants did not resist arrest or retaliate to violent force. After five months, the provincial commissioner ordered a settlement forfeiting governmental right to collect taxes for one year. Again, Gandhi appeared to be a 'just' effective tactician and champion, whose non-violent creed could be used effectively in an Indian setting.

As if to prove that *satyagraha* was not confined to rural cases, Gandhi had been asked to intervene in an industrial dispute on behalf of mill workers at a textile factory in Ahmedabad in March 1918 before going to Kheda. Here workers demanded a 50 percent wage increase, but the mill owner – Ambalal Sarabhai, himself a rich supporter of Gandhi – would only countenance 20 percent. Gandhi sanctioned a strike for a 35 percent wage increase after the owners refused to go to arbitration *but* only on certain conditions: no violence, no intimidation of scabs, no begging and no yielding. At a mass meeting, workers overwhelmingly voted to pledge themselves to these conditions. The employers imposed a lockout for two weeks and then said they would only allow a return to work of those who accepted the initial 20 percent wage rise. A fortnight with no income and no prospect of one caused some workers to relent. Frustration blew up against strike breakers but also against Gandhi: a striker bitterly commented that Gandhi and his associate Anasuya Sarabhai – sister of Ambalal, a Gandhian disciple who had set up night schools for mill workers – 'come and go in their car', 'eat elegant food', and could not understand the agonies of the starving.[10]

As violence threatened, Gandhi continued to forbid militant picketing by workers but instead began his first political fast or hunger strike, stating 'I cannot tolerate for a minute that you break your pledge. I shall not take any food nor use a car till you get a 35 percent increase.'[11] He broke his fast after three days when the strikers voted to continue their pledge *and* the mill owners agreed to go to arbitration, which led to the workers finally being awarded 35 percent.

In each of these cases, we see a deepening of Gandhi's convictions based on ideas imbibed from the writings of Thoreau, Tolstoy, Ruskin – and powerful illustrations of the strengths of his approach of mass non-violent direct action – but also his strategy based on self-discipline, individual suffering and compromise. These three experiences came to epitomise Gandhi's tactics and propel him to national leadership. In each instance highlighted, his version of peaceful 'mass action' by ordinary people won the day. However, as a leader it is noticeable that once workers and peasants were themselves in action, it is clear that he did not want them to go further, or to go beyond utilising the methods prescribed by himself. These campaigns also see for the first time Gandhi's use of fasting as a weapon with which to discipline unruly elements.

These early victories in Gujarat and rural Bihar explain why earlier scholarship credited Gandhi with providing political leadership and instituting social reform. As Judith Brown notes, 'Although Champaran was ripe for public agitation when Gandhi arrived … What actually occurred was the result of Gandhi's intervention, with his very personal range of interests and type of leadership.'[12] Yet the complex class dynamics of Gandhi's social base – revealed by the strike at the textile factory in Ahmedabad – are worth examining in further detail. In 1867 (before Gandhi was born), the province of Bihar had seen the first indigo disturbance at the Lalsaraiya factory, where peasants refused to grow indigo. The factory bungalow caught fire, with the planters blaming the tenants. The commissioner of Patna recognised that indigo cultivation brought no profit but caused actual loss to the tenants. The court (in close connection with the planters) made the tenants pay reparations. Yet if peasant agitation – often violent – in villages had marked colonial rule and pre-colonial India for centuries, the Indian peasantry was not a homogenous entity. There were many divisions based on the size of land holdings. David Hardiman, in his study of Kheda district between 1917 and 1934,[13] identified rich peasants as holding more than 15 acres of land; middle peasants between 3 and 15 acres and the poor peasantry owning less than 3 acres. In addition to this, there were tenant farmers and sharecroppers. In Kheda, a village-based system entailed that organisations had been formed to jointly own a village and to share responsibility in some fixed proportion for the land revenues. The community having collective ownership were the *patidars*, who belong to a caste quite specific to Gujarat. This community was held together by the village *panchayat* (assembly of village elders), with marriage links and caste connections. They also took the name Patel as a community to mark their caste and social status, and did not constitute landless labourers or poor peasants. This class difference in the peasantry is more transparent when we consider the man who invited Gandhi to Champaran, Rajkumar Shulka, son of a prosperous Brahmin cultivator.[14] He was a money lender, who earned 2,000 rupees a month from interest.[15] Hardiman argues that it was the bulk of middle peasants who provided support for Gandhi's *satyagraha* in Kheda. This does not repudiate these protests as petty bourgeois, but allows us to appreciate and understand the complex and contradictory class composition of rural India and the social base and appeal of Gandhi's village *satyagrahis*.

A comparison can be made with Barry Pavier's study of the rebellion of the Telangana peasants during the 1940s which identifies the early stages of this movement as 'multi-class' and how the cadre of the Andhra society was initially made up of 'rich' or 'middle' peasants, whilst later in 1948 it was mostly 'agricultural labourers and poor peasants' who came to the fore.[16] The sociologist D.N. Dhanagare also noted how those at the heart of the Telangana uprising were 'unquestionably the poor peasants and landless labourers'.[17]

Gandhi's involvement in Champaran and Kheda were significant as examples of his initial activity on home ground, but his attitude in each of these scenarios was one of paternalism. In Champaran, he lectured the villagers on personal hygiene as well as raising the issue of cow protection and education. His short time in this village meant these issues could not be implemented at the time but it does signify Gandhi's evolving political outlook. In Ahmedabad, his *hartal* was not a strike in the conventional sense. There were no mass pickets of strikers or attempts to win over those workers who wavered. The emphasis was on the sacred pledge of non-violence and following his leadership. This included appeals to the employers to treat their workers well. The moment the activity threatened to spiral out of control, with attacks on strike breakers, Gandhi intervened to try and call a halt to the movement through launching his own hunger strike. Consequently, Gandhism often acted as a brake on popular initiative and militancy from below.

Trusteeship

Gandhi's attitude to the masses was then very contradictory. In regard to peasants, he would champion their demands and organise them on the condition that they remain peaceful, were respectful of landowners and obedient to his tactics. If they had the temerity to demand the confiscation of private property, then they were deemed to be ungrateful, unruly and unworthy. No matter how forceful his denunciation of colonial rule and industrial developments, Gandhi's philosophy was imbued with paradoxes. He was against industrialisation and in *Hind Swaraj* wrote that 'it would be folly to assume that an Indian Rockefeller would be better than the American Rockefeller', but he made alliances with and relied upon Indian capitalists, who aspired to become 'Indian Rockefellers' and a new post-colonial ruling elite who had no qualms in embracing industrial techniques and exploiting workers.[18] The industrialists Sir Ratan Tata and Ghanshyam Das Birla were instrumental in Gandhi's financial and political base.[19] Sir Ratan Tata donated Rs. 25,000 to Gandhi in November 1909 to support his Non-Co-operation Movement in South Africa. This was the first of three generous donations to Gandhi's work.

G.D. Birla, however, was the *Mahatma*'s most generous financial supporter. While Birla has been described as a devotee of Gandhi, the relationship between the two men was more one of collaboration than of one-sided devotion. Gandhi's campaigns were made possible by drawing from Birla's vast financial resources, whilst Birla benefited from the social and religious prestige which his association with Gandhi brought him, as well as an enhancement of his economic power and influence. Gandhi gave his blessing to the abundant wealth of Birla with his teaching on 'trusteeship', a concept which asserted the right of the rich to accumulate and maintain wealth, as long as some of the wealth was used to benefit society.

Gandhi apparently borrowed the concept of trusteeship from the writings of the nineteenth-century American millionaire steel magnate and 'robber baron' Andrew Carnegie, who had used trusteeship to promote capitalism over socialism. In 1889, Carnegie wrote an article proclaiming 'The Gospel of Wealth', which called on the rich to use their wealth to improve society. Nineteenth-century philanthropy was quite pervasive on both sides of the Atlantic. In Britain, Joseph Rowntree was concerned with social problems and his schemes to fund and provide homes for his factory workforce were typical of voluntary social policy before state legislation was introduced.

Gandhi's belief in the simple virtues of farming and the apparent 'equilibrium' of peasant life – though perfectly logical strategically, given the overwhelmingly large size of the peasantry in colonial India – underestimates the degree of social and economic exploitation inherent in rural communities, and the resulting different interests and outlook that existed between richer and poorer peasants. Similarly, with workers and employers, Gandhi's tactics had all the hallmarks of his earlier compromise and conciliation in South Africa. The notion of trusteeship was used to dissipate workers' anger and prevent them from *fighting as workers*, for their own independent interests. The emphasis was on rights *but* also responsibilities, and his stress on the obligations of workers and peasants was pivotal. So, although Gandhi could claim, 'What the two hands of the labourer could achieve, the capitalist would never get with all his gold and silver',[20] he could also insist in the true spirit of trusteeship that 'capitalists are amenable to conversion.'[21]

Gandhi's use of trusteeship applied to ruling princes as much as it did to wealthy industrialists and large landlords. He advised ruling princes to engage in constructive work, such as to try and establish *Ramraj*, the ideal rule of Ram, the hero of the *Ramayana* in their territories. In this Gandhi was not alone. Several early nationalist leaders found lucrative employment in the service of princely states. Barbara Ramusack points to the influential Tamil congressman, C.P. Ramaswami Aiyar, acting as 'constitutional adviser' to the state of Travancore in South India, while Nehru's father Motilal, along with other lawyers, continued to provide legal services for princes up to the early 1930s.[22] It is striking how, upon Gandhi's return to India in 1915, he advocated a policy largely of non-interference within these states for almost two decades. This may be due to a nativist sympathy for his ancestral roots within princely kingdoms but is perhaps more likely to be as a result of his desire to maintain good relationships with elite, conservative groups.

Caste and Untouchability

The question of caste oppression in India is perhaps best highlighted by the so-called 'untouchable' *Dalits* – landless agricultural labourers whose hereditary occupations were held to be polluting because they involved dealing with animal carcasses or skins, clearing up bodily excretions and dirt, and disposing of the dead – who have suffered horrific oppression over generations as a result.[23] Caste is held to be a quintessentially Indian institution rooted in religious teachings and considered to be timeless. This idealised notion is not particularly helpful in analysing caste, any more than the simple utterance that class has always existed. Conversely, caste cannot simply be reduced to class either. Caste is made up of two features existing in medieval and early modern Indian society: *varna* and *jati*. The first, divides society into four great hereditary categories of priests, warriors, merchants and peasants. This is not that dissimilar to the four great estates of medieval Europe: feudal barons, clergy, urban merchants and the mass of the working population. In India, the brahmins, the priestly group, would provide religious legitimacy to the warrior caste in order to rule. *Jati* distinctions are based upon occupational groupings which are also held to be hereditary where members inter-marry and dine only with each other. As in Europe, there are potters, weavers, millers and bakers, and surnames come to be associated with these trades, so in India the brahmins define themselves as 'pure' and practice vegetarianism to distinguish themselves from those who work with animal products, human excrement, or money. Other caste groups eventually come to associate vegetarianism as a high-status trait and seek to emulate forms of behaviour to further distinguish themselves from the mass of the population.[24] High-caste groups have used access to resources, religious sanctity and their control of state institutions to enforce their power over subordinate groups, particularly labourers – urban and rural, including those defined as the bottom of the heap – the untouchables. Caste does not equate to class, but neither is it totally unconnected from it. It is the interaction between the two that helps to further our understanding of how caste evolved. Even today, caste oppression and the curse of untouchability blights India. According to the Indian National Crime Records Bureau, a crime is committed against a *dalit* by a non-*dalit* every sixteen minutes; every day, more than four *dalit* women are raped by caste men; every week, thirteen *dalits* are murdered and six *dalits* are kidnapped. A serious and effective revolutionary strategy for India has to be rooted in the complete eradication of caste and untouchability which the caste system facilitates.

Gandhi's concerns for the plight of low-caste people and untouchables stemmed from his opposition to untouchability, which by the 1920s he held to be a 'rotten part or an excrescence ... Men like me feel that untouchability is no integral part of Hinduism.'[25] It was a 'blight' that had to be eradicated. And he went further in stating 'I would far rather that Hinduism died than that untouchability lived.'[26] These were remarkable words for a caste Hindu and to this end, Gandhi led a campaign for *dalit* rights in the 1930s. It was part of his constructive programme for social reform which included the promotion of *khaddar* (home spinning), social uplift and Hindu-Muslim unity. In 1933, he undertook a nine-month tour of some 12,500 miles during which he campaigned for the opening-up of wells, temples and roads to *dalits*. He carried a begging bowl to raise money for the movement and cleaned latrines with *bhangis*, the lowest category of untouchable community whose occupation was cleaning latrines. He called on caste Hindus to purge themselves of their prejudices as he attempted to challenge the prejudice that forbade untouchables from entering temples by trying to introduce a temple entry bill at the beginning of 1933. For a short time, this appeared to have a remarkable cathartic-like impact. In cities, small towns and rural areas, *brahmin* Hindus were observed embracing untouchables on street corners, allowing them access to restricted wells and 'talking up' the Gandhi mantra that untouchables were *harijans* (children of God). Muriel Lester went out to India in 1934 to accompany Gandhi on his anti-untouchability tour. Whatever the limitations of this campaign, she noted with admiration how Gandhi walked for long hours and held up to seven open-air meetings daily. Lester was clearly impressed by his stamina and determination to soldier on.[27]

But Gandhi encountered much resistance from orthodox-caste Hindus. They disrupted his meetings and in June 1933 a bomb was thrown at him in Pune. In March of the following year, Gandhi went to Bihar, which had been struck by an earthquake. On meeting with victims, he declared to the world that the earthquake was 'divine chastisement' for the evils of untouchability.[28]

These were brave and, in the context, quite revolutionary sentiments and activities. But Gandhi's treatment of untouchables was not without ambiguity. In 1932, he established a paper *Harijan* (Children of God). The title was somewhat patronising and chosen by Gandhi, not by *dalits* themselves. Nevertheless, Birla the industrialist was the founding president of the *Harijan Sevak Sangha* (Servants of Untouchables Society), an organisation founded by Gandhi in 1932 to tackle untouchability and to champion the upliftment of *dalits*. The very fact that a powerful and extremely rich industrialist should be president of such an association is quite revealing and startling.

Though the temple entry bill of 1936 was passed in Travancore state, it only called for the lifting of restrictions formalised under colonial rule, not the enforcement of entry. Additionally, Gandhi's campaign called for untouchables to go around the temple and not into it and he admonished them for their lack of hygiene and poor sanitation and insisted that they forego the 'impure' habits of meat-eating and alcohol. As with other issues, Gandhi was more concerned with moral indignation and limited social reform that was delinked from any systematic analysis of the structures of power and class. Thus opposing untouchability did not mean advocating the *abolition* of caste. Gandhi's essentially philanthropic approach simply wanted caste Hindus to acknowledge and accept untouchables into the wider fold of Hinduism and to treat them more kindly – in other words, to ameliorate their conditions, but not the source of their oppression.

Gandhi's approach was tested from the left by Bhimrao Ramji Ambedkar, the great *dalit* leader of the 1930s. Dr Ambedkar was from the Mahar caste of Maharashtra. Ambedkar campaigned for separate electorates for untouchables in the early 1930s to fight for *dalit* rights and representation, and initially the British granted this after the 1931 Second Round Table Conference. Ambedkar characterised the problem of untouchability and caste more generally in political terms and sought a political solution based on untouchables acting as their own agents to demand rights and not to be subsumed within Congress. Gandhi saw this as 'the vivisection' of the Hindu community, and he embarked upon a fast unto death to have this revoked. Such was the outcry that even Ambedkar was forced to buckle under the weight of emotional and political blackmail. In negotiations with Ambedkar, Gandhi insisted that he 'would not bargain away their rights for the kingdom of the whole world'.[29] A fast that began at noon on 20 September 1932 ended five days later, with Gandhi getting his way.

The issue itself, however, would remain a central one, thanks in part to Ambedkar's unrelenting campaigning efforts. In 1934, Ambedkar was supposed to deliver a speech in Lahore, on the 'Annihilation of Caste'. This was not directed at Hindu fundamentalists or extremists, but at those who consider themselves liberal and moderate, those whom Ambedkar called 'the best of Hindus'.[30] Ambedkar, in his 1944 tightly argued pamphlet *Which is Worse? Slavery or Untouchability?* concluded that there was no doubt that untouchables were in a worse position than slaves. And he went on to state that the chasm between caste Hindus and untouchables was deep because it was both 'religious *and* social', whereas that between Hindus and Muslims, Hindus and Sikhs, or Hindus and Christians is purely religious alone: 'The chasm between the Hindus and the Untouchables must spell political disaster for the Untouchables because the relationship between the two is that of master and slave.'[31]

Eleanor Zelliot's rich work on untouchables suggests that the mathematics of caste politics was a major consideration for Gandhi. She reports a conversation between Gandhi and Sardar Patel as recorded by Gandhi's secretary, Mahadev Desai, on 21 September 1932, the second day of his 'fast unto death', in opposition to proposals – backed by Ambedkar – that *dalits* should be allowed their own election and representation. Gandhi was horrified by the idea of separate electorates for different sections of Indian society. Thus he declared that 'for all other communities', separate electorates 'will still leave room for me to deal with them, but I have no other means to deal with "untouchables"', thus demonstrating what Perry Anderson has called the 'mathematics of caste politics' was perhaps more imperative than religious or national unity.[32] In the same conversation, Gandhi added his firm belief that separate electorates 'will create division among Hindus so much that it will lead to blood-shed. "Untouchable" hooligans will make common cause with Muslim hooligans and kill caste Hindus.'[33] These were the real fears lurking behind

Gandhi's fast of 1932, about which Ambedkar quite rightly stated that it 'was nothing noble' and 'a foul and filthy act' and the 'worst form of coercion'.[34] The fast had been fully weaponised by Gandhi as part of his *satyagraha* armoury. Abstaining from food in the full glare of world publicity was to prove a most effective tactic in bringing Ambedkar and the *dalits* to heel.

Gandhi hoped that moral invective would be sufficient to overcome untouchability but insisted that caste was an essential part of Hinduism. Whilst his campaigns were earnest and sincere, the failure to understand caste politically and its role in oppressive and exploitative practices and institutions rendered Gandhi's approach ineffective in firmly dealing with this form of extreme inequality.

Women

Paradoxes and inconsistencies are sharper still when we move from untouchability to consider Gandhi's attitudes towards women. He mercilessly castigated men for their repression of women,

> of all the evils for which man has made himself responsible, none is so degrading, so shocking or so brutal as his abuse of the better half of humanity to me, the female sex, not the weaker sex. It is the nobler of the two, for it is even today the embodiment of sacrifice, silent suffering, humility, faith and knowledge.[35]

Gandhi attacked the commodification and objectification of women, insisting that 'wives should not be dolls and objects of indulgence' and appealing to the men in Congress to 'see that women became equal partners in the fight for Swaraj'.[36] He opposed child marriage and championed the rights of widows to control their own fate. Compared to most of his contemporaries, these statements were a positive endorsement of women's liberation. His campaigns provided space for women to be visibly active and engaged in the fight for freedom. However, the role that Gandhi assigned for women was as 'a true helpmate of man in the mission of service'.[37] Service is the operative word: since for Gandhi, women symbolised the 'honour' and 'virtue' of the nation. He believed that men and women possessed distinct qualities as a result of biology. Both of them have separate spheres in societies and specific roles in the making of the Indian nation, for they were essentially complementary to each other.

Men were seen by Gandhi as naturally aggressive and selfish, and women were passive, self-sacrificing and pure. Thus women were more suited to the domestic sphere, particularly engaging with family life and motherhood. In the domestic space – he argued, that is, as wife and mother – women manifest feminine qualities unsurpassable and sometimes superior to masculine ones. Women are self-reliant, courageous, patient and pure, and have a capacity to endure suffering. His models for women lay in the figures of the Hindu goddesses Sita and Draupadi, who epitomised courage and strength but also service to the community. These moral qualities belonged to the spiritual realm. Gandhi's ideal was his mother's life of penance, continual fasts and austere vows. As Madhu Kishwar notes, it is striking how Gandhi did not favour the Rani of Jhansi as a symbol of both a woman's individual strength and the cultivation of women's spiritual and moral courage. The Rani was a fighter who led from the front during the 1857 Rebellion, riding on horseback to physically capture British soldiers. However, this image did not tally with Gandhi's choice of a certain kind of feminine courage, in preference to other kinds of strength and heroism.[38] Such direct action, employing force if necessary, did not correspond to activity that was 'disciplined' and 'ordered', but entailed instead conforming to traditional gender roles.

From around 1919 onwards, Gandhi encourages the production of *khadi* (handspun cloth), made by spinning, as a symbol of self-reliance and regeneration, and also as a form of '*dharma*' or duty for upper-class, urban women in order to demonstrate their solidarity with the poorer women in the countryside. Thus, the *charkha* – the spinning wheel – came to represent a unitary bond that highlighted Gandhi's consideration of class/caste dynamics in his movement for female advancement, and the pursuit of national independence. Spinning also represented, as Kishwar notes, a 'bridge connecting the private, domestic life to the economic, political life' of Indian women.[39] The act of spinning and the production of *khadi* were encouraged as female contributions to the national struggle throughout the entirety of the movement. However, in the early 1930s with the onset of Gandhi's civil disobedience movement, there came a substantial increase in active participation that was no longer exclusively limited to the domestic sphere, for example the boycotting and picketing by women of liquor and foreign cloth shops. These non-violent boycotts and picketing activities were initiated by women themselves but still fitted with Gandhi's world-view of womanhood. Even at major protests, women were expected to nurse the male *satyagrahis* when they were struck down by police charges. Once again, therefore, although Gandhi was forceful in condemning the wrongs inflicted upon women by men and society, his views contain many ambiguities and contradictions. He was not so much concerned with changing the material conditions for women's emancipation as their 'moral' condition. Yet again, stress is placed upon feminine virtue, and ethical upliftment, to service the 'nation'. The conflation of women with the nation is itself highly suspect, as it invests women with embodying 'national honour'. In this manner, the 'nation' can lay claim to women and therefore deny women their own agency in defining their liberation.

Conclusion

Gandhi clearly cared deeply about the issues of inequality and in his own idiosyncratic manner sought ways to redress historic wrongs and map a path towards more social justice for the peasantry, industrial working class, untouchable community and women. In his various campaigns, he was willing to put himself at risk and prepared to go on hunger strike or to prison for his beliefs regarding these questions. Overall, despite his hatred of injustice, he identified problems as stemming from ignorance, indiscipline and lack of spiritual solidarity. This is why his prognosis for conflict was to emphasise rights and responsibilities. This poses the question of social inequality in moral tones and does not begin to question the very fabric of society. This helps explain not only the limitations of his campaigns for social justice, but also indicates a strategy based on the preservation of existing class society as opposed to its eradication. The tensions between mass action that he epitomised, and the social conservatism rooted in much of his support base of Indian business interests and landlords, would underpin his political outlook. It also informed his attitude to nationalism, and the alternative radical politics which would soon emerge and that would pose a challenge to his doctrine of *satyagraha* and *ahimsa*.

4

Nationalist Leader: 1919–29

The end of the First World War saw an upsurge of nationalism internationally. In India, the Congress's constitutional approach was to give way to more radical activity and mass agitation throughout the 1920s and 1930s, and Gandhi would be central to this shift. His first national action was a protest against the Rowlatt Act, which resulted from the Sedition Commission of 1917 on wartime anxieties over revolutionary conspiracies in India. British fears can be gleaned from the following extract from 1918:

> All these plots have been directed towards one and the same objective, the overthrow of British rule in India. Sometimes they have been isolated; sometimes they have been interconnected; sometimes they have been encouraged and supported by German influence ... it is not surprising that, in dealing with conspiracies so elusive and carefully contrived, Government has been compelled to resort to extraordinary legislation.[1]

On 18 March 1919, the Government of India passed the Anarchical and Revolutionary Crimes Act (Rowlatt Act), dealing with sedition and revolutionary conspiracies; it was essentially an extension of the Defence of India Act of 1915 which had allowed for wartime measures of internment and sedition. Under this Act, political cases could be tried without juries and suspects described as 'revolutionaries likely to menace the security of India'[2] interned without trial. Strict controls were placed on the press with many publications deemed seditious, including Gandhi's *Hind Swaraj*. The Act was criticised by Indians who called it the 'Black Act', echoing anger against the South African Asiatic Act a decade before. Coming in the wake of the end of the First World War, the Rowlatt Act was seen as poor reward for loyalty displayed and sacrifices made in Britain's war effort. Some 1.3 million Indians had served in the First World War with 47,000 killed and 65,000 wounded.[3]

A further cause of anger was the fact that in the same year the British had passed the Government of India Act, based on the Montagu-Chelmsford Report, which made provision for an expansion of Indian members to be represented in the legislature. A system of dyarchy was introduced whereby health, education, local government, industry and agriculture were transferred to the legislature, which included Indian members. Departments such as law and order, finance, land revenue and irrigation were retained by the executive, dominated by British members. This body and the British governor could overturn and veto legislative decisions and the franchise was limited to those with a certain amount of property. So these were limited reforms. Ten years earlier, separate electorates had been introduced for Muslims but were now extended to Sikhs, Europeans and Anglo-Indians, part of a longer-standing British imperial 'divide and rule' policy designed to crystallise sectarian identities.

Slow progress on legislative reform and the Rowlatt Act coming in the aftermath of the First World War were seen as placing a 'libel on Indian loyalty'. All Indian members in the legislature voted against the Bill but it was rushed through by the majority British members. Many Indian council members resigned in protest, including Mohammad Ali Jinnah whose response summed up the mood, when he wrote to Viceroy Lord Chelmsford that it was an unwarranted uprooting of the 'fundamental principles of justice' and a gross violation of the 'constitutional rights of the people'.[4]

Gandhi warned the government that if the Bill was introduced, he would be forced to protest peacefully. The following pledge was drafted on 24 February 1919 and signed by Gandhi, barrister Vallabhbhai Patel of the Congress and Anasuya Sarabhai, for the women's branch of the Home Rule League:

> Being conscientiously of the opinion that the Bills … are unjust, subversive of the principle of liberty and justice and destructive of the elementary rights of individuals on which the safety of the

> community as a whole and the State itself are based, we solemnly affirm that ... we shall refuse civilly to obey these laws and such other laws as a Committee to be hereafter appointed may think fit ....[5]

In his accompanying letter to the Viceroy, Gandhi was at pains to point out that his decision had not been taken lightly, as he had 'passed many a sleepless night over it'.[6] In spite of this 'regret', he called for a national *hartal*, which was a stay-away from work where *satyagrahis* would engage in prayer and fasting on the day. Activists were also encouraged to court arrest by circulating and reading banned publications in public.

The revolutionary potentialities – including the potential for revolutionary violence – unleashed by Gandhi's militant leadership, despite his own best efforts to keep within peaceful, constitutional channels, can be seen by what happened next. The original date set for the *hartal* was 30 March 1919, but later pushed back to 6 April 1919 by Gandhi. Some areas, such as Delhi, were not aware of the change in date and there were multiple outbreaks of resistance in some areas. The first outbreak of violence occurred in the Punjab on 10 April when a protest was held outside the residence of the Deputy Commissioner of Amritsar to demand the release of two popular nationalist leaders: Satyapal, a Hindu who had served in the Royal Army Medical Corps during the First World War and Saifuddin Kitchlew, a Muslim barrister. Both preached non-violence but were forbidden to speak publicly under the Rowlatt provisions. Michael O'Dwyer, the lieutenant-governor of Punjab, decided to deport major agitators from the province. Both leaders were arrested and removed to a secret location. A protest was held by supporters and the crowd was fired on by military police, killing several protesters. In response, several banks and other government buildings, including the town hall and the railway station were attacked and set on fire. The violence continued to escalate, culminating in the deaths of three Europeans including government employees and civilians. There was retaliatory firing on the crowd from the military several times during the day, and between eight and twenty people were killed.[7]

To understand why there was so much resentment in the Punjab to the Rowlatt Act, one must remember that one-half of the Indian Army during the First World War had been drawn from this region – a region that had proved indispensable for the Raj's army recruitment ever since the 1857 Rebellion, when the Punjab had generally remained loyal to the British. The concept of 'martial races' had been developed and utilised by the British since the shock of the 1857 uprising to depict Punjabis and Pathans as brave, hardy and warrior-like, whereas Bengalis by contrast were labelled as effeminate and lazy. Punjabi loyalty to the Crown was taken for granted, and the scientific racism it was steeped in could rationalise Indian subordination to British rule. As the military historian Jeffrey Greenhut asserts, the concept of martial races had an 'elegant symmetry' in that it posited intelligent, educated Indians as cowards, whilst those 'defined as brave were uneducated and backward', thus leaving the combined qualities of intelligence and courage with the British officer class![8] In this way, the 'martial races' theory neatly dovetailed with every racist stereotype to buffer colonial armies.

In contrast to Gandhi's relative ignorance of racism in Victorian England, during the war Indian soldiers stationed in Europe had been subjected to segregation, curfews and other restrictions. In his fictional account of Indians sent to France, *Across the Black Waters*, the novelist Mulk Raj Anand refers to the 'unwritten law that no sepoy was to be seen on familiar terms with the women in this country'. The English 'did not like ... the brown-skinned Indians to look at white women'.[9] Even when Indian soldiers were wounded and brought to hospitals on the south coast, concerns over white nurses tending to 'native' soldiers led to 'absolutely inflexible rules' keeping them within hospital precincts.[10] Even on rare occasions of recreation, segregation ruled. In London, Cook's Tours organised trips for small groups of Hindu, and, separately, Muslim soldiers. The supervised tours allowed tourist combatants an hour's shopping at a department store and a ride on the Underground, as well as escorted visits to royal and other tourist sites in the capital.[11] No such supervision, restrictions, or rules governed the soldiers from the white dominions in any theatre of war. Little wonder that so many Indians and especially Punjabis felt that the Rowlatt Bill was an act of bad faith by an empire towards a region that had served it so well. By 13 April 1919, the British government had decided to place most of the Punjab under martial law and Brigadier General Reginald Dyer was brought in to take charge.

The Amritsar Massacre and its Aftermath

On 13 April 1919, the same day General Dyer took charge of the Punjab, thousands of people gathered in the Jallianwala Bagh near the Golden Temple to attend the city's traditional fairs. It was *Baisakhi* – both a harvest festival and the Sikh religious New Year – and people from surrounding villages and small towns attended. At 4.30 p.m., Dyer marched a group of ninety British Indian Army soldiers, mostly Gurkhas, Punjab rifles, Pathan infantry, Dogra regiment and Baluchi regiment, into the park accompanied by two armoured cars carrying machine guns. The vehicles remained outside the main gate as the Bagh entrance alleys were too narrow.[12] Dyer ordered troops to open fire without warning and to direct fire towards the densest sections of the crowd. He continued the firing, approximately 1,400 rounds in all, until the troops' ammunition was exhausted. Official records put the figures at 379 killed (337 men, 41 boys and a 6-week-old baby) and 1,200 injured, but the real figures are estimated to be much higher.[13] The massacre sent shockwaves throughout India, but in a further act of humiliation, Dyer imposed a 'crawling order' on the street in Amritsar where a European schoolteacher had been assaulted by Indians. Any Indian wishing to walk in the street between 6 a.m. and 8 p.m. was made to crawl the 200 yards on all fours, lying flat on their bellies. In response to the Hunter Commission that had been set up to investigate the massacre, Dyer stated that he had gone to the Bagh with the deliberate intention of opening fire if he found a crowd assembled there: 'I think it quite possible that I could have dispersed the crowd without firing but they would have come back again and laughed, and I would have made, what I consider, a fool of myself.'[14]

There was outrage in India at both the massacre and Dyer's defence. Though Dyer was criticised in India and in Britain and he was removed from his role, he nevertheless came home to a hero's welcome, where the British press lauded him as 'the man who saved

India'.[15] The *Morning Post*, a conservative, pro-imperialist newspaper, which later merged with the *Daily Telegraph*, launched a fund for Dyer and raised £26,000, a huge sum at the time, within a month. It supported Dyer's action on the grounds that the massacre was necessary to 'Protect the honour of European Women'.[16] In addition a 'Thirteen-Woman Committee' was constituted to present 'the Saviour of the Punjab with the sword of honour and a purse'.[17] Large contributions to the fund were made by civil servants and by British Army and Indian Army officers. This was in stark contrast to the victims of Dyer's carnage. The families of the victims killed at the Jallianwala Bagh had to fight for government compensation. In the end, they received Rs. 500, for each victim, then equal to £37 10*s* 0*d*.[18]

Outrage in Britain was expressed by among others the Liberal Secretary of State for India Edwin Montagu, who called it 'a grave error in judgement'. In the House of Commons, he asked, 'Are you going to keep your hold on India by terrorism, racial humiliation, subordination and frightfulness?'[19] Even Winston Churchill, Secretary of State for War, called the massacre 'an episode without precedent or parallel in the modern history of the British Empire ... an extraordinary event, a monstrous event, an event which stands in singular and sinister isolation ... the crowd was neither armed nor attacking.'[20] Rabindranath Tagore, the Nobel Poet Laureate, returned his knighthood in protest, stating 'a great crime has been done in the name of law in the Punjab.'[21]

Although Gandhi had called for self-purification through praying and fasting in the aftermath of the massacre, he was not permitted to enter the Punjab and instead was arrested and escorted to Bombay by police. News of his arrest angered the crowds gathered in Bombay to meet him. They were charged by police and some were trampled. In Ahmedabad, angry textile workers and others had attacked government buildings such as the revenue collector's office, the telegraph office and the railway station. Two or three Europeans had been killed alongside scores of Indians, with over a hundred wounded.[22] Gandhi addressed a meeting outside his Sabarmati Ashram in Ahmedabad on 14 April 1919, stipulating that events happening in his name were shameful and 'those who have been responsible for them have thereby not honoured me but disgraced me. A rapier run through my body could hardly have pained me more.'[23] On the same day in a letter to the secretary to the viceroy, he described the Ahmedabad events as 'utter lawlessness bordering almost on Bolshevism' and the news that 'Englishmen and women have found it necessary to leave their bungalows and to confine themselves to a few well-guarded houses. It is a matter of the deepest humiliation and regret for me.'[24] He even used the phrase 'Himalayan miscalculation' to describe the Rowlatt *satyagraha* and called off the *hartal* immediately.

Though critical of British action in Amritsar, Gandhi's main ire was reserved for fellow Indians who in his eyes were not ready for his brand of non-violence. They needed to be trained in all its principles before embarking on any further action. Some of those attempting the whitewashing of the British Empire today have tried to blame Gandhi himself for Amritsar. Nick Lloyd argues that 'Gandhi's *satyagraha* pledge committed its signatories to refuse to obey the Rowlatt Bills, but this was impossible *unless one actually became a terrorist.*'[25] Lloyd further charges Gandhi with 'revolutionary objectives designed to overthrow government legislation' and as such the protests constituted a 'threatening conspiracy'.[26] There is an element of truth of course to such an argument, in the sense that Gandhi's mass actions, in the context of brutal imperialist domination, constantly threatened to overspill into revolutionary responses from the masses – despite all of his own subjectively reformist intentions. As in Ahmedabad, pressures between stated intentions and the reality of the situation on the ground could not always tally. Nonetheless, the Amritsar Massacre has become a byword for colonial brutality and repression, and in India it is remembered as the watershed that irrevocably put Indian nationalists on the path to independence. It marked a turning point in relations between India and Britain, and would lead Gandhi to become more resolute in his commitment to Indian nationalism.

Rising Nationalism, Empire Patriotism and the Muslim League

As the First World War ended, the great powers of Britain and France had divided the spoils of four former empires between them, particularly the former Ottoman lands across the Middle East. Armistice also brought pressure up on the imperial powers from new nationalist movements. The 'Wilsonian moment' referred to Woodrow Wilson's 'creed' of the right of 'every people … to choose the sovereignty under which they shall live'. Another source of pressure on imperialist powers came from the Russian Revolution of 1917, which demanded the right of nations to self-determination.[27] If the First World War had resulted in some quite fundamental changes in India's relationship to Britain, demands for Indian representation and autonomy precipitated mobilisations for political change in India itself, and it is to these mobilisations and their organisational aspects that we will now turn.

The All-India Muslim League, founded in 1906, was initially made up of wealthy Muslim landlords, mainly from the United Provinces (UP) in northern India. Identification with British imperial power was symptomatic of patrician nationalist politics. Thus the League's objectives included the promotion of 'loyalty to the British government, to protect and advance the political rights and interests of Mussalmans of India and respectfully represent their needs and aspirations to government'.[28]

Empire patriotism, as we have seen, epitomised the young Gandhi in South Africa and continued in the run-up to the First World War. In a speech in Patna on 25 May 1918, Gandhi made clear his view that India should provide men for the war and *not* make it contingent on self-rule as 'any calamity that overtakes the Empire is one that overtakes India as well.'[29] These views reflected the class basis of the middle classes, with their elite nationalism wedded to constitutional reforms, more interested in finding accommodation with imperial rule than in fighting for genuine national liberation.

Annie Besant and the Home Rule League

One individual who did not support the British war effort was Annie Besant, a theosophist from Britain whom Gandhi had known in London. Her early life had been characterised by left-wing causes and the fight for socialism. In London, Besant had been close to George Bernard Shaw and joined the Fabian Society. She was closely associated with Edward Aveling, translator of Karl Marx's works into

English and lover of Eleanor Marx. Under such influence, it was not surprising that she supported the match workers' strike in 1888 at Bryant and May's factory in east London. She was later influenced by spiritualism and the desire to fuse the religious practices of Eastern and Western traditions.

Besant had been a vocal campaigner for Irish Home Rule and after settling in India as war broke out, unlike Gandhi, she echoed an Irish nationalist slogan, declaring, 'England's need is India's opportunity.' As editor of the *New India* newspaper, she attacked the colonial administration of India and called for clear and decisive moves towards self-rule. As with Ireland, the government refused to discuss any changes while the war lasted. In 1916, Besant launched the All India Home Rule League along with the militant nationalist, Bal Gangadhar Tilak, who had earned the nickname 'Lokmanya [Tilak]' (beloved of the people). Modelling itself on Irish nationalist practices, this was the first political party in India to have regime change as its main goal. The Home Rule League worked all year round building a structure of local branches, which enabled it to mobilise demonstrations and public meetings to agitate for home rule. Under wartime ordinances, Besant was arrested in June 1917 and interned at a hill station, where she defiantly flew a red-and-green flag.

This had an impact on Congress and the Muslim League, who in spite of their differences, met at a joint session in the northern city of Lucknow in December 1916 to unanimously agree to campaign for Dominion status – the 'Lucknow Pact'. By the end of 1917, the combined membership of the Home Rule League and the Muslim League stood at 60,000 and they were using newspapers and public meetings to press home their demand and widen the campaign.[30] Sensitive to such developments, the Secretary of State for India Edwin Montagu, on 20 August 1917, stressed that the aim of Great Britain was to give India more administrative competence as well as the 'gradual development of self-governing institutions with a view to the progressive realisation of responsible government in India as an integral part of the British Empire'.[31] This policy was a continuation of the Minto-Morley Reforms of 1909, but it was also a recognition of the role Indians had played during the First World War. It allowed more provincial control, but at different levels, according to province and the local conditions in each one.

The Khilafat *Movement and Building Hindu-Muslim Unity*

Another new development was the emergence of the *Khilafat* movement, a pan-Islamic protest campaign at the British and French recognition of Kemal Atatürk's abolition of the Ottoman Caliphate based in Istanbul. To its founders and followers, the *Khilafat* was not a religious movement but rather a show of solidarity with their fellow Muslims in Turkey, and a protest at the prospect of the British ever conscripting Muslims in India to fight against their Turkish counterparts.[32] However, religious sentiment was aroused by the fear of Islam's holy sites coming under the control of Western imperial forces. The *Khilafat*'s main base was in India, where it was launched by Maulana Mohammad Ali, an Oxford-educated journalist, and his brother Shaukat Ali. Maulana had spent four years in prison for advocating resistance to the British and support for the Caliphate. The organisation based in Lucknow, published the *Khilafat* Manifesto in 1920, which called upon the British to protect the Caliphate and for Indian Muslims to unite and hold the British accountable for this purpose.[33]

The All-India Muslim League did not support the *Khilafat* movement, but Gandhi for various reasons did become a supporter, which elevated the *Khilafat* movement's leaders into the role of spokesmen for the wider Muslim community. Gandhi was friends with the Ali brothers and there was an automatic unity of interests and philosophy as religion was central to both parties. Moreover, the championing of oppressed groups was essential to Gandhi's prognosis for Indian nationalism and so Hindu-Muslim unity was a central objective to that end.[34] Gandhi understood that such a united front against the British Empire had to be fought for and the issue of the Caliphate as an anti-British issue could both bring Muslims into the nationalist movement and simultaneously be used to redirect Congress into being a mass movement focused on a popular cause.

Gandhi's own religiosity meant that he held all faiths to be equal, believing that they were different paths to the one god and salvation.

He stated 'What does it matter that we take different roads so long as we reach the same goal?'[35] But he was also acutely conscious of the fact that Muslims were a minority, whose grievances and the discrimination suffered by them had to be addressed. Hence his championing of the *Khilafat* movement was crucial to aiding Hindu-Muslim unity and forcing the nationalist movement to politically identify with a 'Muslim' cause – even though it brought criticism from Jinnah, who saw this as further evidence of Gandhi intermingling politics with religion. Yet Gandhi's leadership over this issue meant that at the Nagpur session of the Indian National Congress on 30 December 1920, the following resolution was proposed and agreed upon: '[The British] Government … has forfeited the confidence of the nation by its utter disregard of the sacred sentiments of the Mussulmans in India and the outraged feelings of the whole of India regarding the wanton atrocities of the Punjab administration during the satyagraha year.'[36]

In July 1921, Maulana Mohammad Ali along with other leaders of the *Khilafat* was arrested for holding the view that it was religiously unlawful for the Muslims to continue in the British Army. Gandhi as well as the Congress supported Mohammad Ali and issued a manifesto.

The Non-Co-operation Movement

Gandhi was now fully aware of the need to address multifaceted grievances. Popular outrage at the Amritsar Massacre and subsequent events, despite Gandhi calling a halt to the Rowlatt action, had not dissipated. Consequently, the Non-Co-operation Movement was launched at the Allahabad meeting of the INC in June 1920, to right the three 'wrongs': the 'Sikh' wrong experienced at the massacre of Amritsar, the 'Muslim' wrong of the abolition of the Ottoman Caliphate, and the general wrong of colonial rule.

Gandhi's wider programme of non-co-operation involved the surrender of the titles and offices and resignation from nominated posts in the local bodies. The non-co-operators were to boycott government duties, *Durbars* and other functions, and they were to withdraw their children from government schools and colleges and establish national schools and colleges. They were to boycott British courts and establish private arbitration courts; they were to use *swadeshi* (homemade) cloth. Truth and non-violence were to be strictly observed by non-co-operators. In audaciously declaring *Swaraj* within one year as their goal, Congress under Gandhi's leadership seemed to be chiming with the wider global radical mood of 1919, exemplified by the Wilsonian moment and the founding of the Communist International.

The non-co-operation campaign emulated the *Swadeshi* campaign of 1905, based in Bengal where the strategy of boycotting all foreign goods and only purchasing indigenous products had been so successful in reversing the partition of Bengal in 1911. The immediate results were quite spectacular. In the first months, 9,000 students left schools and colleges and joined more than 800 national institutions that had sprung up all over the country. By early 1922, an estimated 100,000 students had left the government colleges and enrolled in national ones. Congress politicians resigned from newly elected provincial councils; solicitors gave up law practices; and alcohol shops were picketed. Protests against forest regulations in Madras attracted the support of landless peasants and *adivasis* (indigenous) communities. The most successful item of the programme was the boycott of foreign cloth, as Gandhi espoused the virtue of *khadi* homespun cloth. The value of imports of foreign cloth almost halved, falling from Rs. 102 crores in 1920–21 to 57 crores in 1921–22, hitting tax revenues.[37]

Non-co-operation seemed to capture the mood of the masses. It was the first nationwide political agitation of the nationalist period, not just a local campaign like Gandhi's previous *satyagrahas*. Critically, the Non-Co-operation Movement achieved a level of political unity between Hindus and Muslims in India, and saw a process of politicisation begin to take place among many Muslims as a result of their being part of a mass nationalist movement on a national scale.

In spite of this momentum, the more elite figures in the Indian nationalist movement remained aloof, and by March 1921 only 24 title-holders (out of more than 5,000) had surrendered their honours and only 180 lawyers had given up their practices. Candidates stood for all but six of the 637 seats in the legislative council and assembly elections in November 1920, and although polling was low in many places, it did not prevent the new legislatures coming into being or Indian ministers taking office under the new constitution.[38] As is often the case with mass movements, there can be a degree of popular unity at the outset while things are going forward, but political arguments and differences soon emerge over strategy and tactics – in this case over the role of violence in the struggle. The two contentious flashpoints around which arguments raged came in August 1921, with the Mappila Rebellion, and then on 5 February 1922 with the Chauri Chaura incident.

The Mappila Rebellion

In late August 1921, a rebellion broke out in the Malabar region of south-west India where up to 10,000 armed Mappila peasants rose against British authority. The immediate spark was state repression, when the British district magistrate banned a meeting of a local Muslim leader from Malabar in February 1921. When the leader indicated that he would defy the order, the speaker and *Khilafat* leaders were arrested and sentenced to six months' imprisonment. Protests erupted but soon subsided without incidence. Initially, Malabar was a region relatively immune to Gandhi and the wider Congress movement. Even the Home Rule League and All-India Muslim League historically had next to no influence here.[39] But this had changed after the Nagpur Congress when, in January 1921, the Keralan Congress Committee and the Malabar *Khilafat* Committee pledged support for non-cooperation. The local tenants' conference called for non-cooperation against landlords over land tenureship and was therefore in line with Gandhi's campaign. This demonstrates how non-cooperation had given rise to a number of grievances coming to fruition, including those of poor peasants. Colonial land-tenure policy and high taxation resulted in anger against the landlord class, who were predominantly high-caste Hindus, whereas the small tenant farmers, peasants and landless labourers were predominantly Muslim. So, the Mappila Rebellion had a combination of economic, agrarian and communitarian factors being played out.

In late July 1921, another protest took place over a dispute between a landlord's agent and a *Khilafat*-supporting Mappila tenant. By the beginning of August 1921, protest numbers were building up, as thousands of demonstrators, sporting skullcaps with *Khilafat* badges and some in *khadi* shirts armed with knives, spears and swords, assembled in the village.[40] Again, the events ended without violence, but the fear of economic and religious grievances propelling a protest movement from below signalled a danger for the British, as evidenced here: 'the crowd at Pukkottur had been heard to express a desire or determination to add the heads of Mr. Hitchcock and myself to the bag ... I feel powerless with my present force ... we have peace now on a precarious tenure only if we make no move.'[41]

Acting on his fears, the magistrate and police evacuated European women from Ernad district and troop reinforcements of Gurkhas were ordered in, despite the lack of violence. As troops searched houses to make arrests, many more people massed on the streets. When they refused to disperse, they were charged at with bayonets and fired upon and martial law was imposed by 25 August 1921.[42] Initial minor clashes between police and *Khilafat* activists turned into more serious outbreaks with police stations, court and government treasuries being taken over by Indian protesters. The insurgents used guerrilla tactics to out-manoeuvre government forces and managed to hold control of the southern *taluks* (administrative areas) of Ernad and Walluvanad for several months. It took the authorities six months to crush the rebellion, at the end of which 2,339 Mappilas were killed and a further 1,652 wounded.[43] Unofficial estimates of Mappila casualties were much higher and nearly 6,000 were captured. By contrast, government casualties numbered 43, with 126 wounded. The government was merciless in its revenge for such flagrant insurgency: over 24,000 Indians were convicted, with nearly 200 hanged. A further tragedy was the death by asphyxiation of 70 out of 100 prisoners loaded into a closed railway carriage. This had been made 'practically airtight' as a result of fine wire gauze, which had been painted over and was clogged with paint and dust.[44]

During the rebellion, there were rumours of violence against Hindus with reports of 600 Hindus killed and forced conversions of 2,500 others.[45] As Arnold argues, such incidents provoked fear that non-cooperation and the *Khilafat* could lead to violence and increased communalist tensions.[46] But in November 1921, there were also protests against the visit of the Prince of Wales with demonstrations and riots in Bombay, which involved Hindus, Muslims and Parsis, suggesting that struggles from below could unite people across communitarian lines against a common enemy. Here again, clashes with the police left 58 people dead and 381 wounded.[47] And even in Malabar, three of the hundred loaded into the doomed rail carriage were Hindus.[48] These instances are significant as there has been a tendency to interpret the causes of the Mappila Rebellion in crude communalist terms. The advantage for the British in seeing this episode through the lens of religion was made crystal clear by Governor of Madras Willingdon, when he confided to the viceroy that the Malabar trouble had been 'a blessing in disguise' for the government, 'for the Hindu is really frightened and has begun to doubt more than ever the reality of Hindu-Muslim *entente cordiale*.'[49] Gandhi also interpreted the rebellion through a religious lens, but one that had been provoked through an indifferent political authority that was happy to see inter-Indian violence. Officially, the British blamed non-cooperation in general and Gandhi in particular.

More significantly, Gandhi – though ostensibly committed to the unity of Hindus and Muslims as one people cut from the same cloth – saw the Muslims of Malabar as possessing 'a fiery temperament', and prone to being 'easily excitable'[50] due to their Arab heritage. Gandhi believed that 'the outbreak would not have occurred had the message of non-violence been allowed to reach them',[51] so echoing his stance over the 'Himalayan' blunder a few years earlier. On the violence against Hindus, Gandhi proclaimed that Hindus and Muslims 'would have jointly appeased the Moplahs', but that even if Muslims had supported the Mappila violence then 'Hinduism would have relied upon its creed of non-violence and turned every Mussalman into a friend, or Hindu valour would have been tested and tried.'[52] This clearly indicates Gandhi's firm belief in the theory of Hinduism as inherently superior to any other creed, despite his general opposition to traditional brahmanical doctrines. So he could utter the following:

> The Moplahs were never particularly friendly to the Malabar Hindus. They had looted them before ... They were kept in utter darkness by the government and neglected both by Mussalmans

> and Hindus. Being wild and brave but ignorant, they have mistaken the mission of the Khilafat and acted in a savage, inhuman and irreligious manner.[53]

The elitism in Gandhi's method is here clear: he is enlightened, educated, aware and knowledgeable enough to be a genuine *satyagraha*; he feels some middle-class elements of society are ready for this, but the great unwashed masses are ignorant, uneducated, ruled by irrational passions and require the guidance of a benevolent teacher.

The Chauri Chaura Incident

The second incident took place in the United Provinces in north India in the village of Chauri Chaura where, on 4 February 1922, protesters answering the call for non-cooperation, were demonstrating against high food prices in the local marketplace, thus again underlining how non-cooperation fed into a mood of local discontent over material conditions. The demonstrators were beaten back by local police with some of their leaders arrested and locked up at the Chauri Chaura police station. In response, a protest against the police was called and on 5 February 1922, some 2,000–2,500 protesters gathered in front of the police station demanding the release of their leader. Armed police were dispatched to control the situation while the crowd started shouting anti-government slogans. Initially, the police fired warning shots into the air, but this only agitated the crowd, who began to throw stones at the police.[54]

The Indian sub-inspector then ordered the police to open fire directly on the crowd, and three protesters were killed and several others wounded. This infuriated the demonstrators who set the *chowki* (police station) ablaze, killing all of the Indian policemen trapped inside. Most were burned to death though several appear to have been killed by the crowd at the entrance to the *chowki* and their bodies thrown back into the fire. Twenty-two policemen and the son of a policeman were killed.[55] As with the Mappila Rebellion, government repression was brutal. In a trial lasting eight months, 228 people were charged with 'rioting and arson'. Of these six died while in police custody and 172 were sentenced to death. On 20 April

1923, the Allahabad High Court reviewed the death verdicts; 19 death sentences were confirmed and 110 were sentenced to prison for life, with the rest sentenced to long terms of imprisonment.[56]

As before, Gandhi was distressed by the violence, organised supposedly in his name. Under his instruction, the Congress issued the following resolution at its Bardoli session: 'The Working Committee deplores the inhuman conduct of the mob at Chauri Chaura in having brutally murdered constables and wantonly burnt the Police *Thana* and tenders its sympathy to the families of the bereaved.'[57] So the protestors were a 'mob' and the concern was for the bereaved of the policemen, not for activist casualties. As we have noted, Gandhi's position was always to condemn violence, but he was particular about who was to blame for the violence.

In the aftermath of the Chauri Chaura incident, on 12 February 1922, Gandhi called a halt to the Non-Co-operation Movement and suspended civil disobedience. Gandhi undertook a fast for five days as penance for what he considered a violent crime committed in his name. He was arrested and sentenced to six years' imprisonment but released in February 1924 on health grounds. Gandhi also now abandoned the *Khilafat* movement due to violence, which saw the main leaders of the *Khilafat* movement all arrested. Gandhi's withdrawal of support represented a massive blow to the *Khilafat* movement, leading to a further splintering of its leadership. The *Khilafat* movement now lost momentum and was disbanded in 1924 after the Caliphate itself was abolished, meaning that there was no longer an organised force pushing for a unification of Indian Muslims as a political constituency within the wider Indian nationalist movement.

Gandhi's Leadership

The divisions among the *Khilafat* leaders only reinforced the fact that Gandhi had now established himself as the dominant, commanding figure both within the Congress and the wider Non-Co-operation Movement, and some even now talked of Gandhi's 'dictatorship'. As well as being to the fore of the Non-Co-operation Movement, Gandhi had helped to transform the Congress into a mass party with an annual membership fee, re-organised into provincial committees based on the language spoken, and with a 15-member 'Working Committee' elected as the executive head. This expanded the membership and also the social base of the Congress and transformed it away from its elite gathering associations.

Yet while helping transform the Congress away from elitism, as we have seen, Gandhi's own thinking contained a strand of elitism. On both Chauri Chaura and the Mappila Rebellion, Gandhi blamed not only himself but also Indians for not being 'ready', rather than hold the police and authorities to account for the bloodshed. Gandhi's tone was patronising and elitist, precisely what in the past he had taken the Congress to task for. According to Richard Johnson, Gandhi argued that the violence left the twin pillars of imperialism – the ideological and the military justifications for continued rule – intact and as such it was the 'anti-imperialist terrorists' who had provided the British with ideological and military legitimacy.[58] Gandhi genuinely believed that independence could have been achieved in 1922 had it not been for the violence at Chauri Chaura, as can be seen from his article, 'My Friend, the Revolutionary':

> I respectfully contend that their sacrifice, nobility and love are not a waste of effort, but being ignorant and misguided, do and have done more harm to the country than any other activity. Their reckless disregard for the lives of their opponents has brought on repression that has made those that do not take part in their warfare more cowardly than they were before … The masses are not prepared for the repression that follows in the trail of revolutionary activities and unwittingly strengthen the hand of the very Government which the revolutionaries are seeking to destroy. It is my certain conviction that had the Chauri Chaura murder not taken place the movement attempted at Bardoli [a major *satyagraha* campaign in Gujarat] would have resulted in the establishment of Swaraj.[59]

The Rowlatt *satyagraha* and the non-cooperation campaigns had thus succeeded at least in bringing people together for a short while, testament to how Indian national unity was a critical plank of Gandhi's theology and political outlook.

There were of course critics of Gandhi's strategy. Tagore, a former admirer, described non-cöoperation as 'political asceticism'.[60] Tagore was vehemently opposed to notions of pious suffering, making a virtue out of misery as opposed to focusing on real social and political emancipation. Tagore also came to be highly critical of what he perceived as the 'cult of the charkha', the spinning wheel, whereas Gandhi saw this as providing useful work for India's mass rural and urban populace. Additionally, Gandhi did not expect everyone to spend the entire day spinning, but that every Indian should give 'everyday only thirty minutes to spinning as sacrifice for the whole nation'.[61] Gandhi believed spinning could deal with the problems of idleness and unemployment. It was useful work that he believed provided a service to the nation. Just as *khadi* was indigenous, spinning relates to Gandhi's views on industrial development and his romanticised notion of some idyllic past that India should strive towards achieving. Tagore saw in this the levelling-down of all into some pre-ordained uniformity that denied genuine creativity of thought and activity, let alone any sense of individuality. That is why he castigated the very principle of spinning: 'instead of removing poverty or achieving Hindu-Muslim unity, or leading to *swaraj*, it was more likely to paralyse the reasoning power of the people and perpetuate their habit of reliance on the *guru* or some magical *mantra*.'[62]

The *mantra* lay in Gandhi's inflexibility and the total obedience he expected from his followers. Gandhi was an authoritarian, as acknowledged even by Nehru in his *Autobiography*, where he referred to Gandhi's 'Kingliness' that compelled a willing obeisance from others.[63] He adds that Gandhi was 'consciously and deliberately meek and humble. Yet he was full of power and authority, and he knew it and at times he was imperious enough, issuing commands which had to be obeyed.'[64]

The Class Basis of Gandhism

A short public correspondence, with all letters published in the Indian press, with Shapurji Saklatvala, the Indian Communist MP for Battersea North in London, in 1927 over questions of industrialisation and livelihoods of workers and peasants demonstrates some of the problems and limits of Gandhi's concept of trusteeship and his wider programme for championing workers and peasantry.[65] Saklatvala questioned him on the value and viability of spinning as employment. Gandhi had stated that two annas' worth[66] per day was sufficient for peasants engaged in the *charka* movement. Saklatvala picked up this point, and harangues Gandhi stating 'would India have given you any importance, would India have allowed you to take the political leadership, would India have poured in lakhs of rupees in response to your demands if you had said that you wanted all this only for the purpose of adding Rs. 2 a day to the income of barely three percent of the Indian peasantry?'[67]

Saklatvala tried to make the case for the All-India Trade Union Congress, which Gandhi was reluctant to support in the belief that they antagonised employers by preaching 'class warfare'. The crux of this debate was over the reluctance of the Ahmedabad textile workers to join the AITUC. Saklatvala believed the federation would be stronger as a national trade union body representing workers from all corners of the country. The Ahmedabad workers' leadership was controlled by Anasuya Sarabhai, from a wealthy family of industrialists and business people, and her brother was one of the mill owners who had made an anonymous donation of Rs. 13,000 to Gandhi's Sabarmati Ashram. Anasuya herself had opened a school for poor women and worked for the improvement of conditions for women and the poor more generally. Clearly, a section of indigenous industrial magnates supported Gandhi's programme as a tradition of philanthropy existed, such as the Birla family discussed in previous chapter.

Saklatvala insisted on the right of workers to be organised and to challenge and fight for their rights against their exploitation, as militant and active workers. Gandhi's response is telling, 'I do not regard capital as the enemy of labour.'[68] He was not against labour organisation but campaigned for it on 'Indian' lines, or as he put it more candidly, 'my lines'.[69] Gandhi's benevolence and paternalism can be demonstrated by his analysis of the state of the Indian labour movement. 'Labour in India is still extremely unorganised',[70] Gandhi noted, adding that 'the Labourers have no minds of their own when it comes to national policy or even the general welfare of labour itself.'[71] He insisted that labour had no cohesion, no mutual ties and was entirely divided. Gandhi's own personal attitude to strikes in general was made explicit in 1921 when he wrote strikes 'do not fall within the plan of non-violent non-cooperation':[72] 'In India we want no political strikes ... We must gain control over all the unruly and disturbing elements ... We seek not to destroy capital or capitalists, but to regulate the relations between capital and labour. We want to harness capital to our side. It would be folly to encourage sympathetic strikes.'[73] His policy in the Ahmedabad dispute was clearly not 'anti-capitalistic'; instead, the underlying philosophy was one of moral reform and class conciliation, to

> take from capital labour's due share and no more, and this is not by paralysing capital, but by reform among labourers from within and by their own self-consciousness; not again through the cleverness and manoeuvring of non-labour leaders, but by educating labour to evolve its own leadership and its own self-reliant, self-existing organisation. Its direct aim is not in the least degree political. Its direct aim is internal reform and evolution of internal strength.[74]

The chief reason for Saklatvala writing to Gandhi in such a public manner was of course in part recognition of the fact that by 1927 Gandhi and his ideas now had a tremendous influence over millions of Indians, but this was to no avail and Gandhi kept the AITUC and the Ahmedabad mill workers union completely separate.

Conclusion

This chapter has demonstrated how Gandhi became a national figure in 1919, a profile that was sustained throughout the 1920s. Such was Gandhi's stature that he had assumed the effective leadership of the Congress, and indeed served as its president from 1924 to 1929. The freedom struggle assumed an all-India character under his leadership and at midnight on 31 December 1929, the Indian National Congress raised the tricolour flag of India on the banks of the Ravi River at Lahore. On 26 January 1930, the Congress, led by Gandhi and Nehru, publicly issued the Declaration of Independence, or *Purna Swaraj*. The declaration included the readiness to withhold taxes, and the statement boldly declared:

> We believe that it is the inalienable right of the Indian people, as of any other people, to have freedom and to enjoy the fruits of their toil and have the necessities of life, so that they may have full opportunities of growth ... We believe therefore, that India must sever the British connection and attain *Purna Swaraj* or complete independence.[75]

The nationalist movement, as represented by the Congress, had its membership expand from 80,000 to 450,000 by 1929. Gandhi had truly become a national figure and in this decade, he had succeeded in bringing everyone together.

But there were also weaknesses and problems. Gandhi's conclusion about the outcome of the 1919 *hartal* was that it was a blunder of 'Himalayan magnitude', because of the premature nature of a population that he perceived to be unprepared and ignorant of his particular brand of non-violent resistance. As in every instance discussed above, rather than placing the blame at the door of the British, he arrogantly lectured Indians. But the fact that millions had answered his call to stay away from work marked the beginning of Gandhi's emergence as a new national leader of the masses. Over the next year, Gandhi organised the Congress inquiry into the Punjab, presided over the *Khilafat* conference in Delhi and was entrusted with drafting a new constitution for Congress. By October 1919, he assumed the editorship of two weekly publications, *Navajivan* and *Young India*. The constitution of Congress was also radically changed to make it a mass-based organisation, with the clear objective of achieving *Swaraj* and committed to non-violent non-cooperation as the means to achieve this. Gandhi had certainly come a long way in less than a decade after his return to India.

5

Global Icon: 1929–39

In 1919, the British government had declared that a parliamentary commission would be sent to India in ten years' time to examine the effects and operations of the constitutional reforms, and to determine whether India was ready for further reform. However, anxious to prevent a possible Labour government from making its own appointments to such a commission, the Conservative government decided in late 1927 to advance the date of the commission and appoint a trusted committee of seven MPs headed by Sir John Simon. This action was interpreted as an outrageous insult and betrayal of the promise to increase Indian participation in government, as not a single Indian would sit on the Simon Commission. As a result, a wide cross-section of Indian political opinion agreed to organise a boycott because they felt that the commission would ignore Indian criticism of the 1919 reforms. The Simon Commission left England in January 1928. Almost immediately upon its arrival in Bombay on 3 February 1928, its members were confronted by throngs of protesters shouting 'Simon go back', although among the crowds there were also some supporters, who saw the commission as the next step on the road to self-governance.[1] A strike began and many people turned out to greet the commission with black flags. Similar protests occurred in every major Indian city that the seven British MPs visited. Nationalist anger and disappointment over the issue would help place Gandhi once again onto the political stage as the major player.

Further constitutional reform was necessary because a growing number of nationalist politicians saw the 1919 system as ineffective. Frustration at British high-handedness in the legislature was adding to growing disenchantment with the British government. But the prospect of disunity made Indian nationalists fearful of challenging the British Raj. Motilal Nehru and the moderate T.B. Sapru convened an All Parties Conference and proposed that they draft an alternative constitutional plan.

Presented in September 1928 as the Nehru Report, it conceived of India as a federation of British India and the Princely States, enjoying the same status as the white Dominion States of the British Empire. It departed radically from the 1919 system by giving power to the central government and making it responsible to the electorate. It granted religious freedom to Muslims and other minorities and offered to create new provinces in Sind and the North-West Frontier where Muslims were in the majority, but recommended the abolition of separate electorates for Muslims. Criticism of the Nehru Report reflected the prevailing divisions within Congress. Orthodox Hindus and Muslim associations predictably opposed it as well as younger radical Indians such as Jawaharlal Nehru and Subhash Chandra Bose, who favoured total independence. Motilal Nehru pleaded with Gandhi to attend the annual Congress meeting in Calcutta in December 1928 because he felt that Gandhi was the best person to heal the rifts between the different factions. Gandhi's role as conciliator is one of the keys to understanding why he played such a central role in the nationalist movement. However, Gandhi failed to conciliate the leaders of the Muslim League, who felt the Nehru Report was a moment Mohammad Ali Jinnah referred to as the 'parting of the ways'.[2]

Shaken by the boycott of the Simon Commission, before the publication of the Nehru Report, the British government stated that Indian opinion would henceforth be considered, and that the natural outcome of the constitutional process would be dominion status for India. But things were not to go smoothly for British imperial officials, for Gandhi would soon take it upon himself to shake things up once again.

The 1930 Salt March

'That year, 1930, was full of dramatic situations and inspiring happenings; what surprised most was the amazing power of Gandhi to inspire and enthuse a whole people. There was something almost hypnotic about it, and we remembered the words used by Gokhale about him: how he had the power of "making heroes out of clay"'.[3]

Nehru's hagiographic description of Gandhi's qualities is indicative of how far Gandhi had travelled. He had moved from being a local to national leader and 1930 would mark his arrival as a truly global figure. Gandhi used his mixture of nationalism and mass action in the civil disobedience movement from 1930 to 1934. This included the famous 1930 Salt March, when he walked 240 miles from Ahmedabad to the coastal town of Dandi with 78 male volunteers. Under the 1882 Salt Act, the British had a monopoly on salt, levying a tax that all had to pay. Upon arrival at Dandi on 6 April 1930, Gandhi issued a statement to the world's press saying that, although the government had not interfered with the march, 'the wanton disregard shown by them to popular feeling and their high-handed action leave no room for doubt that the policy of heartless exploitation of India is to be persisted in at any cost.' The only interpretation he could put on the non-interference in the march was that 'the British Government, powerful though it is, is sensitive to world opinion' which would 'not tolerate repression' of civil disobedience 'so long as disobedience remains civil and therefore necessarily non-violent'. He would now test whether the government would 'tolerate the actual breach of the salt laws by countless people'.[4]

Gandhi picked up a lump of muddy salt and declared 'With this, I am shaking the foundations of the British Empire.'[5] After boiling it in seawater to produce illegal salt, he implored his followers to do likewise 'wherever it is convenient'.[6] The effect was dramatic as 2,000 people bathed in the sea at Dandi with Gandhi to pick up salt and so declare the salt laws broken.[7] Mass civil disobedience spread throughout India as millions broke the salt laws by making salt or buying illegal salt.

As in previous campaigns, Gandhi wrote to Viceroy Lord Irwin; on 2 March 1930, beginning his letter with 'Dear Friend,' Gandhi explained why he viewed British rule as a 'curse' and outlined some of the abuses and excesses of the British administration. These included obscenely high salaries for British officials, taxes on alcohol and salt, the eccentric land revenue system, and the importation of foreign cloth.[8] Gandhi warned that unless the viceroy was willing to make changes, he would begin a programme of civil disobedience. He added that he wished 'to convert the British people to nonviolence and thus make them see the wrong they have done to India'.[9] This letter was not made public for a week and only his closest confidants were privy to Gandhi's thoughts. When his plan for the march was finally announced on 5 March 1930 Nehru was not impressed: 'We were bewildered and could not fit in a national struggle with common salt',[10] whilst another colleague compared the proposed protest to striking a 'fly of the salt act' with a 'sledgehammer, of satyagraha'.[11] When Lord Irwin and his British advisers learned the specifics of the plan, they found the idea ridiculous, with Irwin writing 'at present the prospect of a salt campaign does not keep me awake at night.'[12] The British press saw his plan as 'childishly theatrical' and they hoped that the movement would die out if it was ignored.[13] Such attitudes demonstrated a sense of detachment from the quotidian lives of ordinary Indians. No concessions were forthcoming, so plans were made for the Salt March. Firstly, the route needed to be mapped, so some of Gandhi's trusted followers were tasked with this. They wanted the Salt March to go through villages where Gandhi could promote sanitation, personal hygiene and abstention from alcohol, as well as the end of child marriages and untouchability.

Since hundreds of followers would be marching with Gandhi, he sent an advance team of *satyagrahis* to help the villages along the path prepare, making sure that food, sleeping space and latrines were provided. In addition, correspondent and newspaper agencies from dozens of Indian, European and North American newspapers, along with film crews, descended upon India to bear witness to the drama and began covering the event.[14] This clearly indicates how Gandhi had become a master of media and stage management, directing his *satyagraha* with precision. He had drawn lessons from previous protests he had initiated, and was determined to set the scope, and prescribe methods and intended outcomes. He did not want unruly elements taking matters into their own hands and risk another 'Himalayan blunder'.

At 6:30 a.m. on 12 March 1930, Gandhi and 78 dedicated followers began their trek from his Sabarmati Ashram in Ahmedabad. They wore sandals and clothes made of *khadi* and each carried a woven bag containing a bedroll, a change of clothes, a journal, a *takli* (small support spindle for spinning), and a drinking mug. Gandhi, now 61, had a bamboo staff. The attire and accessories give clear indication as to the nature of this protest. Progressing between 10 to 15 miles a day, they walked along dusty roads, through fields and villages, where they were greeted with flowers and cheers. Throngs joined the march until thousands were with him when he reached the Arabian Sea at Dandi. Daily on the trek, Gandhi required each marcher to pray, spin and keep a diary. He continued to write letters and news articles for his papers. At each village, Gandhi collected information about the population, educational opportunities and land revenue. This gave him facts to report to his readers and to the British about the conditions he witnessed.

Just as non-cooperation fed into wider grievances, the civil disobedience campaign became a movement mobilising greater numbers of people and provided an outlet to much wider and deeper discontent against the British. As protests erupted elsewhere and spread, they generalised to wider opposition to British rule. Unpopular forest laws were defied in Maharashtra, Karnataka and Central provinces. Gujarati peasants refused to pay tax and Bengalis in Midnapore led a campaign refusing to pay a tax to keep the *chowkidar* (local village guard).[15] The British responded quickly, moving to arrest local leaders and lieutenants of Gandhi, but not for the moment touching Gandhi himself. In Peshawar, a *satyagraha* was led by a Muslim Pashtoo disciple of Gandhi, Ghaffar Khan (known as the Frontier Gandhi in colonial India), who had trained a 50,000-member army of non-violent activists called *Khudai Khidmatgar* (Servants of God).[16] On 23 April 1930, Ghaffar Khan was arrested. A crowd of *Khudai Khidmatgar* gathered in Peshawar's *Kissa Khani* (Storytellers) Bazaar. The British ordered troops to open fire with machine guns on the unarmed crowd, killing an estimated 200–250. The Pashtun *satyagrahis* acted in accord with their training in non-violence, willingly facing bullets as the troops fired on them. One British Indian Army regiment refused to fire at the crowds. The entire platoon was arrested and many received heavy penalties, including life imprisonment.[17] The British responded with more laws, including censorship of correspondence and declaring Congress and its associate organisations illegal, and had incarcerated over 60,000 people by the end of April 1930. None of these measures slowed the movement, as middle-class women joined the ranks of civil disobedients, manufacturing and selling salt throughout India. Usha Mehta, an early Gandhian activist who ran an underground radio station in the 1940s, remarked that 'Even our old aunts and great-aunts and grandmothers used to bring pitchers of salt water to their houses and manufacture illegal salt. And then they would shout at the top of their voices: "We have broken the salt Law!"'[18]

The symbolism of salt was not lost on Gandhi: it was a basic necessity to every household and the idea of an alien power taxing an indigenous product was too good an issue to pass up. Gandhi included the salt issue as part of his eleven-point programme for this *satyagraha*, which also demanded a reduction of land revenue assessments, cuts in military spending and the imposition of a tariff on foreign cloth. Gandhi planned a raid on the Dharasana Salt Works in his native Gujarat but on 4 May 1930, he was arrested and imprisoned, ostensibly pending trial near Pune. Despite this, and with his blessing, the raid was executed by a 76-year-old retired judge and with Gandhi's wife Kasturbai leading the march. Both were arrested before reaching Dharasana and sentenced to three months in prison. So, on 21 May 1930, Sarojini Naidu, a woman poet and freedom fighter, took charge and marched approximately 3,000 *satyagrahis* peacefully to the Salt Works. They carried 'implements to effect trespass into the compound, such as ropes, wire cutters and wooden planks'.[19] On arrival they said prayers, and Naidu, addressing the crowd, insisted that 'Gandhi's body is in jail but his soul is with you. India's prestige is in your hands. You must not use any violence under any circumstances. You will be beaten, but you must not resist: you must not even raise a hand to ward off blows.'[20] Naidu recalled how, as the crowd approached the barbed wire, they started chanting, '*Inquilab Zindabad! Inquilab Zindabad!*' (Long Live Revolution!).[21]

The British response was brutal and immediate – police and soldiers began to beat up protesters with steel-tipped *lathis* (clubs).[22] This is another iconic image depicted in Attenborough's film which illustrated how this incident globalised the Indian struggle and attracted international attention. As the United Press correspondent Webb Miller reported at the time:

> Not one of the marchers even raised an arm to fend off the blows. They went down like ten-pins. From where I stood I heard the sickening whacks of the clubs on unprotected skulls. The waiting crowd of watchers groaned and sucked in their breaths in sympathetic pain at every blow. Those struck down fell sprawling, unconscious or writhing in pain with fractured skulls or broken shoulders. In two or three minutes the ground was quilted with bodies. Great patches of blood widened on their white clothes. The survivors without breaking ranks silently and doggedly marched on until struck down. When every one of the first column was knocked down stretcher bearers rushed up unmolested by the police and carried off the injured to a thatched hut which had been arranged as a temporary hospital.
>
> There were not enough stretcher-bearers to carry off the wounded; I saw eighteen injured being carried off simultaneously, while forty-two still lay bleeding on the ground awaiting stretcher-bearers. The blankets used as stretchers were sodden with blood.
>
> At times the spectacle of unresisting men being methodically bashed into a bloody pulp sickened me so much I had to turn away … I felt an indefinable sense of helpless rage and loathing, almost as much against the men who were submitting unresistingly to being beaten as against the police wielding the clubs …
>
> Bodies toppled over in threes and fours, bleeding from great gashes on their scalps. Group after group walked forward, sat down, and submitted to being beaten into insensibility without raising an arm to fend off the blows. Finally the police became enraged by the non-resistance … They commenced savagely kicking the seated men in the abdomen and testicles. The injured men writhed and squealed in agony, which seemed to inflame the fury of the police … The police then began dragging the sitting men by the arms or feet, sometimes for a hundred yards, and throwing them into ditches.[23]

Though a lengthy statement, the eyewitness account above does demonstrate the level of force used by the British, which had remained undiminished since Amritsar and previous protest movements. It is worth bearing in mind that the 'enraged' police were Indians albeit, following the orders of their British superiors. The fact that an American correspondent was reporting these events demonstrates the extent to which Gandhi's campaigns had reached an international audience thus furthering the globalised projection of his methods.

By now Dharasana had become a symbol of resistance. On 1 June 1930, another Congresswoman, Kamaladevi Chattopadhyaya, led a raid of 15,000, including women and children, to the salt pans in Wadala, where they began collecting handfuls of salt. Chattopadhyaya was arrested but her 7-year-old daughter carried their banner as the raid continued; more fundamentally, salt was being manufactured, packed in small amounts and sold in bazaars, all illegally. Gandhi had not permitted any women to accompany him on the march to Dandi, but women were present everywhere on his route. He did not expect women to break the salt laws and thought that they should confine themselves to picketing alcohol shops. But women had other ideas. Margaret Cousins, a British campaigner wrote, 'women must ask that no marches, no imprisonments, no demonstrations organised for the welfare of India should prohibit women from a share in them.'[24] And it is significant that out of the 5,000 people who welcomed Gandhi while he was on the way to Dandi, about 2,000 were women. As Manini Chatterjee observes, 'thousands upon thousands of women in all parts of India, not just in big cities but also in small towns and villages, became part of the satyagraha struggle.'[25]

Unlike his previous campaigns, the Salt campaign has been seen as a predominantly 'Hindu' *satyagraha* and the lack of significant Muslim participation has been noted as an underlying factor to explain Muslim disengagement from Gandhi and Congress. A telegram from colonial officials, reporting Gandhi's arrest on 5 May 1930, states that in 'Bombay troops were posted at strategic points to prevent possible disturbances.' And though Congress had called a two-day *hartal*, 'many Muhammadans and Parsees had kept their shops open.'[26] Bipan Chandra writes that the 'participation of Muslims in the Civil Disobedience Movement was certainly nowhere near that in 1920–22.' And his explanation for this was that 'the appeals of communal leaders to stay away, combined with active Government encouragement of communal dissension to counter the forces of nationalism, had their effect.'[27] By this he means the boycott of the civil disobedience campaign by the Muslim League. However, there is also evidence that the participation of Muslims was not insignificant, either. In Bengal, middle-class Muslim support for Gandhi's campaign was quite important in Senhatta, Tripura, Gaibandha, Bagura and Noakhali and in Dacca, Muslim students and shopkeepers as well as people belonging to the lower classes extended support to the movement. Middle- and upper-class Muslim women were also active. The Muslim weaving community in Bihar, and in Delhi and Lucknow the lower classes of Muslims, were effectively mobilised as were many others in different parts of the country.[28] Similarly, a biographical account from 1951 describes in vivid detail a *hartal* that took place in Ahmedabad following Gandhi's arrest in May 1930 which involved Muslims and Hindus who shut down mills and shops;[29] in Peshawar, a predominantly Hindu regiment refused orders to fire on unarmed, predominantly Muslim, demonstrators.[30] Similarly, in Bombay a riot had broken out in a Muslim neighbourhood which police tried to quell by firing. According to Reynolds, high-caste Hindus tended to the care of wounded Muslims from the riot and those brought over from the Dharasana Salt protests.[31] So in spite of growing communal tensions, the salt campaign under Gandhi's leadership still had the capacity to offer communal unity, despite the divisions amongst elite politicians.

The unexpected power of this mass movement – drawing in women as well as men, the interaction of the social discontent and greater nationalist aspirations, giving a glimpse of communal unity – and the momentum it had developed as it started to generalise nationally, won a victory when it forced the British to finally release Gandhi from prison on 26 January 1931. Viceroy Irwin was desperate to end the salt-tax boycott and so offered talks with Gandhi. Rather than ensure that the magnificent momentum of the Salt March and civil disobedience continued to deepen and proceed to 'fight to the finish' for Indian self-rule, as Gandhi had promised in January 1930, he would take up Viceroy Irwin's offer, and in classic reformist fashion bring the movement to an end, in return for the chance for him to participate in the next round of talks about constitutional reform in London.

The Gandhi-Irwin Pact and the Second Round Table Conference

The very idea of Gandhi – who had seemingly single-handedly almost accidentally plunged British India into a new state of crisis – entering into talks with Viceroy Irwin had horrified much of conservative public opinion back in imperial Britain. Winston Churchill now famously scorned Gandhi, complaining bitterly that

> It is alarming and nauseating to see Mr Gandhi, a seditious Middle Temple lawyer, now posing as a fakir of a type well known in the east, striding half naked up the steps of the viceregal palace, while he is still organising and conducting a campaign of civil disobedience, to parlay on equal terms with the representative of the Emperor-King.[32]

David Lloyd George, incandescent with rage, derided the 'extraordinary spectacle of the Government of India drinking tea with treason and actually negotiating with sedition'. Understanding the potential revolutionary danger represented by Gandhi, Churchill further believed that Gandhism and all it represented, would 'have to be grappled with and finally crushed'.[33]

The Gandhi-Irwin Pact, which would eventually result from these talks in early 1931, meant that in exchange for an end to the boycott, Irwin agreed that the Raj would release all the prisoners taken during the salt upheaval, allow residents of coastal areas to make their own salt, and allow non-aggressive picketing of shops selling alcohol or foreign cloth. Gandhi's success in negotiating this deal was in part down to his personal charm. A respect and even fondness had developed between Irwin and Gandhi as demonstrated by a personal letter Irwin wrote to Gandhi following their settlement. In this he writes of his 'very great thanks' to Gandhi 'for all you have done, while we have been working together during these last difficult days'. He speaks of what a 'great privilege' it had been to meet and get to know Gandhi and that 'history may say you and I were permitted to be instruments in doing something big for India and humanity.'[34] When an official asked if Gandhi was tiresome during the negotiations, Irwin retorted, 'Some people found Our Lord very tiresome',[35] thus underscoring their bond. Since the Gandhi-Irwin Pact did not actually end the salt tax, many have questioned the efficacy of the Salt March. Others realise that the Salt March galvanised all Indians into wanting and working for independence and brought worldwide attention to their cause. After his 'parleying' with the viceroy, Gandhi was invited to attend the Second Round Table Conference in London in 1931. Although he represented the Congress, Gandhi found he was just one out of 112 delegates. Sixty-nine other Indians represented other parities in British India and 23 represented the princely states alongside 20 representing the British government.[36] This brought home the harsh truth of the realpolitik dominating colonial policy. Gandhi was seen as a leader of the Congress but this organisation was by no means regarded as a united party representing all Indians. This state of affairs suited the British, who used differences manifested through religion to foster disunity, citing Muslim separate electorates, even though this had actually been granted by the British themselves.

The British offered no progress towards self-rule; though it was agreed that individual families could procure salt for domestic purposes, the salt law was still in place and no significant gains were made on the other points of Gandhi's 11-point programme. However, Gandhi was free and he was talking to the viceroy as an equal for the first time on behalf of India. There was dissent from radical voices such as Jawaharlal Nehru and the Bengali Congress leader, Subhash Chandra Bose, who clearly felt that their advantage had to be driven home. However, Gandhi firmly believed in a 'peace with honour' for both sides, in the same way as he had negotiated in South Africa with Smuts. Compromise was the hallmark of Gandhi's tactics, even though to reach such a compromise he had to both mobilise the masses and ensure that their actions did not lead to the overthrow of the authorities. The price of his partial victories was to be measured in the bashed-in heads and broken bodies of his non-resisting followers.

Gandhi Abroad

Gandhi arrived in London for the Second Round Table Conference on 12 September 1931 and stayed for three months in the UK. During this time, he met with a range of political and civic leaders, including the actor Charlie Chaplin; he spoke to Indians living in Birmingham and addressed Indian students in London and Cambridge; he visited Eton and Oxford, and gave several interviews and statements to newspapers.[37] Since the Salt March, Gandhi had become an international celebrity, appearing on the cover of *Time* magazine on two occasions within ten months: first on 31 March 1930, and again as *Time*'s 'Man of the Year' on 5 January 1931.[38] His fame preceded him everywhere and people flocked to see the 'saint'. He was welcomed with curiosity and warmth.

Early biographers of Gandhi's life and his ideas were all admirers and several of them were members of the Friends of India Society, such as Reginald Reynolds, founder of the society and more famously known for his book *The White Sahibs in India* (1937), a strident attack upon British imperialism. This society was associated with the Quakers and perhaps not surprisingly during the 1930s many left radicals, non-conformists and pacifists in Europe were drawn to Gandhi. Part of their role was to raise public awareness of British injustice in India and make the case for British solidarity for the Indian cause of self-government. Along with loyal Gandhi followers such as Henry Polak and Horace Alexander, the socialist Fenner Brockway and Marxists such as Sylvia Pankhurst and Shapurji Saklatvala were also members. The Friends of India effectively ceased to function after the outbreak of war in 1939, but during its nine-year existence it published news from India about colonial atrocities in its publication, *India Bulletin*.

Reynolds had travelled to India in 1929 and had been present with Gandhi at the time of the salt campaign. He had travelled to Ahmedabad, Lahore, Bombay and to the south before leaving in 1930. In his 1931 work, *India, Gandhi and World Peace*, Reynolds makes the case for Gandhi being a revolutionary, claiming that *satyagraha* stands in opposition to both imperial violence and revolutionary violence,[39] and that '*satyagraha* is the antithesis of fear, since it is the opposition of the unarmed to the armed.'[40] The Preface from Reynolds's book provides a sense of how the Friends of India viewed Gandhi as representing a 'revolution' where

> a new society is in the making; India is in the throes of a rebirth. The East and the West have given of their best; Eastern and Western idealism have freely and joyously intermingled to create this glorious vision and to lay the foundation deep in freedom, equality and non-violence. Truly, therefore, this is a Revolution greater than all other revolutions that have gone before.[41]

'The failure of his movement would mean, not our success, but that of the Third International or of war-lords of the Chiang Kai Shek variety',[42] wrote Reynolds in conclusion, stressing his fear of revolutionary violence on the one hand in India and alluding to the counter-revolutionary violence in China when Communists were massacred by the nationalist Kuomintang. Radical liberals in Britain like Reynolds looked to Gandhi's ideas and practice as offering a 'third way' between revolution and counter-revolution, a more acceptable strategy of non-violence to bring about mass change.

Whilst in London during the conference, Gandhi stayed at Kingsley Hall in Bow and Muriel Lester recalls how the 'people of Bow were amassed in the streets and inside Kingsley Hall, awaiting their guest'.[43] Gandhi was invited into the homes of working-class families who took this little man in a loincloth to their hearts. One worker who lived opposite Kingsley Hall would often meet Gandhi walking, as the night shift worker left for his shift at 1.30 a.m. His summation of Gandhi goes a long way to explaining his appeal: 'He never missed once; regular as clockwork he wos. Now, that wot I admire in the man. He must have got weary, but he never gave up. I'm not religious myself, but ....'[44] This common touch endeared Gandhi to many, but particularly to the people of the East End.

Gandhi was invited to Lancashire to meet with employers and workers in the mills. His friend Charles Freer Andrew, who had met Gandhi in South Africa, had made the arrangements. This could have been a difficult call, particularly as the Indian boycott of British cotton was causing hardship for workers in the mill towns of north England.

In March 1931, 24,000 out of 90,000 looms in one weaving town had closed and another 46,000 had stopped indefinitely – one in three cotton workers was unemployed.[45] But Gandhi gladly accepted the invitation stating his intention was to 'remove any misunderstanding' in the 'minds of the people of Lancashire'.[46] He travelled north on 25 September 1931 and spent two days as the guest of non-conformist industrialists (see Figure 6). On his approach:

> A crowd numbering three or four thousand people assembled at Darwen Station … when the train was heard to be entering the station, there was a babel [*sic*] of eager voices, and every eye was focused on the station exit, but hopes were quickly dashed to the ground and the crowd was greatly disappointed when the first passenger to see the gathering shouted, 'You can all go home. He got off at Spring Vale [*sic*].'[47]

Such stories are testament to Gandhi's sincere desire to 'get to know the people of England'. He was certainly made more welcome among

Figure 6 Women workers from the cotton mill in Darwen, Lancashire, greet Gandhi on 26 September 1931. Photo taken by Manshull for the *Daily Herald*.

Source: Wikimedia Commons, the free media repository.

working-class people than among the rich and powerful rulers of the Empire. Gandhi's visit to Buckingham Palace for tea with King George V is much lauded as evidence of Gandhi's acceptance into high society, but before the meeting, the British monarch referred to Gandhi as 'the rebel fakir ... behind all the attacks on my loyal officers!'[48]

In reality, Gandhi understood very little, if anything, about the philosophy or political traditions of the left. In a letter to Stanley Baldwin dated 7 October 1934, the pacifist Muriel Lester stressed of Gandhi that 'he doesn't know anything about real socialism. He is 50 years behind the times on that subject.'[49] Indeed, on his way back home to India, Gandhi stopped off in Europe, spending five days in Switzerland with the left-wing writer Romain Rolland. Though the latter had been an ardent admirer of Gandhi a decade before, believing that the principles of *satyagraha* would provide 'Eurasian collaboration' that would 'redeem the West from its suicidal violence',[50] Rolland had become more influenced by Marxism, as fascism had taken root in Italy. He now warned Gandhi of the evils of fascism, but undeterred and unconvinced, Gandhi accepted an invitation to visit fascist Italy and also stated his intention to meet with Mussolini. In response to Rolland's pleas, Gandhi declared, '[I]f the Pope wants to see me I shall go. As for Mussolini, I do not think he wants to see me, but if he does I shall go without hesitation. But it will not be in secret.'[51] Gandhi did indeed now go to Italy and is pictured meeting with fascist youth (see Figure 7). Gandhi was so feted in Europe that perhaps it is not surprising that many a politician desired to meet him. He had been invited to Italy by Luigi Scarpa, the former Italian Consul in India, and Gandhi very much desired to meet the Pope and clearly Il Duce. The former Gandhi was not able to meet, but he did visit the Sistine Chapel, where the crucifix, like the New Testament three decades before, moved him deeply.

But Gandhi did meet Il Duce on 12 December 1931. In response to Rolland, Gandhi stated, that 'Mussolini is an enigma to me. Many of the reforms he has made attract me. He seems to have done a great deal for the peasantry. Of course, the iron glove is there. But allowing that force is the basis of Western society, Mussolini's reforms deserve an impartial study.'[52] Obviously, Gandhi's enthusiasm for Mussolini

Figure 7 Gandhi meeting young fascists in Rome on 17 December 1931 whilst on a visit to Italy to meet the Pope and Mussolini.

Source: © Getty Images, Popperfoto.

was tempered by the dictator's questionable tactics, but his curiosity was clearly evident as he continued admiringly to describe him:

> [Mussolini's] care of the poor people, his opposition to overurbanisation, his attempt to bring about coordination between capital and labour, seem to me to demand careful attention … My own fundamental doubt of course abides in that these reforms are forced. But that is true even of democratic institutions. What strikes me is that behind Mussolini's ruthlessness is the motive of serving his people. Even behind his bombastic speeches there is a ring of sincerity and burning love for his people. It also seems to me that the bulk of the Italians like Mussolini's iron rule.[53]

Their meeting lasted some twenty minutes and of course Mussolini inquired about the Round Table discussions and the possibility of further agitation against the British. Gandhi was shrewd enough to be aware that his visit could be misinterpreted, and though Scarpa had stated that he was inviting Gandhi in a personal capacity, he understood that 'the Italian Government is behind it and Scarpa is its instrument.'[54] But he held Consul Scarpa to be 'a cultivated man, who knows the Indians',[55] and that is why he felt 'obliged to take literally'[56] his statement. He had no conception of how, in spite of individuals being educated, cultivated and possessing impeccable manners, this did not necessarily imply sincerity or lack of treachery.

Gandhi had no sympathies with fascist Italy, and a generous reading would argue that this was before Hitler's Nazis came to power in Germany, and Gandhi just wanted to see for himself the reality of this apparent new fascist society in the making in Italy. But the Italian escapade does illustrate how Gandhi was never anchored in political tradition, except perhaps a kind of Victorian liberalism. He did not appreciate, let alone fully understand, the politics of the twentieth-century fascist right and the Marxist left.

Just as previously, Gandhi's charitable attitude and favourable disposition towards elites in political circles was in sharp contrast to his edicts towards subaltern groups. Whilst he felt a certain affinity with working-class communities in Lancashire and London's East End, he scolded them for being confrontational with their employers: 'I told the workers that the remedy is to fight not against capitalism but against themselves.'[57] Rolland, though still a friend to Gandhi, was clearly as frustrated by his naïvete and ignorance on this matter as he was over his meeting with Mussolini. In the same correspondence, Rolland and Gandhi have a dialogue over labour and capital. Rolland is passionate about the right of workers to act collectively to gain concessions and win their demands. He writes:

> In reality the workers are not united, as the capitalists have their intrigues: they foster divisions and buy 'blackleg' labour. In this case, the minority of perceptive and energetic workers who understand the situation feel justified in forcing the masses to form this unity. This is the *dictatorship of the proletariat*, the conscious proletariat in the interests of the proletarian mass whose support it obtains by force.[58]

This was anathema to Gandhi, who retorted 'I am totally against this.' His simple reason being 'it would mean Labour seizing Capital, and seizing Capital is the wrong way of going about it.'[59]

Even on the question of revolt against colonial conquest, Gandhi's emphasis was on abstract moral principles, that divulge a certain detachment from reality, as seen in the following article from 1938, which discussed Mussolini's brutal 1935 war on the people of Ethiopia (previously called Abyssinia):

> But if the Abyssinians had adopted the attitude of non-violence of the strong, i.e., the non-violence which breaks to pieces but never bends, Mussolini would have had no interest in Abyssinia. Thus if they had simply said: 'You are welcome to reduce us to dust or ashes but you will not find one Abyssinian ready to co-operate with you', what would Mussolini have done? He did not want a desert. Mussolini wanted submission and not defiance, and if he had met with the quiet, dignified and non-violent defiance that I have described, he would certainly have been obliged to retire.[60]

It did not seem very radical to expect Africans to acquiesce in the face of brutal imperialist violence and terror from a fascist 'civilising mission' in one of the continent's last independent states – a state which had a proud tradition of successful resistance to Italian empire-building dating back to the Battle of Adwa in 1896.

A further example of his conservatism was that of Gandhi's response to the arrest, trial and execution of Bhagat Singh. Singh was a socialist revolutionary from the Punjab who joined the Hindustan Republican Association (HRA), a radical group, which under his leadership later became the Hindustan Socialist Republican Association (HSRA), formed with his fellow revolutionaries Chandrashekhar Azad and Sukhdev Thapar. He established contact with the members of the Kirti Kisan Party (workers' peasant party) and started contributing regularly to its magazine, the *Kirti* (*Worker*). As a student, Bhagat Singh was an avid reader interested in European nationalist movements, but inspired by writings of Marx and Engels, his political ideologies took shape and he became more inclined towards a socialist approach. A taste of Singh's politics can be gleaned from the following:

> By *Revolution* we mean that the present order of things, which is based on manifest injustice must change. Producers or labourers, in spite of being the most necessary element of society, are robbed by their exploiters of their labour and deprived of their elementary rights. The peasant who grows corn for all, starves with his family; the weaver who supplies the world market with textile fabrics, has not enough to cover his own and his children's bodies; masons, smiths and carpenters who raise magnificent palaces, live like pariahs in the slums. The capitalists and exploiters, the parasites of society, squander millions on their whims.[61]

It is easy to see why Singh was dubbed 'an inspiration not a person' by Subhash Chandra Bose. Singh had been placed on trial in 1929 for the murder of a British police officer in Lahore. In late 1928, Singh and his comrades had planned to assassinate the British police superintendent responsible for the *lathi* charge on the popular nationalist leader Lala Lajpat Rai (who had died of a heart attack in the aftermath). Though they killed the wrong man, Singh and one other comrade came out of hiding to be arrested for avenging Lala's death, by exploding two bombs in the Central Legislative Assembly in Delhi in April 1929. Charged with murder, the 23-year-old Bhagat Singh was found guilty and on 23 March 1931, at 7:30 a.m., was hanged in Lahore Jail with his comrades Shivaram Rajguru and Sukhdev Thapar. It is said that the trio proceeded quite cheerfully towards the gallows while chanting their favourite slogan: '*Inquilab Zindabad*' and 'Down with British imperialism'.

Gandhi has been criticised for not making sufficient efforts to save Singh's life and obtain a commutation of the death sentence. However, he did write to the viceroy on 4 May 1930, a year after Singh's arrest, condemning the use of special tribunals held in camera: 'Is it any wonder if I call all these official activities a veiled form of Martial Law?'[62] And again on 31 January 1931, in Allahabad, he spoke against the sentence stating that those 'under a death sentence should not be hanged … that is my personal opinion and we cannot make their release a condition.'[63] Herein lies the problem. By early 1931, the Gandhi-Irwin talks were in place and the suspicion that his parlays with the viceroy took precedence over the execution of a much-loved nationalist leader remain. This seemed even more so when, on 18 February 1931, Gandhi asked for a suspension of the sentence and not commutation. Gandhi's adherence to non-violence meant he disapproved of Singh's methods and in spite of efforts at talks with the very cultivated and earnest Irwin, Singh was still executed.

Gandhi's conciliatory approach to his opponents made him a useful tool for imperial interests. His emphasis on negotiations, making concessions so that both sides in battle feel they have gained something, as well as turning the other cheek in the face of state violence, endeared him towards certain sections of imperial Britain, who preferred his short-lived non-violent *satyagraha* to any prolonged militant strategy. This point was well understood by the great Italian revolutionary Antonio Gramsci, who observed of Gandhi that elevating 'spiritualism' over 'materialism' leads to an 'exaltation of purely spiritual values, etc., to passivity, to non-resistance, and to non-cooperation – but in reality, it is a debilitating and diluted form of resistance, the mattress against the bullet.'[64] This approach would be most telling in his attitude towards the left inside Congress.

The Rise of the Left and the Meerut Conspiracy Case

Gandhi had so far in his campaigning faced little competition or challenge to his leadership or ideas within India from the left, but in the aftermath of the inspiration of the Russian Revolution, increasing numbers of Indian radicals would be attracted by the politics of revolutionary socialism and the Communist International. The Communist Party of India (CPI) had been formed in 1920 in Tashkent by a group of radical Indian students, including Manabendra Nath Roy, referred to as M.N. Roy.[65] Roy was a Marxist philosopher, an Indian nationalist and an anti-colonial cosmopolitan. He had been influenced by the works of Marx, Engels and Lenin, and concluded at an early age that only armed struggle could liberate India from the yoke of colonial rule. Roy had been invited to the Second World Congress of the Communist International in Moscow in 1920, where he met with Lenin and discussed Lenin's *Theses on the National Question*, written in 1913. Through this dialogue, Roy formulated his own ideas as a supplement to Lenin's *Preliminary Draft Theses on the*

National and the Colonial Questions.[66] Roy was such a gifted and deeply intellectual person that in 1936 Nehru would say, 'I was attracted to him by his remarkable intellectual capacity.' Roy was arrested in July 1931 and charged with sedition for 'conspiring to deprive the King Emperor of his sovereignty in India'. The trial was held in camera and he was sentenced to twelve years' imprisonment. So severe was state censorship of the proceedings that Roy's defence statement had to be smuggled out of India to the US before it could be printed and published. The following gives a flavour of his unrepentant stance:

> The oppressed people and exploited classes are not obliged to respect the moral philosophy of the ruling power ... *A despotic power is always overthrown by force.* The force employed in this process is not criminal. On the contrary, precisely the guns carried by the army of the British government in India are instruments of crime. They become instruments of virtue when they are turned against the imperialist state.[67]

Though Roy was appreciative of the fact that Gandhi did relate to ordinary people through his attire, language and even the uses of religion, he nevertheless astutely argued 'I do not share the view that our struggle for freedom, ever since 1920, is the creation of Mahatma Gandhi. On the contrary, Mahatma Gandhi is a creation of the Indian masses.'[68] This point illustrates well the conundrum that is Gandhi: his individual agency was important at critical junctures because he had the ability to articulate grievances of the masses in a popular manner, something that totally eclipsed mainstream national leaders. But Gandhi had emerged as a leader precisely because he also possessed the ability to unite the myriad class forces involved in Indian nationalism. This was effective when the movement was going forward, but such a coalition was inherently unstable, as wider interests of the disparate sections would come to the fore as activity was halted. This was the key problem of a nationalist movement combining the bourgeoisie, middle classes and masses. Gandhi became the axis for their collaboration, which was intrinsically laden with friction. In this sense, his leadership position was created more by the situation, than by himself and Roy's astute observation firmly recognises that Gandhi was the product of the movement.

In the aftermath of the impact of the Russian Revolution, and amidst growing disillusion among many younger radical nationalists with Gandhi's strategy of compromise and negotiation from above, new forces and currents began to emerge to the Left. As Paul Le Blanc notes:

> Roy's efforts to explain Bolshevism elicited Gandhi's outright rejection. 'Insofar as it is based on violence and a denial of god, it repels me,' the Mahatma responded. 'I am an uncompromising opponent of violent methods even to serve the noblest of causes … I desire to end capitalism almost if not quite as much as the most advanced socialist or even communist. But our methods differ, our languages differ.'[69]

As with Roy, the Communist Party of India from its very beginnings was under scrutiny from state authorities[70] and it was a proscribed organisation for much of its history. The biggest legal case its activists faced give some idea of the difficulties the party operated under. Thirty-one of its leading members were arrested in 1929, among them three members of the All-India Congress Committee and a Bombay Provincial Secretary of the Congress.[71] They were put on trial, on charges which carried a maximum penalty of transportation for life, in what came to be known as the Meerut Conspiracy Case; the trial lasted until January 1933.[72]

Nehru, as president of the All-India Trade Union Congress at the time, sent letters to the British Trades Union Congress appealing for assistance and asserting that the trial was an attempt by the Government of India to 'break the power of the labour and trade union movement' and therefore presented a threat much wider than just to the Communists.[73] In his summation, the High Court judge admitted that the accused were not charged with 'having done any overt illegal act in pursuance of the alleged conspiracy'.[74] But he found them guilty, sentencing all but four to varying terms of imprisonment. The Communists' legal team was comprised of Nehru, and other figures who were going to play a leading role in the Congress.

This is testimony to the ability of Communists to work jointly with activists in the labour movement and Congress – even though the Congress as a party (and for that matter Gandhi himself) did not take up the defence of the Meerut 'conspirators'.

The harnessing of this type of wider unity by the Communists would prove to be invaluable to the left as the 1930s progressed. By the mid-1930s, many activists in India were disillusioned and frustrated with Gandhi for repeatedly calling off the militant campaigns of civil disobedience. Even Nehru describes how he 'felt angry' at Gandhi's 'religious and sentimental approach to a political question', and wondered 'after so much sacrifice and brave endeavour, was our movement to tail off into something insignificant?'[75] Activists were further incensed that a section of Congress wanted to resume the constitutional path by taking part in elections, through the revival of the now defunct Swaraj Party.[76]

The Congress Socialist Party (CSP) was established in March 1934 as a grouping of Congress members who remained an integral part of that organisation. Its founding objective was 'the achievement of complete independence, in the sense of separation from the British Empire, and the establishment of a socialist society';[77] its leading members included Minoo Masani, Jayaprakash Narayan (known as 'J.P.') and Yusuf Merherally. Masani and Narayan had been in prison at Nasik jail during the Civil Disobedience campaign and decided to form a socialist grouping within the Congress upon their release, a decision which received support from Nehru, who welcomed 'the formation of socialist groups in the Congress to influence the ideology of the Congress and the country'.[78] In July 1935, Masani had visited London, where he had meetings with Stafford Cripps, the then leader of the Socialist League, with the Communist former MP Shapurji Saklatvala and some Indian students who were behind the formation of the All-India Progressive Writers' Association.[79] The CSP was formed and Communist Party members were admitted on an individual basis from January 1936.[80]

Subhash Chandra Bose was another important figure at this time. An articulate, flamboyant and charismatic individual from Calcutta, he was able to command the allegiance of young radicalised youth from both within and outside the Congress who were desirous for social change and mass militant action to achieve it. Like many before him, Bose had been sympathetic to Gandhi's campaigns when they mobilised large numbers in opposition to the British, but again like many, he became mistrustful of Gandhi's tactics and his ability to demobilise action and settle for concessions. As he put it in June 1933:

> We had been engaged in a non-violent war with the British Government – for the attainment of our political freedom. But today our condition is analogous to that of an army that has suddenly surrendered unconditionally to the enemy in the midst of a protracted and strenuous campaign. And the surrender has taken place, not because the nation demanded it – not because the national army rose in revolt against its leaders and refused to fight – not because the supply of the sinews of war was cut off – but either because the Commander-in-Chief was exhausted as a result of repeated fasting or because his mind and judgement were clouded owing to subjective causes which it is impossible for an outsider to understand.[81]

Bose, who had studied and travelled in Europe extensively, was firmly of the view that 'mine enemies' enemy is my friend'. To that end he made overtures to the Axis powers. Bose was not a fascist, but wanted to take advantage of Britain's woes vis-à-vis Nazi Germany – something the Indian nationalist leadership was not prepared to do. As Nehru put it at the time, 'no enemy of the United Kingdom [is] necessarily our friend.'[82]

Although Bose never joined the CSP, he was very supportive of its efforts and he was elected Congress president in 1937, which further galvanised efforts of left-wingers, much to the chagrin of more conservative members. As president, he not only denounced British rule but quoted Lenin, praised the Communist Party of Great Britain, and again stressed the favourable situation for Indian nationalism with another inter-imperialist conflict looming:

> I have, therefore, been pressing for a dynamic move from our side – for an ultimatum to the British Government demanding Purna

> Swaraj ... there is no sign of any intention on your part or on the part of the Gandhian group to utilise the international situation for our benefit ... I feel that either we should take international politics seriously and utilise the international situation for our benefit – or not talk about it at all.[83]

Such talk was anathema to Gandhi, and when Bose decided to stand again for president, Gandhi moved against him. In October 1938, he wrote to a confidant, 'There is bound to be some difficulty this time in electing the president.'[84] Gandhi pulled strings within the Congress's conservative faction to persuade Nehru or Maulana Azad to stand, but they both declined. Bose won the position again in 1939 with the support of the left and other radical currents within the Congress, despite opposition from Gandhi.[85] This was a significant victory for the left. However, it did not last long, since Gandhi, refusing to respect the democratic decision of his own organisation, worked like a classic bureaucrat behind the scenes to undermine Bose and the left. A resolution was drawn up stipulating that the president nominates a Working Committee in accordance with the wishes of Gandhi. The two principle bodies of Congress – the Working Committee and the All India Congress Committee (AICC) – did not support the president. As both bodies had a majority of Gandhites, they declared 'no confidence' in Bose and threatened to withdraw from Congress bodies if Bose did not resign. Bose was left alone on the Working Committee with only his brother Sarat as the other member. Nehru himself was pressured into voting against Bose. Thus the stage was set for a showdown at the All-India Congress session in Tripuri in early 1939. Attended by 200,000 people, Bose's resolution calling for an ultimatum against the British over independence was defeated overwhelmingly and Gandhi had won.[86] Pained by the lack of support shown by his comrades, particularly Nehru, Bose wrote more in sorrow than anger to Nehru, 'for some time past you have become completely biased against me ... since the presidential election, you have done more to lower me in the estimation of the public than all the twelve ex-members of the Working Committee put together.'[87]

Several years later, Nehru admitted that he had let Bose down and that, even though he agreed with Bose, 'Gandhi was India. Anything which weakened Gandhi weakened India.'[88] Bose was removed as president of the Congress in February 1939.

The Muslim Mass Contact Campaign

The Second Round Table talks failed to resolve any issues and the civil disobedience movement had been demobilised further by Gandhi's refusal to launch anything on the scale of 1930. The year 1935 saw the introduction of the Government of India Act that extended the franchise to 35 million Indians through direct elections. Though mass action had drawn to a halt since the collapse of the civil disobedience campaigns, the sustained pressure of the movement had produced more constitutional change. Preparation for the general election of 1937 would see a serious attempt to build Hindu-Muslim unity from below by left activists within Congress. The Muslim Mass Contact Campaign, as it was called, was based on appealing to Muslims as poor peasants who had more in common with their Hindu brethren than with the leaders of the Muslim League (AIML). It involved recognition that appeals to religious sentimentality and tolerance were not sufficient and, in this respect, implied criticism of Gandhi's methods, which could be viewed as bringing religion into the centre of the political arena and relying upon elites to forge unity. The CPI had raised its own criticism, arguing that 'the Congress programme had to be denuded of all sentimental trimmings … The object for which the Indian people will fight … should be found in their immediate surroundings – in their huts, on the land, in the factory. Hungry mortals cannot be expected to fight indefinitely for an abstract ideal.'[89]

This bottom-up approach attempted to forge unity between ordinary Indians on the basis of class interests that could over-ride those based on communitarian identity. Congress notices were distributed in rural and urban areas in Urdu. A circular from Nehru in March 1937 urged provincial Congress committees to

> make a special effort to enrol Muslim Congress members, so that our struggle for freedom may become even more broad based than it is … there is no difference between the Muslim masses and the Hindu or Sikh or Christian masses in the country. Differences only come to the surface when we think in terms of the handful of upper class people.[90]

The campaign's first major test came in a by-election in July 1937 in the Jhansi-Jalaun-Hamirpur constituency of United Provinces (UP). Congress stood Nisar Ahmad Khan Sherwani as its candidate against the ML's Rafiuddin Ahmad. This was quite a high-profile exercise with many Congress workers sent to campaign in the area,[91] some of whom were detained and arrested. This approach of appealing directly to Muslims on a class basis was in sharp contrast to Gandhi's insistence of moral unity based on appeals to religious symbolism.

The Muslim League strongly criticised the mass contact policy, with Jinnah declaring it 'as fraught with very serious consequences'.[92] The League had not performed well in the provincial elections held that year and so this election was a test case for them, as they had not been challenged in this manner before. The ML candidate won with 58.7 percent, but Congress received almost 2000 votes, so Nehru felt vindicated by the campaign and argued that 'there is a strong band of Muslim workers all over the province who are determined to fight reaction and to support the Congress.'[93]

In 1937, the first elections were held in the Provinces, resulting in Congress Governments being returned in almost all Provinces.[94] The Muslim League won 106 seats, 6.7 percent of the total, whilst Congress won 707 seats, 44.6 percent of the vote. Among the 864 seats assigned 'general' constituencies, Congress contested 739 and won 617. Of the 125 non-general constituencies contested by Congress, 59 were reserved for Muslims and in those the Congress won 25 seats, 15 of them in the entirely Muslim North-West Frontier Province. Neither the Muslim League nor the Congress did well in the Muslim constituencies. While the Muslim League fared better in Muslim seats from the non-Muslim-majority provinces, its performance was less impressive in the Muslim-majority provinces such as Punjab and Bengal.

Conclusion

With the collapse of the Civil Disobedience campaign, Gandhi withdrew from national politics to focus on his constructive programme for social reform including advocacy of *khaddar* (home spinning) and renewed efforts to gain temple entry for untouchables (in the aftermath of his falling out with Ambedkar). Congress leaders resumed constitutional concerns as Gandhi's style was becoming more ascetic, with the utilisation of Hindu mythology and symbols becoming hegemonic in his campaigns, speeches and approach. The development of Cow Protection Societies had fed developments towards Hindu fundamentalism with the growth of extremist organisations such as the *Rashtriya Swayamsevak Sangh* (RSS – National Volunteer Organisation), a middle-class and middle-caste group formed in 1925 and united by fear and loathing of other social groups, most notably Muslims.

In every instance, Gandhi initiated mass action in order to change mass consciousness, and, in every case, the moral force of non-violence propelled the freedom movement forward as it became larger, broader and deepened as activists radicalised after each successive wave. It was this that drew masses of young people towards Gandhi and this is what marks his intervention as seminal in the interwar years. But it was also the case that at each stage, as the movement became more militant, the weakness and limitations of Gandhi's strategy were revealed. Just as he instigates and leads from the front, he quickly backtracks and calls a halt to activity when he felt it was veering off course. The desire for compromise and readiness for conciliation, reveals the constant tension that lay at the heart of Gandhi's approach. He was much more interested in controlling events than propelling them forward to involve more numbers with increasing militancy. When he did take the position of making an ultimatum, it was in relation to forces from below and to the left of him as opposed to those at the top of society. As he once put it, 'I can no more tolerate the yoke of Bolshevism … than of capitalism … mobocracy is autocracy multiplied [a] million times.'[95] Efforts to defend Gandhi's strategy from the left have been provided by Bipan Chandra, who theorised Gandhi's technique as rooted in an understanding of the semi-hegemonic character of the colonial state. Accordingly, the political passivity of the masses was a basic factor in the stability and safety of colonial rule. In order to prosecute successful struggle, the masses had to be mobilised. And Gandhi tried to do this: 'A major objective of the movements of the Gandhian era was to bring the masses into active politics and political action.'[96] Chandra describes Gandhian strategy as 'Struggle-Truce-Struggle', in which peasants, workers, businessmen, professionals, women, landlords are all participants in a grand coalition of popular resistance under the leadership of Gandhi and his non-violent approach.[97]

This strategy assumed that a mass movement could not be carried on indefinitely because the masses would be exhausted after some time. So, they need 'breathing time' and space to consolidate, recuperate and gather strength for the next round of struggle. This space was critical to help build the self-confidence of the nationalist movement politically, psychologically and physically, as the colonial state still possessed a state apparatus, a monopoly on state violence and therefore the 'considerable capacity to crush a movement'.[98] Chandra characterises colonial India as a 'semi-democratic state' possessing 'semi-hegemonic' and semi-authoritarian' features, a state that uses the trappings of a parliamentary system but was ruthless enough to 'crush all opposition except to the extent that they permitted it'.[99] Consequently, Gandhi's method of withdrawing from struggle forms an inherent part of an intelligent strategy of political action based on the masses. This was the ideal approach towards the liberal authoritarian regime that was British imperial India. The argument follows that this strategy would not have been effective under an absolutist authoritarian system that routinely used violence with no legal redress. Semi-democratic spaces opened up for the Congress to operate, and in periods of a suspension of struggle, time would be spent in constructive works to further help mobilise legal, peaceful mass struggles. Non-violence was essential for the life blood of the movement, as it was linked to the specific nature of British rule in India. Gandhi's reasoning was that if the state used force to crush the movement, it could be exposed as brutal, as in Amritsar and the Salt March *satyagraha*, or it would not be able to implement its laws. Either way, the nationalist movement would win: 'the hegemony of colonial rule or its moral basis was destroyed bit by bit.'[100] Critics of Gandhi tend to blame pressure from the middle classes and Gandhi's own class bias, for his inclination to compromise with imperialism, and/or fear of revolt from below and of forces external to his influence. But in Chandra's view, the critics fail to understand the strategic design of the Gandhian method of struggle.

The use of the Gramscian term 'war of position' seems to provide a Marxist and revolutionary content to Gandhian strategy, in Chandra's interpretation, as the retreats are all strategic rather than a response to colonial initiatives. But in enabling subversive collaboration on a national scale for all Indians, Chandra furthers the notion of nationhood as an all-embracing concept irrespective of class differences and appears to be unaware of how the dynamics of these diverse interests could unravel at critical junctures. Even as the movement retreats, rather than withdrawing into spiritual re-awakening and moral upliftment, effort could be made to build up social forces that could counter divide-and-rule policies; challenge communalism, and build solidarity amongst workers and peasants in the manner of Nehru's mass contact work. Genuine bottom-up activity based on local areas could have provided a beacon for those radical activists who quite rightly were mistrustful of landlords, business leaders, and the high command of the Congress. If momentum had not been lost, independent revolutionary forces to the left could have been galvanised, so that next time the movement would not have to rely upon an 'enlightened' self-appointed leader, such as Gandhi.

Chandra's thesis thus seems to be based upon the all-too-familiar caricature of revolution as predicated on the use of violence for the sake of violence. Clearly, there have been situations when quite cavalier methods were adopted, calling for mass uprisings in an abstract manner, with moral exhortation the only criteria. But serious revolutionaries do not engage in revolution as a by-product of bloodthirstiness. The employment of violence is not the critical function of revolution. A sober and honest assessment of the balance of forces in any given scenario needs to be undertaken. And the question of violence is not dictated by those at the bottom of society. Rather, it is acknowledged that in order to defend gains if the state uses its monopoly of violence to crush revolt, then the masses will need to defend that revolt and not blink first. Despite the attempts to utilise Marxist concepts, Chandra's interpretation risks essentialising the colonial experience in India and consigning the 'masses' to a stage army to be wheeled in and out at the whim of an educated leader. This implies an elitist approach which bears little resemblance to Marxism. As M.N. Roy stated above, it was the masses that made Gandhi. Whether Gandhi was conscious of this fact is hard to test, but what is undeniable is that in all of Gandhi's dealings thus far, a pattern is emerging whereby he assumes leadership and the license to initiate or halt struggles. The basic Gandhian style of leading a movement was 'drawing-in the masses, while at the same time keeping mass activity strictly pegged down to certain forms, pre-determined by the leader, and above all to the methods of non-violence'.[101]

In spite of the glaring weaknesses in strategy and its failure to push home the advantage of the Indian anti-colonial struggle from below, by the mid-1930s, Gandhi was now talking to Viceroy Irwin as an equal, and meeting with international political leaders and the king. In short, he had become truly 'global'. Gandhi had come a long way from Porbandar town, and as the decade drew to a close, war, famine and the unravelling of British rule would test his experiments with truth to their limits.

Figure 8 Gandhi meeting political prisoners at Dum Dum, near Calcutta, on 29 March 1938.

Source: Wikimedia Commons, the free media repository.

6

Fascism, War, Independence and Partition: 1939–48

The onset of war presented another set of challenges to Gandhi. The apostle of peace had previously seemed to condone war, becoming a stretcher-bearer for the British in the Boer War, and even acting as a kind of recruiting sergeant for the British Army in the First World War.[1] Since the end of that conflict, the world faced a new phenomenon: the growing menace of fascism in Europe amid the Great Depression which by 1939 threatened a new world war. For most people on the left – particularly after the rise of Hitler's Nazis in Germany – fascism had to be opposed, violently if necessary, as, for example, during the Spanish Civil War. Gandhi's response to the new danger posed by the rise of fascism, however, was to maintain his faith in non-violence as a strategy of resistance that could work as effectively in Nazi Germany as in British India. In 1938, he publicly advised Jewish people to act as *satyagrahis* and choose self-immolation: 'The calculated violence of Hitler may even result in a general massacre of the Jews ... But if the Jewish mind could be prepared for voluntary suffering, even the massacre I have imaged could be turned into a day of thanks giving and joy that Jehovah had wrought deliverance of the race even at the hand of the tyrant.'[2]

Gandhi hailed the Munich Pact as an act of statesmanship and cautioned the Czechs against armed resistance to the German invasion in the name of non-violence, insisting that they 'refuse to obey ... and perish unarmed in the attempt, for though the Czech may lose his body, his soul and honour are intact.'[3] Two years later, in 1940, he wrote in favour of Pétain's armistice, signalling the French ruling class's surrender to Nazi invasion and occupation as 'brave statesmanship' and further extolled French politicians for showing 'rare courage in bowing to the inevitable and refusing to be party to senseless mutual slaughter'.[4] On 3 July 1940, on the eve of the 'Battle of Britain' and when an invasion by Nazi Germany seemed imminent, Gandhi sent a message to the British War Cabinet, begging them and 'every Briton' to follow his counsel:

> Lay down the arms you have as being useless for saving you or humanity ... Let them (Herr Hitler and Signor Mussolini) take possession of your beautiful island, with your many beautiful buildings ... If these gentlemen choose to occupy your homes, you will vacate them. If they do not give you free passage out, you will allow yourself man, woman and child, to be slaughtered, but you will refuse to owe allegiance to them.[5]

As a sign of his detachment from the political realities of Europe in this period, Gandhi even wrote a letter to Hitler directly on 23 July 1939, where he addressed the Führer as 'Dear friend':

> I must make my appeal for whatever it may be worth. It is quite clear that you are today the one person in the world who can prevent a war which may reduce humanity to the savage state. Must you pay the price for an object however worthy it may appear to you to be? Will you listen to the appeal of one who has seliberately [*sic*] shunned the method of war not without considerable success?[6]

Gandhi's letter never reached Hitler, for the British government intervened to stop it. It is bizarre to imagine that Gandhi thought his writing such a letter would change the perspective of a racist psychopath like Hitler – a great admirer of the British Empire – and someone who in 1937 had bluntly suggested the British government just 'shoot Gandhi'. Gandhi's lack of a response from Hitler did not stop him writing again on 24 December 1940, once again addressing the Führer as 'Dear Friend', for 'I own no foes', and pleading with him against further escalation of the war. 'We have no doubt about your bravery or devotion to your fatherland, nor do we believe that you are the monster described by your opponents', Gandhi wrote.

Gandhi continued to lecture Hitler on the virtues of non-violence, rightly noting that in the context of challenging British imperialism his methods had led to some partial victories:

> We have attained a very fair measure of success through non-violent effort. We were groping for the right means to combat the most organized violence in the world which the British power represents ... We have found in non-violence a force which, if organized, can without doubt match itself against a combination of all the most violent forces in the world. In non-violent technique, as I have said, there is no such thing as defeat. It is all 'do or die' without killing or hurting.[7]

Gandhi's call for world peace was certainly sincere, but naïve in the extreme, as was his call for non-violent resistance to fascism in general, and the Nazi war machine in particular, as the following passage bears witness,

> Hitlerism will never be defeated by counter-Hitlerism. It can only breed superior Hitlerism raised to [the] *n*th degree. What is going on before our eyes is the demonstration of the futility of violence as also of Hitlerism ...
>
> ... today if the Czechs, the Poles, the Norwegians, the French and the English had all said to Hitler: '...We will meet your violence with non-violence. You will therefore be able to destroy our non-violent army without tanks, battleships and airships.' It may be retorted that the only difference would be that Hitler would have got without fighting what he has gained after a bloody fight.[8]

Gandhi was generalising his particular tactic – which fitted his approach of unleashing the masses to exert pressure on the British but not overthrow them. He was insistent upon non-violence as a creed that he elevated to the principle of a moral crusade.

As the world tilted towards total war yet again, British India as a crown possession was committed to defend British interests, and all India's resources and manpower were marshalled towards the defence of the Empire. The viceroy, Lord Linlithgow, thus declared

India for war without consulting a single Indian politician in the provincial councils. The Congress ministers all resigned in outrage at the lack of consultation. In the absence of indigenous representation in the provincial legislature, the colonial state set about prosecuting the war with little opposition but resulting in a colossal impact on India. The priorities of the British state are perhaps most graphically illustrated by the Bengal famine of 1943, which left between 1.5 and 3.5 million dead,[9] and which Nehru called 'the final judgement on British rule in India'.[10] The Famine Inquiry Commission had described Bengal as a 'land of rice growers and rice eaters'.[11] As already noted, the nature of British rule in India was predicated upon draining its society of resources to further the aims of empire, and famines were no different. During the war, eleven times the usual number of soldiers were needed at India's expense. To pay for troops, the money supply required expansion, which produced inflation, which in turn resulted in a flight of currency and subsequent hoarding.[12] The price of rice increased tenfold between May and October 1943, as ordinary Bengalis suffered to obtain a single grain.[13] The situation was made worse by the Japanese occupation of Burma (modern Myanmar), which cut off important supplies of rice from the east, and by the destruction of boats and bridges in East Bengal to inhibit a possible Japanese advance into India.

The callous nature of the colonial response to growing food shortages in Bengal can be measured in the following evidence: ships carrying wheat from Australia docked at Calcutta only to be instructed by Churchill not to and instead to sail on to Europe,[14] believing that sending food amounted to 'appeasement' of the Congress Party.[15] Leo Amery, Secretary of State for India, welcomed this distraction from the movement for independence. The public were 'now absorbed in questions of food and cost-of-living' which might 'infuse a tinge of realism into politics'.[16]And the arch-imperialist Churchill again defiantly declared that the 'famine was their own fault for breeding like rabbits'.[17]

The Outbreak of War and the Quit India Movement

Faced with the outbreak of the Second World War, Gandhi declared himself to be filled with 'greater horror' about this looming conflict than he was about the First World War. With hindsight, he declared 'the greater horror would prevent me from becoming the self-appointed recruiting sergeant that I had become during the last war.'[18] But in this instance he was not a 'loyal rebel', and his calling a halt to agitation for independence, cannot be read as implicit support for the British imperial war effort once again. Gandhi welcomed the resignation of Congress ministers in protest at India being dragged into the war, in the hope that it meant a turn away from constitutional measures. He further hoped that the space vacated by legislative horse-trading would lead to a return to his type of strategy. Accordingly, on 17 October 1940, he embarked on an individual *satyagraha* as a protest against continued British intransigence over the war and encouraged others to do likewise. Once again, his lead struck a chord, and by June 1941 more than 20,000 had been imprisoned but then released. Yet beyond the immediate Congress leadership this peculiarly, individualist campaign proved to be wholly ineffective, and it had fizzled out by the end of 1941.[19] If internal dissent was now mute in India, the British Empire's position in South and South East Asia was, however, increasingly threatened militarily by Japan, an Axis power. The Japanese had declared war on Britain on 7 December 1941 and its army rolled through South East Asia; by 1942 the British had lost Singapore, Malaya and Burma, and the Japanese were now threatening Assam and Bengal.

These losses shattered colonial complacency over India and the wider region, but also angered Indian opinion as retreating British troops commandeered all transport and left Indian migrant workers to trek home through atrocious conditions. Train loads of wounded Indian soldiers returning from the Burmese front intensified the mood of anger and hostility to an alien and meaningless war. Such military defeats heightened colonial officials' fear of internal dissent. In spite of the arch-imperialist Churchill leading a wartime coalition government, the British had no choice but to make a further attempt at obtaining Indian compliance for the war effort. To that end, London dispatched Stafford Cripps to lead discussions with Congress and other leaders on the possibility of independence at some future point post-war, in return for wartime cooperation. The proposals were so flimsy that both the Congress and the Muslim League rejected them as inadequate whilst Gandhi, equally unimpressed, reportedly labelled the Cripps offer a 'post-dated cheque on a failing bank'.[20]

Most of the Indian nationalist movement went along with this – the Communist Party of India was the only organisation of any significance on the left arguing that the colonial liberation struggle should continue unabated amidst what they rightly judged to be an 'imperialist war'. However, when Nazi Germany invaded the Soviet Union in 1941, the Communists switched their position completely to one of support for what was now declared to be a 'people's war'. As prices in India rocketed, the Congress rebel Subhash Chandra Bose now added to the pressure on Britain by fleeing to Japan and taking over the formation of an Indian National Army (INA) comprised of former plantation workers from South East Asia and Indian prisoners of war in Japanese camps in 1943.[21] The INA pledged to fight with the Japanese in order to kick Britain out of India.

Recognising the growing nationalist mood against British imperialism bubbling up from below, on 8 August 1942, Gandhi introduced the Quit India resolution at the All-India Congress Committee held in Bombay. This stipulated that

> every man and woman, who is participating in this movement must function for himself or herself within the four corners of the general instructions issued. Every Indian who desires freedom and strives for it must be his own guide urging him all along the hard road where there is no resting place and which leads ultimately to the independence and deliverance of India.[22]

The British used wartime ordinances to order mass detentions, arrests and imprisonment. As Congress leaders were jailed, the leadership of the Quit India movement transferred to a younger, more militant generation who had been inspired more by Bose than any ethical commitment to non-violence. This changed its character, as activists took to sabotaging factories, bridges, telegraph and railway lines, and other government property.

This movement once again quickly went far beyond Gandhi's control, and was described by Viceroy Linlithgow as by far the most serious rebellion since the 1857 mutiny.[23] It was easy to see why.

From 9 August to 21 September 1942, some areas of north India were virtually under parallel governments, as a younger generation of activists took the lead. Activists attacked some 550 post offices, 250 railway stations, damaged many rail lines, destroyed 70 police stations, and burned or damaged 85 other government buildings. There were about 2,500 instances of telegraph wires being cut. The greatest level of violence occurred in Bihar. The Government of India deployed 57 battalions of British troops to restore order.[24] State repression was swift and brutal. Some 66,000 were arrested, all committees were banned and the press was censored. By the end of 1943, over 90,000 people had been arrested, with the highest figures coming from Bombay Presidency (24,416), United Provinces (UP) (16,796) and Bihar (16,202).[25] This threatened the war effort and the colonial state responded with mass brutal repression, arresting tens of thousands and killing some 2,500.[26] Bengal had been one of the most militant areas and was arguably the strongest nerve centre of the agitation.[27] In 1943, there were numerous acts of sabotage against institutions or offices of colonial rule, including 151 bomb explosions, 153 cases of severe damage to police stations or other public buildings, four police stations destroyed, and 57 cases of sabotage to roads.[28] State authorities made use of public floggings and of torture such as pushing a ruler up the rectum of captured protesters, and Linlithgow ordered aerial bombing against crowds disrupting communication networks in Patna, Bihar.[29]

As with previous anti-colonial protests, Quit India resonated with the Indian masses as it acted as catalyst for wider grievances. In addition to urban revolt, there were strikes by workers in Lucknow, Kanpur, Bombay, Nagpur and Ahmedabad – all large industrial centres critical to Britain's war effort. By 12 August 1942, only 19 of Bombay's 63 mills were functioning.[30] Workers at Tata Steel's giant Jamshedpur plant declared 'they will not resume work until a national government has been formed', while the three-month textile strike in Ahmedabad earned the moniker of 'the Stalingrad of India'.[31]

The historian Bidyut Chakrabarty characterises the second phase of the Quit India movement as one where parallel government seemed to exercise power. For example, in rural Maharashtra, peasants organised to suppress banditry in their area and in doing so, they began to take up peasant power to organise their own affairs.[32] Underground radio stations were established initially as Azad Radio (Freedom Radio). Attempts to broadcast from several places were made but the Bombay transmitter was the most successful, and Congress radio managed to survive for a hundred days following the August movement.[33] In Medinapur District, thousands of protesters gathered to prevent rice stocks being shipped out by mill owners. Three demonstrators were killed by the police and rather than dissipate action, a parallel government was established which banned grain exports, imposed fixed prices on merchants and seized some supplies to distribute to the people.[34] The extent to which Medinapur had gone beyond Gandhi's non-violence was indicated by students who shouted: 'We shall cut off [King] George's head, and finish England with fire and the sword. And hoist Churchill aloft on the point of a spear.'[35]

In addition, Gandhi uttered the famous mantra, '*karenge ya marenge*' ('Do or die'). Gandhi himself was arrested on 9 August 1942 and detained until May 1944, after his wife had passed away, but more importantly, because the British had long feared him dying on their watch. Donny Gluckstein maintains that the above mantra was not designed to be provocative,[36] as the Quit India movement would be prosecuted along non-violent lines. But the words 'Do' or 'Die' imply different meanings and intentions; the first emphasises a militant and combatant challenge to British rule – better to fight than die – whereas the latter emphasises better to live than fight. The following example of a Congress leader Dr Shivpujan Raj illustrates the different approach graphically: 'It is not by killing but by dying that we shall attain our goal. The leader of the nation has ordered this. We cannot violate his wishes.' So, casting their weapons aside, demonstrators marched unarmed on government offices. When they arrived, seven were shot dead, including Dr Raj. The rest chose to 'do' rather than 'die', and the next day they returned to sack the building, a police station, seed store, and railway station (while still chanting Gandhi's name).[37] The fact that Gandhi's name was being invoked does not hide the reality that the movement was acquiring lessons from previous experiences and making tactical judgements on the ground, based on what would propel the movement forward and not halt it in the name of abstract non-violence. As in the past, Gandhi had denounced the movement he initiated as a 'calamity' and 'deplorable destruction' by 'people wild with rage to the point of losing self-control'.[38] This leads Gluckstein to conclude that Gandhi was both a progressive and reformist nationalist who deployed mass activism but feared class struggle and revolution.[39] Mass resistance from below and a deepening militancy was replacing caution. And the person losing control was Gandhi.

Again, a lead given by Gandhi had unleashed a mass of forces on the ground – this time greater than ever before – that would involve people taking the struggle into their own hands and fashioning it in their own image. Although the movement dissipated due to Gandhi's intervention and state repression, what remained significant was that the *spirit* of the Quit India movement was Gandhian, but its *tactics* went way beyond this.

The Muslim League and Quit India

The Second World War led to seismic shifts in the fortunes of the All-India Muslim League (AIML). Mohammad Ali Jinnah was now leader of the League and when Gandhi called on the British to Quit India, the League 'deplored' it and called on Muslims to abstain from any involvement in a movement instigated by the Congress.[40] The same resolution signalled the League's willingness to 'shoulder the responsibility for running the administration and mobilizing the resources of the country for the war effort and for the defence of India',[41] thus echoing statements from the formation of the Muslim League in 1906. The AIML had been founded by elite conservative Muslims from UP and they hoped to prosper under the benevolence of empire. Four decades later, Jinnah exercised a degree of pragmatism and opportunism to declare support for the war effort. With Congress leaders and followers in prison, the situation afforded the Muslim League a space to operate in that proved quite favourable, with the British government providing financial support (by means of advertisements) for their newspaper, *Dawn*.[42]

Frustrated by Gandhi's peculiar religious idioms and Congress's apparent acquiescence to them, Jinnah had left India in 1930 to live in London where he ran a successful law practice. Whilst in London, he attended two of the inconclusive Round Table Conferences. He was persuaded to return to India in 1934 to take over the leadership of the Muslim League as its president. He was also elected by the Muslims of Bombay to be their representative in the Central Legislative Assembly.[43] The lack of electoral success in Muslim-majority areas in the 1937 provincial elections, compared to more local regionalist parties (a government was formed in Bengal only through an alliance with the Krishak Sramik Party), compelled Jinnah to re-think strategy. Over the next two years he would dedicate himself to building the League as a force to be reckoned with. In this endeavour, Jinnah took a leaf out of Gandhi's playbook, which had helped transform Congress away from being purely a party of the elite. Jinnah borrowed from Gandhi's use of religious symbolism to attract a mass audience. He also worked to expand the League into a mass organisation, reducing the cost of membership to two annas ($^1/_8$ of a rupee), half of what it cost to join the Congress. He restructured the League along the lines of the Congress, with provincial branches, subdivided into ward and district organisations that would elect members to the AIML Council. A working committee was established, which appointed all subcommittees.[44] Jinnah also secured the right to speak for the Muslim-led Bengali and Punjabi provincial governments in the central government in New Delhi.[45] By December 1939, the League's membership is estimated to have stood at 3 million members.[46]

Structural and demographic changes combined with an increasing perception by Muslims that they needed a counter-weight to the growth of fringe Hindu chauvinist organisations, such as the Hindu Mahasabha and the increasingly influential *Rashtriya Swayamsevak Sangh* (RSS). Consequently, in 1940, the AIML session at Lahore passed a resolution that called for 'geographically contiguous units' to be

> demarcated into regions which should be constituted, with such territorial readjustments as may be necessary that the areas in which the Muslims are numerically in a majority as in the North Western and Eastern Zones of (British) India should be grouped

> to constitute 'independent states' in which the constituent units should be autonomous and sovereign.[47]

This was an ambiguous and vague resolution that possessed the merit of being all things to all Muslims. Neither partition or any idea about 'Pakistan' were mentioned, but subsequent interpretations have succeeded in imagining in this resolution a demand for partition seven years before it was ever on anyone's horizon. Though two young Punjabi Muslim students at Cambridge had written two pamphlets in 1933 and 1935 coining the name 'Pakistan' (from Punjab, Afghan Province and Kashmir), no one in the Muslim League, least of all Jinnah, took it seriously, dismissing it as a student's pipe-dream.[48]

With the passing of the Lahore Resolution, Jinnah did begin espousing what has come to be termed the 'two-nation' theory of Muslims and Hindus. In 1939, he had already warned the British that 'no declaration should in principle or otherwise be made ... without the approval and consent of the two majority communities of India viz. Musalmans and Hindus.'[49] Five months later, Jinnah fleshed out his two-nation thesis further and on 23 March 1940, he made a speech in Lahore stating that 'Hindus and Muslims belonged to two different religious philosophies, social customs and literature. They neither intermarry, nor [interdine] together, and indeed they belong to two different civilizations based mainly on conflicting ideas and conceptions.'[50] This meant that Muslims were not a minority but a nation, and expected to be treated as such.

Notwithstanding Jinnah's gross oversimplification of a thousand years of Indian history, the early 1940s had produced tensions between the League and the Congress over representation and parity. Gandhi's reaction to the Lahore Resolution was apparently muted; he called it 'baffling', but told his disciples that Muslims, in common with other people of India, had the right to self-determination. Others were more vocal, with Nehru referring to Lahore as 'Jinnah's fantastic proposals', whilst another Congressman deemed Jinnah's views on partition 'a sign of a diseased mentality'.[51] However, Gandhi's response to Jinnah's assertion of two nations was anything but muted: 'I find no parallel in history for a body of converts and their descendants claiming to be a nation apart from their parent stock. If India was one nation before the advent of Islam, it must remain one in spite of the change of faith of a very large body of her children.'[52]

But by the mid-1940s, the Congress could no longer dismiss the League as an irrelevance. The League had lacked a popular touch with which to appeal to the mass of Muslim opinion in India, but Jinnah's re-organisation and the use of religion as a political category for Muslims had catapulted the League into a major player. As early as November 1939, Linlithgow expressed his gratitude to Jinnah for the 'valuable help' he provided 'against Congress claims' and admitted that 'I could claim to have a vested interest in his position.'[53] Not only were the Congress and the League divided during the war, but Gandhi's non-violent strategy had proved to be ineffective in the face of war and internal nationalist divisions. The Muslim League was riven with class tensions, but Gandhi's stifling of open class expressions (in particular with respect to Congress's attempts to build among Muslims) and his apparent pandering to 'Hinduised' idioms meant that Jinnah's attempts to re-launch the League and make an appeal for a 'two nations' theory of Hindus and Muslims had been more successful than it might otherwise have been.

The Left

A further twist came with the Communist Party of India's opposition to the Quit India Movement, on the grounds that the conflict in Europe was a 'people's war', and so Britain – as an ally of the Soviet Union – had to be supported. The largest left bloc in India was thus completely disarmed and impotent during the protests of 1942. In fact, in areas where the CPI had a strong base, their members actively worked to diffuse strikes, demonstrations and walkouts. This did not strengthen their popular support in north India, although their support for the war effort did mean that for the first time they were unbanned, and their organisational efforts enjoyed some success in the cities of rural north Bengal, Kerala and in the princely states of South India. There is much evidence that this position caused friction and anguish inside the ranks of Communist members and sympathisers, as activists organised solidarity for the Bengal Famine Relief based on nationalist sentiment.[54] But alas, the result was that the leaderships of the Congress and the Muslim League went unchallenged from the left.

The Congress, as shown earlier, had always been a mixed bag and its membership quite a motley crew. Although Gandhi's reforms of the 1920s had widened its appeal, so much so that its total membership rose from just over 3 million at the beginning of 1938 to almost 4½ million a year later.[55] However, although its membership now included middle-class, middle-caste peasantry, it still lacked a base among workers, landless peasants, and the mass of untouchables. This is important as it is tempting to casually think Congress had an overwhelmingly mass base under Gandhi. It did not. Nonetheless, the general wider radicalisation of politics throughout the 1930s and 1940s meant that left-wing currents inside Congress – such as the CSP and also members of the CPI – could gain a limited hearing. There was a constant internal battle between right and left for ascendancy and liberals usually sided with the right wing of the party, limiting efforts to mobilise the poor peasantry and industrial working class, as will be illustrated below.

The Indian National Army Trials and the Royal Indian Navy Mutiny

Britain emerged from the war in 1945 a considerably weakened power. Moreover, some 2.5 million Indian soldiers were being decommissioned from the British Army. There were only 40,000 British troops in India at the time and most of them were war weary and eager to get home. Britain's resolve to hold on to its empire was severely diminished, however, not simply due to the war but also due to the successive waves of mass action that Gandhi had initiated, which showed that the push from below for independence was irresistible. Indeed, two developments – independent of Gandhi's direct leadership – indicate this wider mood of resistance and rebellion.

The Indian National Army (INA) had been formed in 1942 and pledged to fight with the Japanese in order to kick Britain out of India. Its leader Bose in a public meeting in Singapore on 9 July 1943 issued the following call to arms:

> Friends! You will now realize that the time has come for the three million Indians living in East Asia to mobilize all their available

> resources, including money and man-power. Half-hearted measures will not do. I want Total Mobilization and nothing less, for we have been told repeatedly, even by our enemies, that this is a total war … Out of this total mobilization I expect at least three hundred thousand soldiers and three crores of dollars [$30,000,000]. I want also a unit of brave women to form a death-defying regiment who will wield the sword which the brave Rani of Jhansi wielded ….[56]

Bose's commitment to making Indian women full partners in the independence struggle is in marked contrast to Gandhi's understanding. Bose did not relegate women to the role of nursing, boycotting alcohol shops and being 'help-mates' to their husbands. Whereas Gandhi prescribed different spheres for men and women corresponding to traditional gendered roles, Bose did not see women as secondary partners to be confined to spinning, caring and non-violence. Under his command, a women's regiment was established numbering a thousand. He called them the 'Rani of Jhansi' regiment, after the nationalist heroine of 1857. Under the leadership of a young Indian doctor living in Singapore named Lakshmi Swaminathan, this regiment saw combat as they fought alongside other INA regiments and Japanese troops against the Indian Army in Burma.[57]

A weakened but vindictive imperial power placed three INA officers on trial at Delhi's famous Red Fort in November 1945, after they had been captured: General Shah Nawaz Khan, Colonel Prem Sehgal and Colonel Gurbaksh Singh Dhillon, a Muslim, Hindu and Sikh respectively. The three INA officers – symbols of intercommunal unity – were represented by Nehru as part of their defence counsel during the 'Red Fort Trial'. Found guilty of 'waging war against the King-Emperor' and sentenced to transportation for life, a popular outcry acclaimed them as national heroes and demanded their release, to which the British reluctantly acceded, thereby revealing their tenuous hold on India.

On 21 and 23 November 1945, a mass demonstration took place in Calcutta. Participants included members of the Congress, the Communist Party and the Muslim League. The police shot more than two hundred people, of whom 33 died. Then the British decided to put on trial only those INA men who were charged with committing murder or brutality against other POWs. However, Calcutta simply exploded when, in February 1946, Abdul Rashid Khan (a Muslim) of the INA was given seven years' imprisonment for murder. The protest by Muslim League students had begun peacefully, but later students of the Congress and Communist Party joined them in solidarity. Both the police and the army were called to put down what came to be known as 'the almost revolution'. This time, nearly four hundred people were shot down, and nearly a hundred killed. Since racial discrimination was rampant in the Royal Indian Navy, Khan's trial gave thousands of Indians the excuse to mutiny.

On 18 February 1946, the Royal Indian Navy mutiny began, encompassing a total strike and subsequent mutiny by Indian sailors on board ship and at shore establishments in Bombay. From here the mutiny spread throughout British India, from Karachi to Calcutta and Madras, with the slogans 'Strike for Bombay', 'Release 11,000 INA prisoners' and '*Jai Hind*' and came to involve 78 ships, 20 shore establishments and 20,000 sailors. It was a tremendous and inspirational action that united Hindu and Muslim sailors, whose grievances entailed poor food rations and lack of career advancement, but also racism at the hands of navy personnel. Such was the feeling that even the Gurkhas (a 'martial' group) in Karachi refused to fire on striking sailors. The mutineers took down the Union Jack and instead hoisted the flags of the Congress, the Muslim League and the CPI onto their ships in a symbolic display of national unity.[58] Thousands of people brought food for the rebels and fraternised at the harbour with the sailors. A general strike in support of the mutiny involved 300,000 across Bombay and united protests spread to Karachi and other areas that were later to be part of Pakistan.

Nehru grasped the significance of these events: 'The whole country is in the throes of serious discontent. We are sitting on the edge of a volcano which may erupt at any moment. A spark set ablaze Bombay, Calcutta and Karachi. These pre-storm conditions are not limited to big cities but are found even in the remotest villages.'[59]

Historians Peter Cain and Anthony Hopkins have noted how, by this stage, 'there was a loss of purpose at the very center of the imperial system. The gentlemanly administrators who managed the

Raj no longer had the heart to devise new moves against increasing odds, not least because after 1939 the majority of the Indian Civil Service were themselves Indian.'[60]

In most school textbooks, the role of non-violence and Gandhi are pre-eminent, and the place of the INA trials and the Royal Indian Naval mutinies are dismissed in a few cursory paragraphs. But to gain a measure of their significance, a letter from 1956 describing the conversation between Clement Attlee, British Labour Prime Minister at the time of independence and Chief Justice P.B. Chakrabarty of the Calcutta High Court who had been governor of West Bengal in 1947, is most revealing and illuminating. Chakrabarty wrote, 'My direct question to him [Attlee] was that since Gandhi's "Quit India" movement had tapered off quite some time ago and in 1947 no such new compelling situation had arisen that would necessitate a hasty British departure, why did they have to leave?' In his reply, Attlee stated 'the principal' reason amongst others was the 'erosion of loyalty to the British crown among the Indian army and navy personnel as a result of the military activities of Netaji, [Subhash Chandra Bose]'. Chakrabarty eventually asked Attlee about the extent of Gandhi's influence upon the British decision to quit India: 'Hearing this question, Attlee's lips became twisted in a sarcastic smile as he slowly chewed out the word, m-i-n-i-m-a-l!'[61]

In a similar vein, Ramesh Chandra Majumdar concludes:

> In particular, the revelations made by the INA trial, and the reaction it produced in India, made it quite plain to the British, already exhausted by the war, that they could no longer depend upon the loyalty of the sepoys [low-ranking Indian soldiers under British command] for maintaining their authority in India. This had probably the greatest influence upon their final decision to quit India.[62]

The magnificent Royal Indian Navy mutiny had not been initiated by Gandhi, and, tragically, Gandhi condemned it. His statement on 3 March 1946 criticised the strikers for mutinying as 'thoughtless and ignorant' and acting without the call of a 'prepared revolutionary party' and without the 'guidance and intervention' of 'political leaders of their choice'.[63] In spite of his general reservations regarding purely constitutional methods, Gandhi betrays his true motives on the mutiny in the following comment, 'If the union at the barricade is honest then there must be union also at the constitutional front.'[64] And finally as if to clarify his notion of freedom, Gandhi insulted the mutineers by declaring, 'That *swaraj* is not to be obtained by what is going on now in Bombay, Calcutta and Karachi.'[65] In addition, the leaders of the Congress and the Muslim League refused to back the mutineers and effectively sabotaged the strike by sending their representatives to broker an agreement. Nationalist leaders feared revolt from below and did their utmost to call off the mutiny. Both Jinnah and Congress leader Vallabhbhai Patel successfully persuaded the ratings to surrender. On 1 March 1946, Patel wrote, 'discipline in the army cannot be tampered with ... We will want [the] army even in free India.'[66]

Not only was the mutiny called off but none of their demands were met, and to add insult to injury, none of the dismissed mutineers were ever admitted into the Indian or Pakistani navies after independence. The shortcomings of Gandhi's reformist approach here and his version of nationalism, based as it was on an appeal to the religiosity of individuals was woefully inadequate when tested at a crucial juncture. The magnificent intercommunal unity on display during the naval mutiny was not to be nurtured by national leaders who vied for territory and power in the final transfer of power as August 1947 approached.

The Road to Partition

Partition in August 1947 witnessed the largest peacetime migration of people ever, with more than 15 million people uprooted, and also one of the most bloody and barbaric, with between 1 and 2 million dead. Some 75,000 women were raped, and many then disfigured or dismembered. From the perspective of the architects of the British Empire, however, as William Dalrymple notes, Partition was in one sense fairly successful. Whereas two hundred years of British rule in India had long been marked by violent revolts and brutal suppressions, the 'British Army was able to march out of the country with barely a shot fired and only seven casualties' on their side![67]

The level of barbarity witnessed in this period should be noted. One historian, Nisid Hajari, writes of how

> Gangs of killers set whole villages aflame, hacking to death men and children and the aged while carrying off young women to be raped. Some British soldiers and journalists who had witnessed the Nazi death camps claimed Partition's brutalities were worse: pregnant women had their breasts cut off and babies hacked out of their bellies; infants were found literally roasted on spits.[68]

The first series of widespread religious massacres took place in Calcutta, in 1946. Alex von Tunzelmann documents atrocities witnessed there by the writer Nirad C. Chaudhuri, who described a man tied to a tramline connector box with a small hole drilled in his skull, so that he would bleed to death as slowly as possible. The writer also related how a Hindu mob stripped a 14-year-old boy naked to confirm that he was circumcised, and therefore Muslim. The boy was then thrown into a pond and held down with bamboo poles – 'a Bengali engineer educated in England noting the time he took to die on his Rolex wristwatch, and wondering how tough the life of a Muslim bastard was'.[69] The American photojournalist Margaret Bourke-White, who had witnessed the opening of the gates of a Nazi concentration camp a year earlier, wrote that Calcutta's streets 'looked like Buchenwald'.[70]

When historians think about the causes for such a catastrophe in a society where a myriad of peoples, traditions and cultures had essentially coexisted for thousands of years, it is clear that it is not sufficient to simply point to a return to irrational age-old hatreds. One has to recall how British imperial policies of 'divide and rule' policy fostered animosity between Hindus, Muslims and Sikhs throughout the period of their rule in India. As von Tunzelmann observes, once 'the British started to define "communities" based on religious identity and attach political representation to them, many Indians stopped accepting the diversity of their own thoughts and began to ask themselves in which of the boxes they belonged.'[71] Yasmin Khan judges that Partition 'stands testament to the follies of empire, which ruptures community evolution, distorts historical trajectories and forces violent state formation from societies that would otherwise have taken different – and unknowable – paths'.[72]

A critical moment here was during the elections to the central and provincial legislatures in December 1945/January 1946. In the last provincial elections in 1937, the Muslim League had performed badly and the Congress had taken the most seats in provincial governments. Wartime opportunism, British support and the use of a populist slogan – 'Pakistan' – would provide a very different result. In the December 1945 elections for the Constituent Assembly, the League won every seat reserved for Muslims. In the provincial elections in January 1946, the League took 75 percent of the Muslim vote, an increase from 4.4 percent in 1937.[73] The result appeared to prove the 'universal appeal of Pakistan among Muslims of the subcontinent'.[74] According to one biographer, this 'was Jinnah's glorious hour: his arduous political campaigns, his robust beliefs and claims, were at last justified.'[75] The Congress dominated the central assembly elections, winning 91 percent of the vote in non-Muslim constituencies. Of the total of 1,585 seats, Congress won 923 (58.23 percent) and the League won 425 seats (26.81 percent of the total), placing it second.[76] The left was represented by the Communist Party of India, which stood 108 candidates, out of whom only eight won a seat. Seven out of the eight seats were reserved for labour representatives. The CPI obtained 2.5 percent of the popular vote,[77] clearly indicating a loss of credibility over its decision not to support the Quit India movement of 1942. In spite of this setback, the Communists did become the third force in terms of the popular vote.

Yet Jinnah's advocacy of the 'two-nation' theory and the still hazy notion of 'Pakistan' now took a decisive turn, and we can see the result in August 1946 when the League, frustrated by negotiations, launched Direct Action Day around the slogan 'Islam in Danger', which unleashed an unprecedented wave of communal riots. People moved, or were forced out of, mixed neighbourhoods and took refuge in increasingly polarised ghettos. Tensions were often heightened by local and regional political leaders. H.S. Suhrawardy, the Muslim League chief minister of Bengal, made incendiary speeches in Calcutta, provoking rioters against his own Hindu constituency, and wrote in a Calcutta newspaper that 'bloodshed and disorder are not necessarily evil in themselves, if resorted to for a noble cause.'[78] In Calcutta, 10,000 were killed in a day. The governor of Bengal, who did not lift a finger to stop the killing (claiming he had neither adequate transport nor troops), described how the streets were 'littered with corpses. I can honestly say that parts of the city ... were as bad as anything I saw when I was with the Guards on the Somme.'[79]

The Calcutta killings were followed by communal riots and killings in east Bengal, Bihar and the United Provinces and then the whole of the Punjab was engulfed from March 1947 onwards. Who was immediately responsible varied from area to area, as fearful Hindus exacted revenge when they heard stories of massacres by Muslims and vice versa. Muslim, Hindu and Sikh communal organisations fed each other's unrest, provoking fear and loathing that was reinforced by every atrocity. While the League urged Muslims to join the National Guards it organised in many provinces, the *Rashtriya Swayamsevak Sangh* declared Hindustan only for the Hindus. RSS propaganda declared, 'Trust not a Muslim ... Muslims are our eternal enemies ... Every Hindu must keep daggers and spears at his home and carry a sharp knife with him.'[80]

Independence and Alternative Futures

As we have seen in our discussion of the Royal Indian Navy mutiny and its widespread support at the base of Indian society, amid all the communal frenzy a different picture emerges which points to an alternative future which might have been won through resistance from below and unity against the common enemy – British imperialism. Country-wide protests saw massive intercommunal unity, particularly in Calcutta where strikes and riots exploded intermittently over a number of months. At the same time, railway, post and government workers threatened national strikes over rising prices. The naval mutiny and the mass protests over the INA trials had the potential to provide the antidote to communal frenzy and to electoral politics – both arenas dictated to by political and religious elites. Gandhi could have genuinely championed a cause of communal unity from below, that could have challenged what he later called the 'vivisection of India'. Alas, five days after the mutiny had begun, he condemned the ratings for setting a 'bad and unbecoming example for India' and declaring that 'a combination between Hindus and Muslims and others for the purpose of violent action is unholy.'[81]

So rather than have unity, further divisions were stoked between late 1946 and the summer of 1947. Likewise, the newly elected Labour government realised they had lost control and began to speed up their exit strategy. On the afternoon of 20 February 1947, British Prime Minister Clement Attlee declared that British rule would end on 'a date not later than June, 1948'. If Nehru and Jinnah could be reconciled by then, power would be transferred to 'some form of central Government for British India'. If not, they would hand over authority 'in such other way as may seem most reasonable and in the best interests of the Indian people'.[82]

In March 1947, Lord Louis Mountbatten had flown into Delhi as Britain's final viceroy. His mission was to hand over power and get out of India as quickly as possible. Attlee had praised previous Viceroy Wavell as a great soldier and man, but did not think old colonial hands were the order of the day and instead believed 'New Men were needed for a new policy.'[83] Nehru feared the 'new policy' seemed to accept Partition, which he saw as leading to the inevitable Balkanisation of India, certain to provoke civil conflict and add to violence and disorder, and lead to a further breakdown of the central authority and demoralisation of the army, the police and the Central Services.[84] Nehru was personally secular, but political expediency governed his actions. He was first to vote for Partition. In a speech in April 1947, Nehru said, he wanted the opportunity to build an India of his conception, adding 'I want that those who stand as an obstacle in our way should go their own way.'[85] In early June 1947, Mountbatten stunned everyone by announcing 15 August 1947 as the date for the transfer of power – ten months earlier than expected. The rush only exacerbated the chaos. Cyril Radcliffe, a British judge who had never before even visited India, was assigned to draw the borders of the two new states and was given barely forty days to remake the map of South Asia. When the borders were finally announced – two days *after* India's formal Independence – no one was happy with the result, least of all Jinnah, who had succeeded in acquiring a truncated nation, separated by a thousand miles of Indian territory – a shadow and a husk, 'maimed, mutilated and moth-eaten', as he famously said.[86]

On the evening of 14 August 1947, in the Viceroy's House in New Delhi, Lord Mountbatten and his wife settled down to watch a Bob Hope movie, *My Favorite Brunette*, whilst Nehru made his famous 'Long years ago, we made a tryst with destiny' speech and Jinnah was sat in Government House in Karachi. But outside the well-guarded enclaves, the horror was well under way. As Nisid Hajari writes:

> Foot caravans of destitute refugees fleeing the violence stretched for 50 miles and more. As the peasants trudged along wearily, mounted guerrillas burst out of the tall crops that lined the road and culled them like sheep. Special refugee trains, filled to bursting when they set out, suffered repeated ambushes along the way. All too often they crossed the border in funereal silence, blood seeping from under their carriage doors.[87]

This was a grim carnival of reaction, with brutal bloody ethnic cleansing akin to that seen in the former Yugoslavia in the early 1990s. Within a few months, the landscape of South Asia had changed irrevocably. In 1941, Karachi, designated the first capital of Pakistan, was 47.6 percent Hindu. Delhi, the capital of independent India, was one-third Muslim. By the end of the decade, almost all the Hindus of Karachi had fled, while 300,000 Muslims had been forced out of Delhi.[88] The changes made in a matter of months remain indelible seventy years later. Yet there was nothing inevitable about Partition.

Indeed, the strike wave unleashed by the Royal Indian Navy mutiny continued with police strikes in April 1946, while threats of an all-India rail strike continued throughout the summer, a postal strike took place in July 1946, as well as a one-day strike in support of the postal workers in Calcutta. The colonial state was literally crumbling, both administratively and militarily, from August 1946 onwards. In November 1946, the Cabinet agreed that the army would not be capable of crushing a mass revolt. The British decided to flee, declaring that Partition was the only way to end the political log-jam in discussions over India's future and the communal violence all round.

Gandhi's Tragedy

After the ignominious ends of the Quit India movement and the Royal Indian Navy mutiny, Gandhi's final tragedy during the final years of his life was his complete inability to prevent the Partition of India and the communal frenzy that accompanied it. He travelled to Noakhali in Bengal to see the horror of hundreds and thousands of dead Muslims and Hindus following the Muslim Day of Action in August 1946. When Partition was announced, Gandhi stayed away from the 'celebrations' of national independence, stating 'let posterity know what agony this old soul went through … Let it not be said that Gandhi was a party to India's vivisection.'[89] On Partition and to those who espoused the removal of Muslims from India, Gandhi retorted, 'Death for me would be a glorious deliverance rather than that I should be a helpless witness of the destruction of India, Hinduism, Sikhism, and Islam.'[90]

Every fibre of Gandhi's body spoke of Hindu-Muslim unity, but some of his pronouncements and actions caused anxiety in Muslim communities. For example, on cow protection, Gandhi held killing cows to be 'sinful', declaring 'When I see a cow, it is not an animal to eat; it is a poem of pity for me and I worship it and I shall defend its worship against the whole world.'[91] In spite of his defence of Muslim rights, statements such as this only provided succour to Hindu chauvinists for whom cow slaughter was and continues to be a stick with which to beat Muslims, particularly during Muslim religious festivals, which required feasting and the sharing of food with the poor. Throughout the 1930s, the Muslim League maintained their distance from Gandhi. For Jinnah, the staunch secularist, Gandhi was a mystic responsible for introducing religion into the political domain. In spite of Gandhi's personal convictions, he presented himself first and foremost as a 'Hindu' figure and this was not merely symbolic, as his pronouncements on cow protection demonstrate. Although he rejected the conflation of religion and nationality, the ambiguity at the heart of Gandhi's ideas and his reluctance and inability to genuinely build and empower a popular movement from below meant that he was powerless as an individual to prevent Partition.

In the final months of Gandhi's life, he undertook two final fasts. In September 1947, Gandhi went to Calcutta and stayed in the home of a Muslim, in the face of arch opposition from Hindu extremists. Here he began his fast unto death with the goal to bring to an end the communal killing which followed the break-up of Bengal. The British proved completely incapable and/or unwilling to police their once glorious empire and as communal violence continued unabated, it was Gandhi's fast that finally ends it. After four days and a stone and half lighter, all the violence stopped.

Then, in January 1948, he fasted for five days, demanding that Pakistan be given the Rs. 55 crores (Rs. 550 million) that it was due from the Indian government as part of the partition plan. His stance on this, and the fast he undertook in Calcutta by staying in Noakhali to help quell communal fires, put him streets ahead of other nationalist leaders, who were more concerned with self-congratulatory gestures as they shared the spoils of office, whilst India burned. Sumit Sarkar has described this as Gandhi's finest hour, and the one fast that had a truly noble sentiment behind it. There is little argument here.

Although Gandhi was able to use his stature, but also his fragility and the emotional toll of Partition to bring a halt to the killing for a short while, he could not re-direct it in any sustainable direction that might have prevented the tragedy of Partition. To achieve that would have required the vision and strategy employed by the naval mutineers to redirect politics in a class direction. The biggest irony of Gandhi's life was perhaps that Partition and independence gave birth to a capitalist state like any other – in fact, two states – with capitalist features of nuclear weapons, wars and immense poverty and obscene wealth, something far removed from the dream of Ram Rajya with which he had once inspired his followers.

Conclusion
Assassination and Legacy

Gandhi was assassinated on 30 January 1948 at Birla House, New Delhi. He was shot three times by Nathuram Godse – a Hindu Brahmin from Maharashtra state – using a Beretta automatic. Just two days before Gandhi had said, 'If I'm to die by the bullet of a madman, I must do so smiling. There must be no anger within me. God must be in my heart, and on my lips. And if anything happens, you are not to shed a single tear ....'[1] According to Manubehn Gandhi, his great-niece who was with him on that fateful day, it was as if he had foreseen his own death. This was not surprising, as there had been five previous assassination attempts.[2]

The assassin, Nathuram Godse, had already been complicit in one such assassination attempt on Gandhi. But on the evening of 30 January, Godse succeeded. Amidst a vast throng of well-wishers, devotees and tourists who mingled freely to catch sight of the 78-year-old *Mahatma*, Godse came forward as if he were a disciple wanting to obtain Gandhi's blessing and then fired at point-blank range. Within moments, Gandhi was dead. This was a declaration of war and statement of intent by the Hindu right-wing fundamentalists rooted in the *Hindu Mahasabha* (Hindu Grand-Assembly) and the *Rashtriya Swayamsevak Sangh* (RSS) and its affiliates. Through this act, Godse and his fellow travellers had committed to a '*Hindu Rashtra*' (nation), something that was complete anathema to Gandhi.

Gandhi had been in Calcutta four months before, following the enormous upheaval of Partition. The Delhi that Gandhi returned to was a refugee site. Gandhi was disgusted with the opportunism he saw in Congress, and up to his death he displayed a principled anti-communalism. While riots raged in Punjab, and 55,000 soldiers failed to stop this, Gandhi told a leader of the Muslim League: 'I want to fight it out with my life. I would not allow the Muslims to crawl on the streets in India. They must walk with self-respect.'[3] Gandhi died for upholding Muslim equality, and Reginald Reynolds wrote that his own first words after receiving the astonishing news of Gandhi's assassination were 'Thank God it was a Hindu.'[4] This was a real fear, as some Muslims had already been attacked. The newly elected Nehru government made sure that news of Godse's culpability was made as public as possible. On 4 February 1948, the state moved with lightning speed to ban the RSS, the Muslim National Guards and the Khaksars, with some 200,000 arrests of RSS cadres.[5]

According to Arvind Sharma, the assassination plans were initiated by Godse and his accomplices in 1947, after India and Pakistan had already started skirmishes over Kashmir. The new, independent government of India, led by Congress leaders, was withholding a payment to Pakistan in January 1948 because Pakistani troops had entered Kashmir. Gandhi opposed the decision to freeze the payment and began a fast-unto-death on 13 January 1948, to pressure the Nehru government to dispatch the payment to Pakistan. The Indian government eventually gave in and reversed its decision.[6] Godse and his colleagues interpreted this as further evidence of Gandhi's appeasement of Pakistan and Muslims.

Their trial, which began in May 1948, was held in Delhi's historic Red Fort, site of the INA trials of 1945. Godse and his co-defendants attempted to use the occasion to justify their action politically by accusing Gandhi of being a better friend to Muslims than caring for Hindus, and blamed him for the sufferings of Partition.[7] Godse blamed Gandhi for continuing to appease Muslims in such a manner 'that my blood boiled and I could tolerate him no longer.'[8] The trial lasted over a year and Godse, along with one accomplice, Narayan Apte, were sentenced to death on 8 November 1949 and hanged a week later on 15 November in Ambala jail. The reason for the unseemly haste is all too self-evident: as with any assassination of a high-profile public figure, the desire to catch and punish the perpetrators was enormous, but there was also fear on the part of the state that, meant to safeguard Gandhi, then wished 'to avoid scrutiny for the failure to prevent the assassination'.[9] Not only was justice swift: Godse's statement was banned by the government and a mass crackdown against the RSS was used to exclude factional rivals within the Congress to Nehru's prime ministerial authority. As Khan observes, this guaranteed the 'ascendancy of secularism and democracy as the legitimate ideological foundation of the Indian state and its constitutional and legal status, notwithstanding grave failures in implementation'.[10]

The Uses and Abuses of Gandhi

George Orwell commented that after his death, Gandhi left a 'clean smell behind', in contrast to most politicians of his time.[11] Gandhi was held by Orwell to be above political horse-trading – the politics of brokerage, the politics of compromise based on naked self-interest. Yet Gandhi's 'clean smell' has not stopped politicians who are already smelling somewhat whiffier invoking Gandhi's name and memory since his death. Prior to becoming president of the United States, then-Senator Barack Obama declared that 'throughout my life, I have always looked to Mahatma Gandhi as an inspiration, because he embodies the kind of transformational change that can be made when ordinary people come together to do extraordinary things.'[12]

Despite his record of drone strikes and bombing of some of the world's poorest people while in office, Obama followed Martin Luther King Jr in being awarded the 2009 Nobel Peace Prize for his 'extraordinary efforts to strengthen international diplomacy and cooperation between peoples'. Even after leaving office, Obama continued to praise Gandhi, noting in 2017 that '"Mobilizing movements starts with a story", he said, adding that it was Gandhi's understanding of India's stories and traditions, his attention to the marginalised voices in Africa, that helped him gather a movement that drove out the world's most successful empire.'[13]

In 2015, a statue of Gandhi was unveiled in Parliament Square in London to mark the hundredth anniversary of his return to India to start the struggle for independence from British rule, with the then British Prime Minister David Cameron paying tribute to 'the universal power of Gandhi's message'.[14] Chancellor George Osborne stated that 'As the father of the largest democracy in the world, it's time for Gandhi to take his place in front of the mother of parliaments. He is a figure of inspiration, not just in Britain and India, but around the world.'[15] Later that year, Cameron and Osborne honoured 'the universal power' of Gandhi's 'inspirational message' in their own way by launching military air-strikes on Syria.

Just as pernicious have been as yet unconfirmed reports that the Indian Prime Minister Narendra Modi's government has given licence to destroy archival files that include those relating to Gandhi's assassination.[16] Whatever the truth of such allegations, one thing remains clear: the RSS has been and continues to be a core ideological component of Modi's Bharatiya Janata Party (BJP).[17] The politics of 'Hindutva' are enshrined within the organisation of the BJP and their vision for a Hindu India is the political project to which the Modi government is committed. The fact of Gandhi's assassin coming from their ranks has proved a difficult path to negotiate for the BJP. After many decades of keeping their distance, there are now tentative moves to try to appropriate the Gandhi mantle for Hindutva. In 2017, on the seventieth anniversary of independence, Modi attempted to cloak himself in the *Mahatma* mythology by trying his hand at a spinning wheel at Gandhi's Sabarmati Ashram in Ahmedabad![18] This attempt at appropriation will not be an easy task for the BJP and is fraught with multiple problems, but it does underline the fact that Gandhi's legacy can be interpreted and abused by many a charlatan.

Gandhi – The Man Behind the Myths

Such tributes to Gandhi by liberal imperialists such as Obama and Cameron are in a sense only possible because of long-standing popular myths about Gandhi himself, and about how the actual struggle for Indian independence was won. If one reads Gandhi's ethical power of persuasion as the overriding critical factor here on the one hand, or else on the other, chooses to portray him as 'a harmless icon', a waif-like figure wandering around India in a loincloth with a staff, it does seem remarkable that one such as he could bring the might of the British Empire to its knees. If, however, we remember that Gandhi was a British-trained barrister, with ample experience of political activity, and accustomed to bargaining, then what emerges is a figure who is shrewd, calculating and extremely clever. This does not mean he was insincere – far from it. Gandhi was totally committed to a united independent India. He wanted an end to the callous treatment meted out to *dalits* and low-caste groups. He wanted women to be treated with respect, free to marry or not, and have financial independence, and he so desperately wanted Hindu-Muslim unity to be the defining feature of a composite Indian nationhood.

Gandhi is perceived as the 'weapon less warrior; a barrister at law who became an advocate of his people'.[19] Traditionally, historical scholarship has seen Gandhi as a remarkable figure that acted as a catalyst and provided leadership to the apolitical, apathetic and inarticulate Indians of South Africa and India. Gandhi certainly played a seminal role in bringing the concerns and grievances of the peasantry centre stage into the body-politic of the Congress. It was Gandhi who was responsible for Jawaharlal Nehru and Vallabhbhai Patel going into villages. Most Indian politicians had never entered a village before, much less talk to peasants or the poor. In this endeavour, Gandhi must take some credit for transforming the elite nature of the Congress into a more democratic party.

However, to emphasise Gandhi's personality as the sole instigator of mass movements and change, gives the individual an enormous amount of power in making history, by assuming that before Gandhi there was nothing. This approach does not help explain the developments of mass movements in the first decades of the twentieth century. It treats the Indian population as an undifferentiated mass and prevents an understanding of which specific constituents provided Gandhi with his support base, why they became politicised and what were the factors for this constituency broadening in the 1920s and 1930s. It is also important to acknowledge that political activity and protests by peasants and untouchable groups pre-date Gandhi, but his (inter)national stature and reputation did provide a national focus for these groups. However, Gandhi's moral vision for a 'perfect' world did not entail oppressed groups overthrowing the society that rests on their oppression, or even an understanding that if they did attempt this, that no ruling class in history has ever previously surrendered its power without a fight.

On violence, even sympathetic scholars have admitted that Gandhi was worried that

> once violence became respectable and organized, the masses would want to use it against their native exploiters, thereby dividing the nationalist movement ... He knew that the poor were angry and frustrated ... He was also aware of their role in the Russian and Chinese revolutions ... and was therefore, deeply afraid that once they were mobilised and their expectations aroused, large scale violence was bound to result which neither he nor the Congress would be able to control.[20]

As we have seen Gandhi abhorred violence, particularly if resorted to by ordinary people, and certainly if it was part of a class struggle against exploitation and oppression – foreign or domestic. This was true in South Africa, Chauri Chaura, Mappila, the Quit India movement and the naval mutinies. On each occasion, Gandhi lectured ordinary people, the subalterns, for not having understood the principles of his *satyagraha* strategy. And on each occasion, those who wielded power and had a monopoly on violence to mete out the full power of the state with no regard for passive resistance, were absolved somehow of responsibility. By treating violence and non-violence as abstract moral precepts, Gandhi effectively left the mass of people defenceless in the face of colonial state brutality and violence. Gandhi had no sense of the insight demonstrated by Frantz Fanon, who did not equate the violence of the oppressed with the violence of the oppressor, either morally or politically.

Gandhi's own ideas for how the oppressed might ready themselves for a mass struggle of civil disobedience stressed not self-emancipation by 'the wretched of the earth', but instead their 'self-purification'. At a speech in August 1921, Gandhi declared:

> We must understand thoroughly what self-purification means. Give up drinking alcohol, smoking ganja and eating opium. Give up visiting prostitutes ... India has not yet understood this principle fully. The day I am persuaded that India has learnt this, the country can become free. Today India lacks the power for peaceful, civil disobedience of laws ... But this power will not come through drinking and debauchery. Therefore give up drinking, give up debauchery. This has a very deep meaning. If you would rather

> have nothing to do with dirty things, you should become pure yourselves.[21]

Gandhi's politics then preached class and caste conciliation and personal salvation through moral and social reform. Fanon, on the other hand, always stressed the bigger fundamental political issue at stake:

> The underprivileged and starving peasant is the exploited who very soon discovers that only violence pays. For him there is no compromise, no possibility of concession. Colonization or decolonization: it is simply a power struggle. The exploited realize that their liberation implies using every means available, and force is the first.[22]

Gandhi's sense of colonial liberation being above all a 'power struggle' was limited. A generous reading of his life can hold to the notion of a contradictory revolutionary and this has some merit. But in the final analysis, his intentions were not to overthrow the system but make it kinder. In this sense, Gandhi comes from a long line of classic reformers, and represents someone whose reformism was rooted in a social conservatism that did not seek the overthrow of capitalism but its taming.

His strident critique of Western society in the pages of *Hind Swaraj* was inspirational. Gandhi's prescription for India was to avoid the forced industrial and urban developments pursued by the colonial state. Instead, he believed India's future lay in its rural heartlands. He advocated self-sufficient village communities that were marked by interdependency and social cohesion. This was not some hippy, kibbutz-style, primitive communism. It was a society composed of rights and responsibilities, with individuals fulfilling their respective economic and social roles to the benefit of all. The notion of trusteeship was at the heart of his vision. This type of integrated, interdependent social unit epitomised to Gandhi all the virtues of a simple rustic life and was devoid of the social conflicts and tensions that marred advanced industrial societies.

In this sense, the enigma of Gandhi is not so perplexing or extraordinary. From Thoreau to Tolstoy to Ruskin, each age has produced opponents and those who question the status quo and even champion civil disobedience against it. Such figures tend to be highly contradictory in their politics, and their legacy complex and contested. Lenin stated of Tolstoy, for example, that his doctrine is 'certainly utopian and in content is reactionary in the most precise and most profound sense of the word'. But Lenin also shrewdly observed how the doctrine of non-violence contained 'critical elements capable of providing valuable material for the enlightenment of the advanced classes'.[23] The strategy such figures propose is often imbued with principles of bourgeois morality, even though many such critics lambast aspects of this same morality. It is noteworthy for its self-righteous tone and emphasis on the power of the individual to change the self and society. The emphasis on moral precepts has all the hallmarks of appealing to a variety of constituents: indigenous elites hankering for political office, middle-class urban professionals desirous to secure careers in the civil service, indigenous industrialists and landed gentry ever eager to keep their workers and peasants in check, comfortable peasant tenant farmers jealously guarding their privileges, as well as the mass of impoverished peasantry, landless labourers and urban working classes who have borne the brunt of colonial oppression. But in appealing to disparate groups, the manner in which mass action is interpreted and acted upon will vary, according to the social forces involved and the interests they represent. In relation to conservative, elite social forces, Gandhi did offer a programme of mass action and political activity that drew in wider layers of activists. But in relation to achieving the world of social harmony without social inequality to which he aspired, his strategy proved sorely lacking in understanding how to direct the mass action he helped initiate and lead.

As this book has aimed to show, Gandhi's 'experiments in civil disobedience' therefore need to be examined critically and in their concrete context. Gandhi was not the first to interweave a range of religious texts, nor will he be the last. Indian intellectuals of the interwar period were indeed drawn to Gandhi, particularly during the Non-Co-operation Movement. But many were frustrated by Gandhian non-violence and thus gravitated towards more radical politics in the 1930s. In commenting on Gandhi's first fast in Ahmedabad following the 'unruly' behaviour of strikers angry at strike breakers, the Keralan Communist E.M.S. Namboodiripad stated that this experiment in civil disobedience had been most successful for the elite nationalists with a phobia of the masses, of which Gandhi was a representative, as it 'showed them that here was a technique of struggle which could at once rally the masses and keep them away from militant actions.'[24] Gandhi's programme had very little that was anti-landlord and anti-business. As Hiren Mukherjee notes, 'the aura of Gandhi's glory lent a certain nobility to a generally timorous bourgeois movement, which prized and utilised his capacity of mobilising the people against foreign rule and at the same time of restricting mass activity within limits thought safe for the men of property.'[25]

The 'Practical Idealist'

The extent to which Gandhi is held as an original thinker and his practice innovative has long been a subject of much contested debate and scrutiny. In 1920, Gandhi himself declared 'I am not a visionary. I claim to be a practical idealist. The religion of non-violence is not meant merely for the rishis and saints. It is meant for the common people as well.'[26] He believed the religion of non-violence to be 'the root of Hinduism'.[27] Gandhi's adherence to this creed meant that under his control, the freedom movement took on a 'religious crusade'.[28] His ashrams and similar experiments were indeed 'sites of struggle' – however, often not in a positive outward-looking sense of helping build a united determined struggle against colonialism, but rather in the sense of being inward-looking, disguising internal divisions, hiding antagonisms, petty jealousies, rivalries and tensions and most of all, in maintaining control from above.

Gandhi's overriding religious faith then was both a source of strength, but also of weakness: 'Whatever conclusions I may have come to in my life, I have not drawn them from history, which played a small part in my education ... all my conclusions are based on my personal experience.'[29] His stress on 'personal experience' also meant he was reluctant to take on board new ways of thinking and theorising about the world around him. He was not then a great intellectual in the sense of someone who has invested time and resources into making a deep study of various philosophies or treatises about the world. As Perry Anderson notes:

> Gandhi did not claim much book learning. In London, he had found his legal textbooks full of interest – a manual on property law 'read like a novel' – but Bentham too difficult to understand. Tracts by Ruskin and Tolstoy were a revelation in South Africa. In prison in India he came to the conclusion that Gibbon was an inferior version of the *Mahabharata*, and that he could have written *Capital* better than Marx. What fixed his attention were the short list of works he had read by the time he came to write *Hind Swaraj*, and a limited number of Hindu classics. When he left South Africa, his basic ideas about the world were essentially complete. Not in more books, but in himself lay truth.[30]

Here it might be worth drawing a contrast with that great admirer of Gandhi, Martin Luther King Jr. Unlike Gandhi, King's religious views did not include proselytising to the unconverted. His faith was important to him but not at the exclusion of finding common cause with activists. He was willing to listen to and learn from non-believers, including atheists.[31] King was not insistent that his was the only and correct way. He was not arrogant and presumptuous like Gandhi, who was used to giving ultimatums, not only to his opponents in government but also to other activists. King understood the necessity of strategically challenging power and the powerful, whereas Gandhi instinctively always wished to negotiate and find common cause with them. The tensions between Gandhi's intentions and outcomes are at the heart of the interplay between the art of revolution and non-violence to achieve this. Gandhi remained at the intersection of such debates with his peculiar strategy of unleashing mass mobilisation, only to curtail it when it contradicted his specific edicts. His campaigns could elicit support from ordinary people, but his support base was firmly middle class, composed of business magnates, landlords, better-off peasants, among others – all of whom occupied a specific class position within Indian society that desired serious reform to colonial structures, but would baulk at mass revolutionary social change if it threatened their property rights and relatively privileged status. Consequently, the social conservatism endemic to such a social base would set limits to the more radical demands of workers, poorer and landless peasants, untouchables and forest dwellers – groups that found themselves at odds with prescriptive Gandhian methods. More critically, Gandhi did not have the politics to break out from this impasse. To do so would require a reassessment of the politics of non-violence in the face of an intransigent imperial order. This evaluation would necessitate serious engagement with political currents of the left that clearly existed and operated in his lifetime. Such an engagement is not predicated on the advocacy of violence but lies in having sufficient political understanding that real power will not cede without a fight and the movement needs to be ready to defend hard-fought-for gains to move forward. Yet Gandhi's attitude to thinkers on the Indian left has demonstrated a flagrant disregard to entertaining any serious interrogation of strategy, or capacity to listen and learn from other activists critical of moral abstractness.

Gandhi's Legacy – Can Love Trump Hate?

A serious strategy to bring about revolutionary change has to go beyond mere moral exhortations to do things differently, even though 'moral force' and 'truth force' must indeed be at the very heart of any movement that aims to change the world. The fact that Gandhi failed to provide a strategic political lead pointing towards a real alternative way forward amid the looming tragedy of Partition, as tensions built up, demonstrates that his method proved lacking. Gandhi himself of course was not personally responsible for the violence of Partition itself, but traditional explanations which refuse to critically account for Gandhi's failings and instead blame those individuals who did not share his vision, or broke with his brand of passive resistance, or still subverted it for their own ends, are not particularly convincing either. As we have noted, the history of the naval mutiny and other protests from below have been marginalised in the story of Partition, in part because it points to a potential alternative to Gandhi's strategy, one based on mass class struggle from below. This is not to imply that Partition could have been averted. But the potential of such movements does provide a glimpse of the 'unknowable' paths that might have resulted.

The legacy of Partition means that today India and Pakistan face each other as nuclear powers. In the past, they have fought two inconclusive wars over the disputed region of Kashmir. In 1971, they fought over the secession of East Pakistan, which became Bangladesh. In this context, not only does Gandhi's vision of Hindu-Muslim unity need to be defended and reasserted, but also there is manifestly a need for a resurgence of new 'experiments in civil disobedience' in both India and Pakistan today. Indeed, in a world that is more dangerous than ever, in economic and environmental crisis with rising inter-imperialist tensions and new proxy wars breaking out, it is not surprising that movements and activists today invoke the name of Gandhi and the principles of non-violence in their campaigns. As Guha states, Gandhi is enjoying more life in death than he ever did whilst alive. To his admirers and supporters, he remains a great figure to provide leadership, while his detractors continue to hail from all sides of the political spectrum. On the right, the RSS, *Hindu Mahasbha* and until recently even the Vishva Hindu Parishad (World Hindu Council) and those around the politics of the BJP have poured scorn on Gandhi's life and memory. On the left, as we have seen, criticism has come from varied quarters, predictably from those in the Communist tradition in India and internationally, but also from the great Indian poet Rabindranath Tagore, Nehru and more recently by the writer and activist Arundhati Roy. The aim of this book has been to try and help activists today grapple with the real life and complex and contested legacy of this enigmatic and contradictory 'non-violent revolutionary', and hopefully to be encouraged to go beyond what Gandhi ever thought possible and engage not only in 'experiments in civil disobedience', but also hopefully in the kind of mass class struggles and socialist revolutions of the future, 'experiments in human liberation' that can genuinely and finally build a new society free of the horrors of war, militarism and racism.

Notes

Introduction

1. Attenborough's Oscar acceptance speech in 1982.
2. https://edition.cnn.com/2018/05/14/middleeast/gaza-uprising-leader-intl/index.html.
3. Quoted in Harry Belafonte with Michael Shnayerson, *My Song: A Memoir*, New York: Vintage Books, 2012, p. 273.
4. Ibid., p. 212.
5. Martin Luther King, Jr, *Stride Toward Freedom*, New York: Harper and Brothers, 1958, p. 85.
6. Ibid., p. 85.
7. Perry Anderson, 'India Trilogy: Gandhi Centre Stage – Why Partition – After Nehru', *London Review of Books*, vol. 34, no. 13, 2012, p. 5.
8. Randolph S. Churchill and Martin Gilbert, *Winston Churchill*, vol. 5, London: Heinemann, 1976, p. 390.
9. Quoted in R.A. Huttenback, *Gandhi in South Africa: British Imperialism and the Indian Question, 1860–1914*, Ithaca, NY: Cornell University Press, 1971, p. 330.
10. This was Einstein's tribute to Gandhi on his seventieth birthday. Quoted from Einstein's *Out of My Later Years*, published in 1940, in Bhikhu Parekh, 'Einstein's Assessment of Gandhi' in *The Round Table: The Commonwealth Journal of International Affairs*, vol. 80, no. 320, 1991, p. 469.
11. J. Nehru, *Selected Works of Jawaharlal Nehru (SWJN)*, New Delhi: OUP, 1987, p. 35.
12. Muriel Lester Papers, File 2/7/3/7, 1926; emphasis added.
13. Mira Behn, *The Spirit's Pilgrimage*, London: Great Ocean Publishers, 1960, p. 40.
14. Letter, 24 July 1925 cited in ibid., p. 63.
15. Jack Dromey, 'Jayaben Desai obituary', *Guardian*, 28 December 2010.
16. C.L.R. James, 'Review of *Gandhi: His Own Story*', *The Beacon*, vol. 1, no. 5, August 1931, p. 19. Even after he became a Marxist, James would still later consider Gandhi one of the four 'greatest statesmen of the twentieth century' alongside Lenin, Mao and Nkrumah. See C.L.R. James, *Nkrumah and the Ghana Revolution*, London: Allison and Busby, 1977, p. 187.
17. Hakim Adi and Marika Sherwood, *The 1945 Manchester Pan-African Congress Revisited*, London: New Beacon Books, 1995, pp. 44–45. See

also Christian Høgsbjerg, 'Remembering the Fifth Pan-African Congress', *Leeds African Studies Bulletin*, vol. 77, 2016, pp. 119–139.

18. James, *Nkrumah and the Ghana Revolution*, p. 131.
19. Full speech in *Commemorating the Centenary of the Birth of Dr Eric Eustace Williams, 1911–2011*, San Fernando, Trinidad: Viren Annamunthodo, 2011, pp. 44–53.
20. Ibid., p. 45.
21. Ibid., p. 52.
22. Nelson Mandela, 'The Sacred Warrior', *Time*, 31 December 1999, http://content.time.com/time/subscriber/article/0,33009,993025-1,00.html.
23. Raymond Quevedo (Atilla the Hun), *Atilla's Kaiso: A Short History of Trinidad's Calypso*, University of the West Indies, St Augustine, Trinidad and Tobago, 1994, p. 143.
24. *Young India*, Ahmedabad, 26 November 1931, p. 369.
25. *Harijan*, Ahmedabad, 17 February 1946.
26. Joseph Doke, *M. K. Gandhi; An Indian patriot in South Africa*, London: Indian Chronicle, 1909.
27. Romain Rolland, *Mahatma Gandhi*, trans. Catherine Groth, New York: The Century Company, 1924.
28. Louis Fischer, *The Life of Mahatma Gandhi*, London: HarperCollins, 1997; *Gandhi: His Life and Message for the World*, London: Penguin, 2010.
29. Reginald Reynolds, *To Live in Mankind: A Quest for Gandhi*, London: Andre Deutsch, 1951.
30. See Judith M. Brown and Anthony Parel, *The Cambridge Companion to Gandhi*, Cambridge: CUP, 2011.
31. http://gandhiserve.org/e/cwmg/cwmg.htm.
32. Judith Brown, *Gandhi's Rise to Power: Indian Politics, 1915–1922*, Cambridge: CUP, 1972; *Gandhi and Civil Disobedience: The Mahatma in Indian Politics, 1928–1934*, Cambridge: CUP, 1977 and *Gandhi: Prisoner of Hope*, London: Yale University Press, 1989.
33. David Arnold, *Gandhi: Profiles in Power*, Harlow: Pearson Education, 2001.
34. David Hardiman, *Gandhi in His Time and Ours*, New Delhi: Permanent Black, 2003.
35. Geoffrey Ashe, *Gandhi: A Study in Revolution*, New York: Heinemann Ltd, 1968.
36. See Bhikhu Parekh, *Gandhi's Political Philosophy: A Critical Examination*, Basingstoke: Palgrave Macmillan, 1989; Bal Ram Nanda, *Gandhi and his Critics*, New Delhi: OUP, 1994; J.T.F. Jordens, *Gandhi's Religion: A Homespun Shawl*, New Delhi: OUP, 2012; Erik H. Erikson, *Gandhi's Truth on the Origins of Militant Non-violence*, New York: W.W. Norton & Co., 1969.

37. Ramachandra Guha, *Gandhi Before India*, London: Allen Lane, 2013. Also *Gandhi: The Years that Changed the World (1914–1948)*, Penguin Random House India, 2018. This second volume focuses on Gandhi's life in India.
38. Kathryn Tidrick, *Gandhi – A Political and Spiritual Life*, London: I.B. Tauris, 2006.
39. Rajmohan Gandhi, *Gandhi: The Man, his People and the Empire*, London: Haus Publishing, 2007; Arun Gandhi and Bethany Hegedus, *Grandfather Gandhi*, London: Atheneum Books, 2014.
40. See Maureen Swan, *Gandhi: The South African Experience*, Johannesburg: Ravan, 1985; Ashwin Desai and Goolam Vahed, *The South African Gandhi: Stretcher Bearer of Empire*, New Delhi: Navayana Publishing Pvt Ltd, 2015.
41. See Faisal Devji, *The Impossible Indian: Gandhi and the Temptation of Violence*, London: Hurst & Co. 2012 and Shruti Kapila, 'Gandhi Before Mahatma: The Foundations of Political Truth', *Public Culture*, vol. 23, no. 2, 2011, pp. 431–448.
42. See, for example, Nalini Natarajan, *Atlantic Gandhi: the Mahatma Overseas*, New Delhi: Sage, 2013.
43. Jad Adams, *Gandhi: Naked Ambition*, London: Quercus, 2010, and Joseph Lelyveld, *Great Soul: Mahatma Gandhi and His Struggle with India*, New York: Alfred A. Knopf, 2011.
44. 'Arundhati Roy Accuses Mahatma Gandhi of Discrimination', *Guardian*, 18 July 2014, https://www.theguardian.com/books/2014/jul/18/arundhati-roy-accuses-mahatma-gandhi-discrimination.
45. Russell Brand, *Revolution*, London: Century, 2014, pp. 91, 324.
46. Attenborough, *Gandhi*, 1982.

1 *Early Life: 1869–93*

1. A *diwan* was the senior administrative authority in many princely states. They also acted as revenue collectors in the Mughal administration and these state roles continued well after the decline and disappearance of the Mughal Empire and into British control of the region.
2. Amalendu Misra, *Identity and Religion: Foundations of Anti-Islamism in India*, New Delhi: Sage Publications, 2004, p. 67. See also R. Gandhi, *Gandhi*, 2004, p. 5.
3. Barbara Ramusack, *Indian Princes and their States*, Cambridge: CUP, 2004, p. 13.
4. Nehru, in 1939, quoted in Ramusack, *Indian Princes and their States*, p. 1.
5. Ramusack, *Indian Princes and their States*, p. 88.
6. Ibid., p. 92.
7. A *Nawab* is almost like a peerage. It was a title conferred upon loyal subjects by Mughal rulers to govern princely states.

8. Doke, *Indian Patriot*, p. 13.
9. Ibid., p. 16.
10. Gandhi, *An Autobiography or the story of my experiments with truth*, Ahmedabad: Navajivan Publishing House, 2002, p. 31.
11. Doke, *Indian Patriot*, p. 17. Gandhi, *An Autobiography*, pp. 4–5.
12. Doke, *Indian Patriot*, p. 17.
13. Ibid., p. 19.
14. Gandhi, *Autobiography*, p. 6.
15. Ibid., p. 14.
16. R. Gandhi, *Gandhi*, p. 17.
17. Doke, *An Indian Patriot*, p. 24.
18. R. Guha, *Gandhi Before India*, pp. 27–28.
19. Gandhi, *An Autobiography*, pp. 25–26. *Ahimsa* means not to harm or injure. It can refer to showing compassion but is also associated with being non-violent.
20. Doke, *An Indian Patriot*, p. 27.
21. Yasmin Khan, 'Gandhi's World', in Judith Brown and Anthony Parel, eds, *Cambridge Companion to Gandhi*, p. 27.
22. Gandhi, *Collected Works of Mahatma Gandhi*, Delhi: Navajivan Press Publications Division, Ministry of Information and Broadcasting, Government of India, 1958, vol. 1, p. 54. All citations are from this hard-copy version and subsequently will be cited as Gandhi, *CWMG*.
23. Gandhi, *An Autobiography*, p. 41.
24. Ibid., p. 47.
25. Ibid., p. 52.
26. Thoreau published *Walden (Life in the Woods)* in 1854. This is a manual on living in natural surroundings, spiritual discovery and self-reliance. For him, personal self-introspection would be the path to true independence.
27. *The Vegetarian*, 7 February 1891.
28. *The Vegetarian*, 28 February 1891.
29. Doke, *An Indian Patriot*, p. 29.
30. Gandhi, Speech delivered by Gandhi to the London Vegetarian Society, 20 November 1931.
31. Ibid.
32. Gandhi, *An Autobiography*, p. 63.
33. Ibid., p. 62.
34. Doke, *An Indian Patriot*, p. 31.
35. Gandhi, *An Autobiography*, p. 63.
36. Ibid., p. 72.
37. Ibid., p. 72.
38. Doke, *An Indian Patriot*, p. 31.
39. Gandhi, *An Autobiography*, p. 91.

2 *South Africa and the Birth of* Satyagraha*: 1893–1915*

1. Doke, *M.K. Gandhi: An Indian Patriot*, p. 35.
2. *Harijan*, 10 December 1938.
3. Gandhi, *Autobiography*, p. 98.
4. David Arnold, *Gandhi: Profiles in Power*, Harlow: Pearson Education, 2001, p. 45.
5. *Natal Advertiser*, 9 May 1893.
6. Quoted in Gandhi, *CWMG*, vol. 1, p. 76.
7. *Natal Advertiser*, 26 May 1893.
8. Arnold, *Gandhi: Profiles in Power*, p. 50.
9. Gandhi, *Autobiography*, p. 130.
10. Gandhi, *The Grievances of the British Indians in South Africa: An Appeal to the Indian Public*, Victoria Jubilee Printing Press, 1896.
11. Arnold, *Gandhi: Profiles in Power*, p. 51.
12. Gandhi, *CWMG*, vol. 5, p. 421.
13. Quoted in Vijay Prashad, *Arab Spring, Libyan Winter*, Oakland: A.K. Press Publishing & Distribution, 2012, p. 250.
14. Vijay Prashad, *Red Star over the Third World*, New Delhi: Leftword Books, 2017, pp. 35–36.
15. Gandhi, *CWMG*, vol. 8, pp. 41–42.
16. Gandhi, *Statement to Disorders Inquiry Committee*, 5 January 1920, in *CWMG*, vol. 16, pp. 368–369.
17. Fischer, *Gandhi: His Life and Message for the World*, p. 35.
18. Hardiman, *Gandhi in His Time and Ours*, p. 76.
19. Devji, *The Impossible Indian*, p. 5.
20. Fischer, *Gandhi: His Life and Message for the World*, p. 38.
21. Interview to *Natal Mercury*, 25 October 1913, in Gandhi, *CWMG*, vol. 12, p. 253.
22. Henry Salt, *Company I Have Kept*, London: Allen & Unwin, 1930, pp. 100–101.
23. *Indian Opinion*, 26 October 1907.
24. *Indian Opinion*, 7 September 1907 and 14 September 1907.
25. 'Civil Disobedience', quoted in *Indian Opinion*, 26 October 1907.
26. *Indian Opinion*, 7 September 1907.
27. Gandhi, *An Autobiography*, p. 127.
28. Leo Tolstoy, *The Kingdom of God and Peace Essays*, trans. and intro. Ayler Maude, London: OUP, 1960, p. 530.
29. *Harijan*, 18 January 1922.
30. Leo Tolstoy, 'Letter to a Hindoo'. This is also referred to as 'A Message to Young India' – https://www.theosophyonline.com/userfiles/A%20Letter%20To%20A%20Hindu.pdf.

31. Ibid.
32. Ibid.
33 Quoted in Fischer, *Mahatma Gandhi: His Life and Times*, p. 74.
34. Gandhi, *CWMG*, vol. 10, p. 369.
35. Gandhi, *An Autobiography*, p. 275.
36. Ibid.
37. Gandhi, *Hind Swaraj or Indian Home Rule*, Ahmedabad: Navajivan Trust, 2006, p. 32.
38. Ibid., p. 39.
39. Ibid., pp. 50–52.
40. Ibid., p. 48.
41. Ibid., p. 39.
42. Ibid., p. 34.
43. Ibid., p. 27.
44. Ibid., p. 26.
45. Frantz Fanon, *Black Skins White Masks*, trans. Charles Lam Markmann, London: Pluto Press, 1986, p. 100.
46. Frantz Fanon, *The Wretched of the Earth*, trans. Richard Philcox, New York: Grove Press, 2004, p. 13.
47. *Hind Swaraj*, p. 78.
48. Ibid., pp. 78–79.
49. Quoted in Fischer, *Mahatma Gandhi: His Life and Times*, p. 74.
50. *Indian Opinion*, 26 May 1906; Gandhi, *CWMG*, vol. 5, p. 326.
51. *Indian Opinion*, 16 September 1914.
52. *The Times*, 5 September 1914, p. 9.
53. Ranajit Guha, *Dominance Without Hegemony: History and Power in Colonial India*, Cambridge, MA: Harvard University Press, 1997, p. 43.
54. Desai and Vahed, *The South African Gandhi*, p. 20.
55. Gandhi, *CWMG*, vol. 2, p. 74.
56. *Notes on Grievances*, 14 August 1896, in Gandhi, *CWMG*, vol. 2, p. 13.
57. *Indian Opinion*, 7 March 1908.
58. Desai and Vahed, *The South African Gandhi*, p. 42.
59. Swan, *Gandhi: The South African Experience*, p. 270.
60. Quoted in Arnold, *Gandhi: Profiles in Power*, p. 49.
61. Gandhi, *Satyagraha in South Africa*, p. 41 – https://www.mkgandhi.org/ebks/satyagraha_in_south_africa.pdf.
62. Swan, *Gandhi: The South African Experience*, p. 44.
63. Ibid., p. 38.

3 *The Champion of the Oppressed Returns: 1915–19*

1. Russell Brand, *Revolution*, p. 324.

2. Ibid.
3. Muriel Lester Papers, File 2/7/3/7.
4. Muriel Lester Papers, File 2/7/1/5.
5. Letter to India Office dated 3 May 1933, Muriel Lester Papers, File 2/7/2/6.
6. This is falling rapidly as only about 66 percent is now rural.
7. http://www.censusindia.gov.in/Census_And_You/old_report/Census_1931n.aspx.
8. Gandhi, *CWMG*, vol. 8, pp. 210–216.
9. Judith Brown, *Gandhi's Rise to Power*, Cambridge: CUP, 1974, p. 59.
10. Quoted in Rajmohan Gandhi, *Gandhi*, p. 199. See also Sumit Sarkar, *Modern India: 1885–1947*, New Delhi: Macmillan, 1983, p. 186, quoted in Meneejah Moradian and David Whitehouse, 'Gandhi's Politics: The Experiment with Nonviolence', (2001), https://isreview.org/sites/default/files/pdf/14-Gandhiexpanded.pdf.
11. Quoted in Rajmohan Gandhi, *Gandhi*, p. 199.
12. Brown, *Gandhi's Rise to Power*, pp. 64–65.
13. David Hardiman. *Peasant Nationalists of Gujarat: Kheda District, 1917–1934*, New York: Oxford University Press. 1981.
14. Brown, *Gandhi's Rise to Power*, p. 65.
15. Tidrick, *Gandhi*, p. 117.
16. Barry Pavier, *The Telangana Movement, 1944–51*, New Delhi: Vikas Publishing House, 1981, p. 191.
17. D.N. Dhanagare, *Peasant Movements in India: 1920–1950*. New Delhi: OUP, 1983, p. 204.
18. Gandhi quoted in Sarkar, *Modern India*, p. 180, quoted in Moradian and Whitehouse, 'Gandhi's politics'.
19. See letter from Gandhi to Birla dated 25 January 1933 on funding for the English edition of *Harijan* in *CWMG*, vol. 53, pp. 140–141. Also, it was Birla House in Delhi where Gandhi spent the last days of his life.
20. Quoted in D.G. Tendulkar, *Mahatma: Life of Mohandas Karamchand Gandhi*, New Delhi: Publications Division, 1960, p. 33.
21. Ibid., p. 159.
22. Barbara Ramusack, *The Indian Princes and Their States*, Cambridge: CUP, 2004, p. 217.
23. *Dalit* is the political term used by untouchables to describe themselves.
24. For a more insightful discussion on caste see Chris Harman, 'Class and Caste', 2004, https://www.marxists.org/archive/harman/2004/xx/caste-class.htm. See also Susan Bayly, '"Caste" and "Race" in The Colonial Ethnography of India', in P. Robb, ed., *The Concept of Race in South Asia*, New Delhi: OUP, 2006, pp. 165–218; Nicholas Dirks, 'Castes of Mind: The Institution of Caste in India', *Representations*, vol. 37, 1992, pp. 56–78;

Sekhar Bandyopadhyay and Suranjan Das, eds, *Caste and Communal Politics in South Asia*, Delhi: K.P. Bagchi & Co., 1993.
25. Tendulkar, *Mahatma*, p. 183.
26. Ibid., p. 128.
27. Muriel Lester Papers, File 2/7/2/6.
28. Quoted in B. Chakrabarty, *Social and Political Thought of Mahatma Gandhi*, New Delhi: Routledge, 2006, p. 101.
29. Gandhi, *CWMG*, vol. 48, p. 298.
30. Arundhati Roy, 'The Doctor and the Saint: Ambedkar, Gandhi and the Battle Against Caste', *Caravan*, 1 May 2014.
31. B.R. Ambedkar, *What Congress and Gandhi Have Done to the Untouchables*, Bombay: Thacker & Co., Ltd., 2nd edition, 1946, originally published in 1945, p. 260.
32. Anderson, 'India Trilogy: Gandhi Centre Stage', p. 9.
33. Quoted in Eleanor Zelliot, *From Untouchable to Dalit: Essays on the Ambedkar Movement*, New Delhi: Manohar, 1992, p. 167. Anderson, 'Indian Trilogy', p. 9.
34. Ambedkar, *What Congress and Gandhi Have Done to the Untouchables*, p. 270.
35. *Young India*, 5 September 1921.
36. Gandhi, *CWMG*, vol. 75, p. 155.
37. Ibid.
38. Madhu Kishwar, 'Gandhi on Women', *Economic and Political Weekly*, vol. 20, no. 40, 5 October 1985, p. 1692.
39. Ibid., p. 1698.

4 *Nationalist Leader: 1919–28*

1. East India (Sedition Committee, 1918), Report of Committee Appointed to Investigate Revolutionary Conspiracies in India, 1918, House of Commons Parliamentary Papers, p. 75.
2. Eugene F. Irschick, *Politics and Social Conflict in South India: The Non-Brahman Movement and Tamil Separatism, 1916–1929*, Berkeley: University of California Press, 1969, p. 133.
3. For an overview of the experience of British colonial troops in the First World War, see T. Ahmed, 'The British Empire and the First World War: The Colonial Experience', *International Socialism*, vol. 152, 2016, pp. 117–140.
4. Jinnah to Chelmsford, 28 March 1919, reprinted in Stanley Wolpert, *Jinnah of Pakistan*, New York: Oxford University Press, 1989, p. 62.
5. 'The Satyagraha Pledge', *CWMG*, Vol. 15, p. 101.

6. Letter to Press on the Satyagraha Pledge, 26 February 1919, *CWMG*, vol. 15, p. 120.
7. Yogesh Chadha, *Gandhi: A Life*, New York: John Wiley, 1999, p. 237.
8. Jeffrey Greenhut, 'Sahib and Sepoy: An Inquiry into the Relationship between the British Officers and Native Soldiers of the British Indian Army' *Military Affairs*, vol. 48, no. 1, 1984, p. 16.
9. Mulk Raj Anand, *Across the Black Waters*, London: Jonathan Cape, 1940, pp. 264, 105.
10. IOR/L/MIL/17/5/2016, Colonel Sir Bruce Seton, 'A Report on Kitchener Indian Hospital, Brighton', 1916.
11. Rozina Visram, *Ayahs, Lascars, and Princes: Indians in Britain 1700–1947*, London: Pluto Press, 1986, p. 128.
12. Punjab Disturbances, April 1919, compiled from the *Civil and Military Gazette*, Lahore.
13. Derek Sayer, 'British Reaction to the Amritsar Massacre 1919–1920', *Past & Present*, no. 131, May 1991, pp. 130–131.
14. Cited in Robert Payne, *The Life and Death of Mahatma Gandhi*, New York: E.P. Dutton, 1969, p. 340.
15. This was phrase used by Rudyard Kipling, quoted in Sayer, 'British Reaction to the Amritsar Massacre', p. 158.
16. *Morning Post*, cited in ibid., p. 158, and in *Jallianwala Bagh Commemoration Volume*, Patiala, 1997, p. 45.
17. Quoted in Sayer, 'British Reaction to the Amritsar Massacre, p. 158.
18. Nigel Collett, *The Butcher of Amritsar: General Reginald Dyer*, London: Hambledon & London, 2005, p. 392.
19. Ibid., p. 380.
20. Ibid., pp. 382–383.
21. *Tribune*, Lahore, 16 April 1919.
22. Rajmohan Gandhi, *Gandhi: The Man, his People and the Empire*, p. 209.
23. *CWMG*, vol. 15, pp. 240–241.
24. Ibid., p. 241.
25. Nicholas Lloyd, *The Amritsar Massacre: The Untold Story of One Fateful Day*, London: I.B. Tauris, 2011, p. 35; original emphasis.
26. Ibid., p. 128.
27. For the full resolution see Vladimir Ilyich Lenin, 'The Right of Nations to Self-Determination', in *Collected Works*, vol. 20, Moscow: Progress Publishers, 1977.
28. Quoted in Premen Addy and Ibne Azad, 'Politics and Society in Bengal', in ed. Robin Blackburn, *Explosion in a Subcontinent*, London: Penguin Books, 1975, p. 116.
29. *CWMG*, vol. 14, p. 406.
30. Arnold, *Gandhi*, p. 107.

31. Quoted in Mortimer Wheeler, *The Cambridge History of India*, Cambridge: CUP, p. 589.
32. A.C. Niemeijer, *The Khilafat Movement in India, 1919–1924*, The Hague: Verhandelingen Institute, 1972, p. 84.
33. Gail Minault, *The Khilafat Movement: Religious Symbolism and Political Mobilization in India*, New York: Columbia University Press, 1982, p. 92.
34. For more on Gandhi's harnessing of religion to bind Muslim political struggles to a broader ecumenical nationalism, see Meghnad Desai, *The Rediscovery of India*, London: Brill Academic Publishers, 2011, pp. 141–142, 146.
35. Gandhi, *Hind Swaraj*, p. 44.
36. 'Draft Resolution on Non-Co-Operation', *CWMG*, vol. 19, p. 183.
37. Arnold, *Gandhi*, p. 121. One crore is ten million.
38. Ibid., p. 120.
39. B.R. Nanda, *Gandhi, Pan-Islamism, Imperialism and Nationalism in India*, New Delhi: OUP, 2002, p. 313.
40. Ibid., pp. 314–315.
41. Quoted in Robert L. Hardgrave, 'The Mapilla Rebellion, 1921: Peasant Revolt in Malabar', *Journal of Modern Asian Studies*, vol. 11, no. 1, 1977, p. 75.
42. Nanda, *Gandhi, Pan-Islamism*, p. 315.
43. Hardgrave, 'The Mapilla Rebellion', p. 91.
44. *Report of the Committee Appointed to Enquiry into the Death of Certain Mappilla Prisoners*, 1922, quoted in ibid., p. 90.
45. Arnold, *Gandhi*, p. 124.
46. David Arnold, *The Congress In Tamilnad: Nationalist Politics in South India, 1919–37*, New Delhi: 1977, pp. 71–76.
47. Arnold, *Gandhi*, p. 124.
48. *Report of the Committee Appointed to Enquiry into the Death of Certain Mappilla Prisoners*, 1922, quoted in Hardgrave, 'The Mapilla Rebellion', p. 90.
49. Willingdon to Reading, 7 November 1921, quoted in Nanda, *Gandhi, Pan-Islamism*, p. 319.
50. 4 September 1921, in *CWMG*, vol. 21, p. 47.
51. *Report of the Thirty-Sixth Indian National Congress held at Ahmedabad on the 27th and 28th December 1921*, Ahmedabad, 1922, p. 114.
52. Gandhi, *Young India*, 29 September 1921.
53. Gandhi, *CWMG*, vol. 21, p. 356.
54. Kathryn Tidrick, *Gandhi: A Political and Spiritual Life*, pp. 176–180.
55. Shahid Amin, *Event, Metaphor, Memory: Chauri Chaura 1922–1992*, Delhi: OUP, 1996, pp. 96–97.

56. M.N. Roy, 'Legal Murder in India', *International Press Correspondence*, vol. 3, no. 9, 24 January 1923; reprinted in G. Adhikari, ed., *Documents of the History of the Communist Party of India: Volume 2, 1923–1925*. New Delhi: People's Publishing House, 1974; pp. 62–64.
57. Gandhi, *CWMG*, vol. 22, p. 377.
58. Richard Johnson, *Gandhi's Experiments with Truth: Essential Writings by and about Mahatma Gandhi*, New York: Lexington Books, 2006, p. 234.
59. Gandhi, *Young India*, 9 April 1925, *CWMG*, vol. 26, pp. 486–487.
60. Letter from Tagore to C.F. Andrews dated 2 March 1921 published in *Modern Review*, Calcutta: May 1921.
61. Gandhi, 'The Poet and the Charkha', *Young India*, 5 November 1925.
62. Tagore, *Modern Review*, Calcutta: September 1925.
63. Nehru, *An Autobiography*, p. 129.
64. Ibid., pp. 129–130.
65. On Saklatvala, see Mike Squires, *Saklatvala: A Political Biography*, London: Lawrence & Wishart, 1990, and Sehri Saklatvala, *The Fifth Commandment: A Biography of Shapurji Saklatvala*, Salford: Miranda Press, 1991.
66. One rupee then was worth between 1*s* 6*d* and 2*s*. An anna is one sixteenth of a rupee.
67. Letter from Saklatvala to Gandhi, 8 March 1927, in *Is India Different? The Class Struggle in India, Correspondence on the Indian Labour Movement and Modern Conditions*, London: Dorrit Press Ltd, 1927, p. 8.
68. Ibid., p. 24.
69. Ibid.
70. Letter to Saklatvala, 10 May 1927, in ibid., p. 25.
71. Ibid.
72. Gandhi, *Young India*, 16 February 1921.
73. Gandhi, *Young India*, 15 June 1921.
74. Ibid., pp. 25–26.
75. Quoted in S. Wolpert, *India*, Berkeley, CA: University of California Press, 1999, p. 204.

5 *Global Icon: 1929–39*

1. Desai, *The Rediscovery of India*, p. 210.
2. Hector Bolitho, *Jinnah: Creator of Pakistan*, London: John Murray, 1954, p. 95.
3. Jawaharlal Nehru, *Mahatma Gandhi*, Bombay: Asia Publishing House, 1965, p. 50.
4. Quoted in Homer A. Jack, ed., *The Gandhi Reader: A Sourcebook of His Life and Writings*, New York: Grove Press, 1994, pp. 238–239.

5. Mahatma Gandhi and Dennis Dalton, *Selected Political Writings*, Indianapolis, IN: Hackett Publishing, 1996, p. 72.
6. Jack, ed., *The Gandhi Reader*, p. 240.
7. Telegram from Governor of Bombay to Secretary of State for India, dated 6 April 1930, IOR: L/PJ/6/1998.
8. See full letter in Gandhi, *CWMG*, vol. 43, pp. 2–8.
9. Ibid., p. 6.
10. Nehru, *Autobiography*, p. 210.
11. Thomas Weber, *On the Salt March*, New Delhi: HarperCollins, 1997, p. 85.
12. Letter to London on 20 February 1930, in Peter Ackerman and Jack DuVall, *A Force More Powerful: A Century of Nonviolent Conflict*, New York: Palgrave Macmillan, 2000, p. 84.
13. Weber, *On the Salt March*, p. 90.
14. Dennis Dalton, *Mahatma Gandhi: Nonviolent Power in Action*, New York: Columbia University Press, 1993, p. 107.
15. Irfan Habib 'Civil Disobedience 1930–31', *Social Scientist*, vol. 25, no. 9–10, 1997, p. 57.
16. Ibid., p. 55.
17. Ibid., p. 56.
18. Quoted in D. Hardiman, *Gandhi in His Time and Ours: The Global Legacy of His Ideas*, New York: Columbia University Press, 2003, p. 113.
19. IOR, L/P&J/6/1998.
20. Sarojini Sinha, *A Pinch of Salt Rocks an Empire*, New Delhi: Children's Book Trust, 1985, p. 64.
21. Ibid., p. 64.
22. Ackerman and DuVall, *A Force More Powerful*, pp. 87–90.
23. Miller's report from 21 May 1930 quoted in Brian Martin, *Justice Ignited*, Lanham, MD and Plymouth, UK: Rowman & Littlefield, 2006, p. 38. See also Webb Miller, *I Found No Peace*, New York: Simon and Schuster, 1936, pp. 198–199; Weber, *On the Salt March*, pp. 446–447.
24. Tara Ali Baig, ed., *Women of India*, 1958; quoted in Rozina Visram, *Women in India and Pakistan: The Struggle for Independence from British Rule*, Cambridge: CUP, 1992, p. 27.
25. Manini Chatterjee, '1930: Turning Point in the Participation of Women in the Freedom Struggle', *Social Scientist*, vol. 29, no. 7/8, July–August, 2001, p. 41.
26. Telegram, IOR: L/PJ/6/1998.
27. Bipan Chandra et al., *India's Struggle for Independence*, New Delhi: Penguin Books, 1989 pp. 282.
28. Ibid., pp. 282–283.
29. Reginald Reynolds, *To Live in Mankind: A Quest for Gandhi*, London: Andre Deutsch Limited, 1951, p. 62.

30. Ibid., p. 62.
31. Ibid., p. 73.
32. Gilbert, Martin, 1976, *Winston Churchill*, vol. 5, London: Heinemann, p. 390.
33. Quoted in Martin Pugh, '*Hurrah for The Blackshirts!' Fascists and Fascism in Britain Between the Wars*, London: Pimlico, 2006, pp. 186–187.
34. Letter from Irwin to Gandhi, 6 March 1931 in Halifax Papers, IOR, Mss Eur. C152, vol. 26.
35. Lord Birkenhead, *Halifax: The Life of Lord Halifax*, London: Hamish Hamilton, 1965, p. 299.
36. David Arnold, *Gandhi*, p. 159.
37. For full itinerary see https://biblio.wiki/wiki/Chronology_of_Mahatma_Gandhi%27s_life/England_1931.
38. *Time*, vol. 17, no. 1, 5 January 1931.
39. Reginald Reynolds, *India, Gandhi and World Peace*, London: Friends of India, 1931, p. 6.
40. Ibid., p. 22.
41. See B.P. Sinha, Preface in ibid.
42. Ibid., pp. 23–24.
43. Muriel Lester Papers, File, 2/7/3/45, p. 6.
44. Ibid., pp. 11–12.
45. Irina Spector-Marks, 'Mr Gandhi Visits Lancashire: A Study in Imperial Miscommunication', *History Honors Projects*, vol. 3, 2008, p. 7.
46. Interview to the Press, 12 September 1931, in *CWMG*, vol. 48, p. 6.
47. 'Darwen Houses Mr Gandhi: At Darwen Railway Station', *Darwen News*, 26 September 1931, p. 10.
48. Quoted in Rajmohan Gandhi, *Gandhi*, p. 332.
49. Muriel Lester Papers File, 2/7/2/19. Lester was not a communist. In 1933, she had written a letter to the India Office in London in which she identified fascism as an extreme but also communism and writes of the West facing 'battering attacks of Communism and Fascism'. And she acknowledged that only Nehru could attempt to neuter the radicalism of the Indian left, believing that Nehru's 'realism and common sense' could prevail over some in CPI. Letter to India Office dated 3 May 1933, Muriel Lester Papers, File 2/7/2/6.
50. Ruth Harris, 'Rolland, Gandhi and Madeleine Slade: Spiritual Politics, France and the Wider World', *French History*, vol. 27, no. 4, 2013, p. 581. Rolland also wrote a short biography of Gandhi published in 1924 as *Mahatma Gandhi.*
51. R. Rolland and M.K. Gandhi, *Romain Rolland – Gandhi Correspondence*, New Delhi: GOI, 1976, p. 175.
52. Letter to Rolland 20 December 1931, *Romain Rolland – Gandhi Correspondence*, p. 241.

53. Ibid., pp. 241–242.
54. Extract from Rolland's diary, December 1931, ibid., p. 175.
55. Ibid., p. 174.
56. Ibid., p. 176.
57. Extract from Rolland's diary, ibid., p. 175. See also Arnold, *Gandhi*, p. 234.
58. Extract from Rolland's diary, *Romain Rolland – Gandhi Correspondence*, p. 219; original emphasis.
59. Ibid., pp. 219–220.
60. Gandhi, *Harijan*, 14 May 1938.
61. Quoted in Kulwant Singh Kooner, *Martyrdom of Shaheed Bhagat Singh*, Chandigarh: Unistar Books Pvt Ltd., 2013, p. 114.
62. Gandhi, *CWMG*, vol. 43, p. 391.
63. Ibid., p. 133.
64. A. Gramsci, *Prison Notebooks*, vol. 3, ed. and trans. Joseph A. Buttigieg, New York: Columbia Univeristy Press, 2007, p. 61.
65. See G.D. Overstreet and M. Windmiller, *Communism in India*, Berkeley: University of California Press, 1959. On M.N. Roy, see Kris Manjapra, *M.N.Roy:Marxism and Colonial Cosmopolitanism*, Delhi, Routledge India, 2010.
66. See John P. Haithcox, 'The Roy-Lenin Debate on Colonial Policy: A New Interpretation', *Journal of Asian Studies*, vol. 23, no. 1, November, 1963, pp. 93–101.
67. *'I accuse!', From the Suppressed Statement of Manabendra Nath Roy on Trial for Treason Before Sessions Court, Cawnpore, India*, with an introduction by Aswani Kurma Sharma, New York: Roy Defense Committee of India, 1932, pp. 11–12; original emphasis.
68. M.N. Roy, *Men I Met*, Bombay: Lalvani, 1968, pp. 27–28.
69. Paul Le Blanc, 'India Yesterday: Development and Revolution', *Links*, 2015, http://links.org.au/node/4584.
70. IOR, L/PJ/12 File 627/29.
71. For full details of those arrested, see R.P. Dutt, *India Today*, Calcutta: Manisha, 1940, pp. 415–417.
72. Ibid., p. 421.
73. See cablegram and letter from Nehru to Walter Critine, Secretary of the British Trades Union Congress General Council, 22 June 1929, in C.H. Philips, ed., *The Evolution of India and Pakistan, 1858–1947, Select Documents*, vol. 5, London: OUP, 1965, pp. 259–260.
74. Quoted in Dutt, *India Today*, p. 421.
75. Quoted in R.C. Majumdar and P.N. Chopra, *Main Currents of Indian History*, New Delhi: Sterling Publishers, 1994, p. 197.
76. Letter from Gandhi to M.A. Ansari, dated 5 April 1934, in *Modern Review*, Calcutta, May 1934, p. 585. The Swaraj Party was formed in 1923 to bring together Congress and *Khilafat* members who opposed Gandhi's

suspension of civil resistance following Chauri Chaura in 1922. But by the mid-1930s, they favoured a parliamentary approach.

77. Constitution of Congress Socialist Party, quoted in J.P. Narayan, *Why Socialism?* Benares: The All-India Congress Socialist Party, 1936, p. 20.
78. Quoted in M. Masani, *Bliss was it in that Dawn … A Political Memoir Up to Independence*, New Delhi: Arnold-Heinemann, 1977, p. 44.
79. T. Ahmed, *Literature and Politics in the Age of Nationalism: The Progressive Episode in South Asia, 1932–56*, New Dehli: Routledge, 2009, p. 69.
80. See J.P. Narayan, *Towards Struggle*, ed. Yusef Meherally, Bombay: Padma Publications Ltd, 1946, p. 170; Lakhanpal, *History of CSP*, pp. 76–77.
81. Subhas Chandra Bose, 'The Anti-Imperialist Struggle and Samyavada', https://www.inc.in/en/media/speech/the-anti-imperialist-struggle-and-samyavada.
82. Leonard A. Gordon, *Brother Against the Raj: A Biography of Indian Nationalists Sarat and Subhash Chandra Bose*, New Delhi: Rupa & Co., 2005, p. 371.
83. Subhash Chandra Bose, and Sisir Kumar Bose, *Congress President: Speeches, Articles and Letters January 1938–May 1939*, New Delhi: Orient Blackswan, 2004, pp. 209–210.
84. Gandhi, 'Letter to Manibehn Patel', dated 28 October 1938, in *CWMG*, vol. 68, p. 72.
85. B.P. Sitaramayya, *The History of the Indian National Congress*, vol. 2, Bombay: Padma Public Tons Ltd, 1947, p. 105.
86. Mihir Bose, *The Lost Hero: A Biography of Subhas Bose*, London: Quartet Books Limited, 1982, pp. 131–132.
87. Bose, *Crossroads*, Calcutta: Asia Publishing House, 1962, p. 115.
88. Mihir Bose, *The Lost Hero*, p. 133.
89. Adhikari, *Documents of Communist Movement*, vol. 2, 1923–25, p. 210.
90. Nehru, *Selected Writings*, vol. 8, p. 123.
91. See Letter to Sherwani in AICC papers, File No. G-61/1937, p. 107.
92. Quoted in Nehru, *SWJN*, vol. 8, p. 150.
93. Ibid., p. 167.
94. Peu Ghosh, *Indian Government and Politics*, New Delhi: PHI Learning, Private Ltd, 2012, pp. 20–21.
95. Gandhi, *CWMG*, vol. 25, p. 531.
96. Bipin Chandra, *Indian National Movement – The Long-Term Dynamics*, New Delhi: Vikas Publishing House, 1993, p. 24.
97. Bipin Chandra, Mridula Mukerjee, Aditya Mukerjee, Sucheta Mahajan and K.N. Panikkar, *India's Struggle for Independence*, New Delhi: Penguin Books, 1988, p. 313.
98. Ibid., pp. 510–511.
99. Ibid., p. 506.
100. Ibid., pp. 514–515.
101. Sarkar, *Modern India*, p. 179.

6 *Fascism, War, Independence and Partition: 1939–48*

1. On Gandhi and pacifism, it is worth noting he always thought it better to fight than to be a coward: 'where there is only a choice between cowardice and violence, I would advise violence', he declared. *Young India*, 11 August 1920.
2. *Harijan*, 26 October 1938.
3. *Harijan*, 15 October 1938.
4. *Harijan*, 22 June 1940.
5. *Harijan*, 6 July 1940.
6. Republished in: https://www.theguardian.com/culture/interactive/2013/oct/12/mohandas-gandhi-adolf-hitler-letter.
7. For the full letter, see Michaël de Saint-Cheron, *Gandhi: Anti-Biography of a Great Soul*, Oxford: Routledge, 2018, pp. 125–128.
8. *Harijan*, 22 June 1940.
9. Crispin Bates, *Subalterns and the Raj: South Asia since 1600*, Abingdon: Routledge, 2007, p. 157; John Newsinger, *The Blood Never Dried: A People's History of the British Empire*, London: Bookmarks, 2006, p. 157.
10. On the famine, see Madhusree Mukerjee, *Churchill's Secret War: the British Empire and the Ravaging of India during the Second World War*, London: Basic Books, 2010.
11. Quoted in Ramkrishna Mukherjee, *The Dynamics of a Rural Society: A Study of the Economic Structure in Bengal Village*, Berlin: Akademie-Verlag, 1957, p. 47.
12. See Donny Gluckstein, *A People's History of the Second World War: Resistance Versus Empire*, London: Pluto Press, 2012, pp. 163–164.
13. Newsinger, *The Blood Never Dried*, p. 157.
14. Shashi Tharoor, *Inglorious Empire: What the British Did to India*, London: Hurst & Company, 2016, p. 160.
15. Patrick French, *Liberty or Death: India's Journey to Independence and Division*, New Delhi: HarperCollins, 1998, p. 188.
16. Quoted in Gluckstein, *People's History of the Second World War*, p. 164.
17. Quoted in Tharoor, *Inglorious Empire*, p. 160.
18. *Harijan*, 30 September 1939.
19. Sarkar, *Modern India*, p. 381.
20. Arnold, *Gandhi*, p. 209.
21. Bose formed the second INA in 1943; the first was formed by Mohan Singh in 1942.
22. The Quit India Resolution quoted in *Modern Review*, September 1942, *Calcutta*, pp. 197–198.

23. Bidyut Chakrabarty, 'Political Mobilization in the Localities: The 1942 Quit India Movement in Midnapur', *Modern Asian Studies*, vol. 26 no. 4, 1992, p. 796.
24. John F. Riddick, *The History of British India: A Chronology*, Westport, CT: Praeger Publishers, 2006, p. 115.
25. Chakrabarty, 'Political Mobilization in the Localities', p. 797.
26. Christopher Bayly and Tim Harper, *Forgotten Armies: Britain's Asian Empire and the War with Japan*, New York: Penguin Books, 2005, p. 248.
27. Some have speculated that this reduced the British War Cabinet's willingness to provide famine aid at a time when supplies were also needed for the war effort: Bayly and Harper, *Forgotten Armies*, p. 286.
28. Chakrabarty, 'Political Mobilization in the Localities', p. 813.
29. Home-Poll, 3/52/1943(1), quoted in Sarkar, *Modern India*, p. 396.
30 Quoted in Gluckstein, *People's History of the Second World War*, p. 169.
31. Sarkar, *Modern India*, pp. 394–395.
32. Chakrabarty, 'Political Mobilization in the Localities', p. 801.
33. See K.K. Chaudhari, *Quit India Revolution: the Ethos of its Central Direction*, Mumbai: Popular Prakashan, 1996, pp. 243–274.
34. H. Sanyal, 'The Quit India Movement in Medinipur District', in ed. Gyanendra Pandey, *The Indian Nation in 1942*, Calcutta: K.P. Bagchi & Company, 1988, pp. 46, 59–60.
35. Ibid., p. 133.
36. Gluckstein, *A People's History of the Second World War*, p. 168.
37. Ibid., p. 170.
38. G. Pandey, 'The Revolt of August 1942 in Easter UP and Bihar' in ed. Pandey, *The Indian Nation in 1942*, p. 156.
39. Gluckstein, *A People's History of the Second World War*, pp. 168–169.
40. AIML conference Bombay, 16–20 August 1942, quoted in *Foundations of Pakistan, All-India Muslim League Documents: 1924–1947*, ed. Syed Sharifuddin Pirzada, vol. 2, Karachi: National Publishing House Ltd, 1970, pp. 395, 398.
41. Ibid., pp. 396–397.
42. *Dawn* began as a weekly newspaper in 1941 and transformed into a daily in 1942.
43. Stanley Wolpert, *Jinnah of Pakistan*, New York: Oxford University Press, 1984, p. 136.
44. Ayesha Jalal, *The Sole Spokesman: Jinnah and the Muslim League and the Demand for Pakistan*, Cambridge: CUP, 1985, p. 41.
45. Ibid., p. 39.
46. R.J. Moore, 'Jinnah and the Pakistan Demand', *Modern Asian Studies*. vol. 17, no. 4, 1983, p. 548.
47. Quoted in *Foundations of Pakistan, All-India Muslim League Documents: 1924-1947*, ed. Pirzada, vol. 2, p. 341.

48. Sarkar, *Modern India*, p. 378.
49. Jinnah to Linlithgow, 5 November 1939, MSS. EUR.F.125/148.
50. Quoted in *Foundations of Pakistan, All-India Muslim League Documents: 1924–1947*, ed. Pirzada, vol. 2, p. 338.
51. Wolpert, *Jinnah of Pakistan*, p. 185.
52. Letter to Jinnah, 15 September 1944, Gandhi, *CWMG*, vol. 78, p. 101.
53. Linlithgow to Zetland, note of interview with Jinnah on 4 November 1939, IOR, L/P&J/8/506. Quoted in Jalal, *The Sole Spokesman*, p. 49.
54. See Talat Ahmed, *Literature and Politics in the Age of Nationalism*, pp. 88–108. Sumit Sarkar also described 1942 as a moment of 'significant nuance, conflict and anguish'.
55. Fischer, *Life of the Mahatma*, p. 428.
56. S.C. Bose, *Selected Speeches of Subhas Chandra Bose*, Delhi: Publication Division, Ministry of Information and Broadcasting, 1962, pp. 185–188.
57. Leonard A. Gordon, *Brothers Against the Raj: A Biography of Indian Nationalists Sarat and Subhas Chandra Bose*, New York: Columbia University Press, 1990, pp. 496–497.
58. Bayly and Harper, *Forgotten Armies*, p. 249. No Indian units had mutinied during the Quit India agitation, and in fact the army and police had remained solid.
59. Quoted in S. Banerjee, 'RIN Mutiny', in Ravi Dayal (ed.), *We Fought Together For Freedom*, Oxford: Westview Press, 1995, p. 235.
60. P.J. Cain and A.G. Hopkins, *British Imperialism 1688–2000*, 2nd ed., Harlow: Pearson Education, 2002, pp. 560–561.
61. Cited in Ranjan Borra, 'Subhas Chandra Bose, The Indian National Army, and The War of India's Liberation', *Journal of Historical Review*, vol. 3, no 4, 1982, reference 46.
62. Ramesh Chandra Majumdar, *Three Phases of India's Struggle for Freedom*, Bombay: Bhartiya Vidya Bhavan, 1967, pp. 58–59; Also see Bates, *Subalterns and the Raj*, p. 178.
63. Bipan Chandra et al., *India's Struggle for Independence*, p. 485.
64. Ibid., p. 486.
65. Ibid., p. 485.
66. Quoted in S. Sarkar, *Modern India*, p. 425.
67. William Dalrymple, 'The Great Divide: The Violent Legacy of Indian Partition', *The New Yorker*, 29 June 2015, https://www.newyorker.com/magazine/2015/06/29/the-great-divide-books-dalrymple.
68. Nisid Hajari, *Midnight's Furies*, Gloucestershire: Amberley Publishing, 2017, p. xviii.
69. Alex Von Tunzelmann, *Indian Summer: The Secret History of the End of an Empire*, London: Pocket Books, 2007, p. 143.

70. Quoted in Amritjit Singh, Nalini Iyer, Rahul K. Gairola, eds, *Revisiting India's Partition: New Essays on Memory, Culture, and Politics*, London: Lexington Books, 2016, p. xv.
71. Alex von Tunzelmann, *Indian Summer*, p. 230.
72. Yasmin Khan, *The Great Partition: The Making of India and Pakistan*, New Haven, CT: Yale University Press, 2007, p. 497.
73. Jalal, *Sole Spokesperson*, pp. 171–172.
74. Wolpert, *Jinnah*, p. 254.
75. Bolitho, *Jinnah*, p. 158.
76. Barbara D. Metcalf and Thomas R. Metcalf, *A Concise History of Modern India*, Cambridge: CUP, 2012, p. 212.
77. Gene D. Overstreet and Marshall Windmiller, *Communism in India*, pp. 236–237.
78. Quoted in Hajari, *Midnight's Furies*, p. 13.
79. Quoted in Victor Sebestyen, *1946: The Making of the Modern World*, London: Macmillan, 2014, p. 331.
80. Quoted in A.I. Singh, *The Origins of the Partition of India*, Oxford: OUP, 1987, p. 186.
81. Quoted in Sarkar, *Modern India*, p. 425.
82. Clement R. Attlee, *As it Happened*, London: William Heinemann Ltd, 1954, p. 183.
83. Ibid., p. 183.
84. Extracts from a note by Nehru to Mountbatten, 11 May 1947, IOR: L/P&J/10/79.
85. Nehru, *Selected Works*, 2nd series, vol. 2, p. 89.
86. Quoted in Rajmohan Gandhi, *Gandhi*, p. 501.
87. Hajari, *Midnight's Furies*, p. xviii.
88. The 1951 Census registered a drop of the Muslim population in Delhi from 33.22 per cent in 1941 to 5.33 per cent in 1951. See Bulbul Sharma, *Muslims In Indian Cities*, New Delhi: HarperCollins Publishers, 2013.
89. Quoted in Sankar Ghose, *Mahatma Gandhi*, New Delhi: Allied Publishers Ltd, 1991, p. 341.
90. Speech at prayer meeting, 12 January 1948, Gandhi, *CWMG*, vol. 90, p. 410.
91. Gandhi, *Young India*, 6 October 1921, p. 36, 1 January 1925, p. 8.

Conclusion: Assassination and Legacy

1. Manubehn Gandhi, *Last Glimpses of Bapu*, Delhi: S.L. Agarwala, 1962, p. 280.
2. For more on these attempts see Teesat Setalvad, *Beyond Doubt: A Dossier on Gandhi's Assassination*, New Delhi: Tulika Books, 2015.

3. Quoted in *A Comprehensive History of India*, ed. P.N. Chopra, Volume 3, New Delhi: Sterling Publishers Private Ltd, 2003, p. 293.
4. Reginald Reynolds, *To Live in Mankind*, p. 98.
5. Yasmin Khan, 'Performing Peace: Gandhi's assassination as a critical moment in the consolidation of the Nehruvian state', *Modern Asian Studies*, vol. 45, no. 1, p. 59.
6. Arvind Sharma, *Gandhi: A Spiritual Biography*, London: Yale University Press, 2013, pp. 27–28, 97, 150–152.
7. Claude Markovits, *The UnGandhian Gandhi: The Life and Afterlife of the Mahatma*, London: Anthem Press, 2004, p. 57.
8. J. Edward Mallot, *Memory, Nationalism, and the Narrative in Contemporary South Asia*, New York: Palgrave Macmillan, 2012, pp. 75–76.
9. Markovits, *The UnGandhian Gandhi*, pp. 57–58.
10. Khan, 'Performing Peace', p. 60.
11. George Orwell, 'Reflections on Gandhi', *Partisan Review*, vol. 16, no. 1, January 1949.
12. https://timesofindia.indiatimes.com/world/us/I-have-always-looked-to-Mahatma-Gandhi-as-an-inspiration-Obama/articleshow/2807399.cms.
13. https://timesofindia.indiatimes.com/world/us/to-start-a-movement-look-to-gandhi-says-obama/articleshow/60782390.cms.
14. https://www.theguardian.com/world/2015/mar/14/new-gandhi-statue-unveiled-in-londons-parliament-square.
15. https://www.theguardian.com/world/2014/jul/08/gandhi-statue-for-outside-parliament.
16. https://www.hindustantimes.com/columns/poison-pen-attempt-to-rewrite-india-s-history-is-dangerous/story-Gev8gloP7OVgzT7fPJgcxJ.html.
17. See Sumit Sarkar et al., *Khaki Shorts and Saffron Flags: A Critique of the Hindu Right*, New Delhi: Sangam Book 1993; Achin Vanaik, *The Furies of Indian Communalism: Religion, Modernity, and Secularization*, London: Verso, 1997; A.G. Noorani, *The RSS and the BJP*, New Delhi: Left Word 2000; Arvind Rajagopal, *Politics after Television: Hindu Nationalism and the Reshaping of the Public in India*, Cambridge: CUP, 2001; Pralay Kanungo, *RSS's Tryst with Destiny*, New Delhi: Manohar, 2003.
18. http://www.asianage.com/india/all-india/140817/panels-in-praise-of-pm-modi-at-gandhis-sabarmati-ashram.html.
19. This is the phrase used by the progressive writer and director, Khwaja Ahmad Abbas, in his play about Gandhi's life in South Africa.
20. Bhikhu Parekh, *Colonialism, Tradition and Reform: An Analysis of Gandhi's Political Discourse*, New Delhi: Sage, 1999, pp. 307, 318–319.
21. Gandhi, *CWMG*, vol. 21, pp. 20–21.
22. Fanon, *The Wretched of the Earth*, p. 23.

23. V.I. Lenin, 'Lev Tolstoi and His Epoch,' *Collected Works*, vol. 17, Moscow: Progress Publishers, pp. 51–52.
24. E.M.S. Namboodiripad, *The Mahatma and the Ism*, New Delhi: Leftword Books, 2010, p. 45.
25. Hiren Mukherjee, *Gandhi: A Study*, New Delhi: People's Publishing House, 1958, p. 200.
26. *Young India*, 11 August 1920, in *CWMG*, vol. 18, p. 133.
27. Ibid., p. 134.
28. Larry Collins and Dominique Lapierre, *Freedom at Midnight*, London: Collins, 1975, p. 32.
29. R. Rolland and M.K. Gandhi, *Romain Rolland – Gandhi Correspondence*, New Delhi: GOI, 1976, p. 179.
30. Anderson, 'Why Partition', *London Review of Books*, vol. 34, no. 14, 19 July 2012, p. 11.
31. Belafonte, *My Song*, p. 297.

Index